Spark for Data Science

Analyze your data and delve deep into the world of machine learning with the latest Spark version, 2.0

Srinivas Duvvuri

Bikramaditya Singhal

Packt>

BIRMINGHAM - MUMBAI

Spark for Data Science

First published: September 2016

Production reference: 1270916

Published by Packt Publishing Ltd.
Livery Place
35 Livery Street
Birmingham
B3 2PB, UK.
ISBN 978-1-78588-565-5

www.packtpub.com

Credits

Authors
Srinivas Duvvuri
Bikramaditya Singhal

Reviewers
Daniel Frimer
Priyansu Panda
Yogesh Tayal

Commissioning Editor
Dipika Gaonkar

Acquisition Editors
Tushar Gupta
Nikhil Karkal

Content Development Editor
Rashmi Suvarna

Technical Editor
Deepti Tuscano

Copy Editors
Safis Editing

Project Coordinator
Kinjal Bari

Proofreader
Safis Editing

Indexer
Pratik Shirodkar

Graphics
Kirk D'Penha

Production Coordinator
Shantanu N. Zagade

Foreword

Apache Spark is one of the most popular projects in the Hadoop ecosystem and possibly the most actively developed open source project in big data. Its simplicity, performance, and flexibility have made it popular not only among data scientists but also among engineers, developers, and everybody else interested in big data.

With its rising popularity, Duvvuri and Bikram have produced a book that is the need of the hour, Spark for Data Science, but with a difference. They have not only covered the Spark computing platform but have also included aspects of data science and machine learning. To put it in one word—comprehensive.

The book contains numerous code snippets that one can use to learn and also get a jump start in implementing projects. Using these examples, users also start to get good insights and learn the key steps in implementing a data science project—business understanding, data understanding, data preparation, modeling, evaluation and deployment.

Venkatraman Laxmikanth

Managing Director

Broadridge Financial Solutions India (Pvt) Ltd

About the Authors

Srinivas Duvvuri is currently Senior Vice President Development, heading the development teams for Fixed Income Suite of products at Broadridge Financial Solutions (India) Pvt Ltd. In addition, he also leads the Big Data and Data Science COE and is the principal member of the Broadridge India Technology Council. He is self learnt Data Scientist. The Big Data /Data Science COE in the past 3 years, has successfully completed multiple POC's and some of the use cases are moving towards production deployment. He has over 25+ years of experience in software product development. His experience spans predominantly in product development in, multiple domains Financial Services, Infrastructure Management, OLAP, Telecom Billing and Customer Care, CAD/CAM. Prior to Broadridge, he's held leadership positions at a Startup and leading IT majors such as CA, Hyperion (Oracle), Globalstar. He has a patent in Relational OLAP.

Srinivas loves to teach and mentor budding Engineers. He has established strong Academic connect and interacts with a host of educational institutions, He is an active speaker in various conferences, summits and meetups on topics such as Big data, Data Science

Srinivas is a B.Tech in Aeronautical Engineering and M.Tech in Computer Science, from IIT, Madras.

At the outset I would like to thank VLK our MD and Broadridge India for supporting me in this endeavor. I would like to thank my parents, teachers, colleagues and extended family who have mentored and motivated me. My thanks to Bikram who agreed me to be the co-author when proposal to author the book came up. My special thanks to my wife Ratna, sons Girish and Aravind who have supported me in completing this book.

I would also like to sincerely thank the editorial team from Packt Arshriya, Rashmi, Deepti and all those, though not mentioned here, who have contributed in this project. Finally last but not the least our publisher Packt.

Bikramaditya Singhal is a data scientist with about 7 years of industry experience. He is an expert in statistical analysis, predictive analytics, machine learning, Bitcoin, Blockchain, and programming in C, R, and Python. He has extensive experience in building scalable data analytics solutions in many industry sectors. He also has an active interest on industrial IoT, machine to machine communication, decentralized computation through Blockchain and Artificial Intelligence.

Bikram currently leads the data science team of 'Digital Enterprise Solutions' group at Tech Mahindra Ltd. He also worked in companies such as Microsoft India, Broadridge, Chelsio Communications and also cofounded a company named 'Mund Consulting' which focused on Big Data analytics.

Bikram is an active speaker in various conferences, summits and meetups on topics such as big data, data science, IIoT and Blockchain.

I would like to thank my father, my brothers Manoj Agrawal and Sumit Mund for their mentorship. Without learning from them, there is not a chance I could be doing what I do today, and it is because of them and others that I feel compelled to pass my knowledge on to those willing to learn. Special thanks to my mentor and coauthor Srinivas Duvvuri, and my friend Priyansu Panda, without their efforts this book quite possibly would not have happened.

My deepest gratitude to his holiness Sri Sri Ravi Shankar for building me to what I am today. Many thanks and gratitude to my parents and my wife Yashoda for their unconditional love and support.

I would also like to sincerely thank all those, though not mentioned here, who have contributed in this project directly or indirectly.

About the Reviewers

Daniel Frimer has been involved in a vast exposure of industries across Healthcare, Web Analytics, Transportation. Across these industries has developed ways to optimize the speed of data workflow, storage, and processing in the hopes of making a highly efficient department. Daniel is currently a Master's candidate at the University of Washington in Information Sciences pursuing a specialization in Data Science and Business Intelligence. She worked on Python Data Science Essentials

I'd like to thank my grandmother Mary. Who has always believed in mine and everyone's potential and respects those whose passions make the world a better place.

Priyansu Panda is a research engineer at Underwriters Laboratories, Bangalore, India. He worked as a senior system engineer in Infosys Limited, and served as a software engineer in Tech Mahindra.

His areas of expertise include machine-learning, natural language processing, computer vision, pattern recognition, and heterogeneous distributed data integration. His current research is on applied machine learning for product safety analysis. His major research interests are machine-learning and data-mining applications, artificial intelligence on internet of things, cognitive systems, and clustering research.

Yogesh Tayal is a Technology Consultant at Mu Sigma Business Solutions Pvt. Ltd. and has been with Mu Sigma for more than 3 years. He has worked with the Mu Sigma Business Analytics team and is currently an integral part of the product development team. Mu Sigma is one of the leading Decision Sciences companies in India with a huge client base comprising of leading corporations across an array of industry verticals i.e. technology, retail, pharmaceuticals, BFSI, e-commerce, healthcare etc.

www.PacktPub.com

For support files and downloads related to your book, please visit www.PacktPub.com.

Did you know that Packt offers eBook versions of every book published, with PDF and ePub files available? You can upgrade to the eBook version at www.PacktPub.com and as a print book customer, you are entitled to a discount on the eBook copy. Get in touch with us at service@packtpub.com for more details.

At www.PacktPub.com, you can also read a collection of free technical articles, sign up for a range of free newsletters and receive exclusive discounts and offers on Packt books and eBooks.

Mapt

https://www.packtpub.com/mapt

Get the most in-demand software skills with Mapt. Mapt gives you full access to all Packt books and video courses, as well as industry-leading tools to help you plan your personal development and advance your career.

Why subscribe?

- Fully searchable across every book published by Packt
- Copy and paste, print, and bookmark content
- On demand and accessible via a web browser

Table of Contents

Preface

In this smart age, data analytics is the key to sustaining and promoting business growth. Every business is trying to leverage their data as much possible with all sorts of data science tools and techniques to progress along the analytics maturity curve. This sudden rise in data science requirements is the obvious reason for scarcity of data scientists. It is very difficult to meet the market demand with unicorn data scientists who are experts in statistics, machine learning, mathematical modelling as well as programming.

The availability of unicorn data scientists is only going to decrease with the increase in market demand, and it will continue to be so. So, a solution was needed which not only empowers the unicorn data scientists to do more, but also creates what Gartner calls as "Citizen Data Scientists". Citizen data scientists are none other than the developers, analysts, BI professionals or other technologists whose primary job function is outside of statistics or analytics but are passionate enough to learn data science. They are becoming the key enabler in democratizing data analytics across organizations and industries as a whole.

There is an ever going plethora of tools and techniques designed to facilitate big data analytics at scale. This book is an attempt to create citizen data scientists who can leverage Apache Spark's distributed computing platform for data analytics.

This book is a practical guide to learn statistical analysis and machine learning to build scalable data products. It helps to master the core concepts of data science and also Apache Spark to help you jump start on any real life data analytics project. Throughout the book, all the chapters are supported by sufficient examples, which can be executed on a home computer, so that readers can easily follow and absorb the concepts. Every chapter attempts to be self-contained so that the reader can start from any chapter with pointers to relevant chapters for details. While the chapters start from basics for a beginner to learn and comprehend, it is comprehensive enough for a senior architects at the same time.

What this book covers

Chapter 1, *Big Data and Data Science – An Introduction*, this chapter discusses briefly about the various challenges in big data analytics and how Apache Spark solves those problems on a single platform. This chapter also explains how data analytics has evolved to what it is now and also gives a basic idea on the Spark stack.

Chapter 2, *The Spark Programming Model*, this chapter talks about the design considerations of Apache Spark and the supported programming languages. It also explains the Spark core components and covers the RDD API in details, which is the basic building block of Spark.

Chapter 3, *Introduction to DataFrames*, this chapter explains about the DataFrames, which are the most handy and useful component for the data scientists to work at ease. It explains about Spark SQL and the Catalyst optimizer that empowers DataFrames. Also, various DataFrames operations are demonstrated with code examples.

Chapter 4, *Unified Data Access*, this chapter talks about the various ways we source data from different sources, consolidate and work in a unified way. It covers the streaming aspect of real time data collection and operating on them. It also talks about the under-the-hood fundamentals of these APIs.

Chapter 5, *Data Analysis on Spark*, this chapter discuss about the complete data analytics lifecycle. With ample code examples, it explains how to source data from different sources, prepare the data using data cleaning and transformation techniques, and perform descriptive and inferential statistics to generate hidden insights from data.

Chapter 6, *Machine Learning*, this chapter explains various machine learning algorithms, how they are implemented in the MLlib library and how they can be used with the pipeline API for a streamlined execution. This chapter covers the fundamentals of all the algorithms covered so it could serve as a one stop reference.

Chapter 7, *Extending Spark with SparkR*, this chapter is primarily intended for the R programmers who want to leverage Spark for Data Analytics. It explains how to program with SparkR and how to use the machine learning algorithms of R libraries.

Chapter 8, *Analyzing Unstructured Data*, this chapter discusses only about unstructured data analysis. It explains how to source unstructured data, process it and perform machine learning on it. It also covers some of the dimension reduction techniques which were not covered in the "Machine Learning" chapter.

Chapter 9, *Visualizing Big Data*, in this chapter, readers learn various visualization techniques that are supported on Spark. It explains the different kinds of visualization requirements of data engineers, data scientists and business users; and also suggests right kinds of tools and techniques. It also talks about leveraging IPython/Jupyter notebook and Zeppelin, an Apache project for data visualization.

Chapter 10, *Putting It All Together*, till now the book has discussed about most of the data analytics components in different chapters separately. This chapter is an effort to stich various steps on a typical data science project and demonstrate a step-by-step approach to a full blown analytics project execution.

Chapter 11, *Building Data Science Applications*, till now the book has mostly discussed about the data science components along with a full blown execution example. This chapter provides a heads up on how to build data products that can be deployed in production. It also gives an idea on the current development status of the Apache Spark project and what is in store for it.

What you need for this book

Your system must have following software before executing the code mentioned in the book. However, not all software components are needed for all chapters:

- Ubuntu 14.4 or, Windows 7 or above
- Apache Spark 2.0.0
- Scala: 2.10.4
- Python 2.7.6
- R 3.3.0
- Java 1.7.0
- Zeppelin 0.6.1
- Jupyter 4.2.0
- IPython kernel 5.1

Who this book is for

This book is for anyone who wants to leverage Apache Spark for data science and machine learning. If you are a technologist who wants to expand your knowledge to perform data science operations in Spark, or a data scientist who wants to understand how algorithms are implemented in Spark, or a newbie with minimal development experience who wants to learn about Big Data Analytics, this book is for you!

Conventions

In this book, you will find a number of text styles that distinguish between different kinds of information. Here are some examples of these styles and an explanation of their meaning.

Code words in text, database table names, folder names, filenames, file extensions, pathnames, dummy URLs, user input, and Twitter handles are shown as follows: "When a program is run on a Spark shell, it is called the driver program with the user's `main` method in it."

A block of code is set as follows:

```
Scala> sc.parallelize(List(2, 3, 4)).count()
res0: Long = 3
Scala> sc.parallelize(List(2, 3, 4)).collect()
res1: Array[Int] = Array(2, 3, 4)
Scala> sc.parallelize(List(2, 3, 4)).first()
res2: Int = 2
Scala> sc.parallelize(List(2, 3, 4)).take(2)
res3: Array[Int] = Array(2, 3)
```

New terms and **important words** are shown in bold. Words that you see on the screen, for example, in menus or dialog boxes, appear in the text like this: "It also allows users to source data using **Data Source API** from the data sources that are not supported out of the box (for example, CSV, Avro HBase, Cassandra, and so on.)"

Warnings or important notes appear in a box like this.

Tips and tricks appear like this.

Reader feedback

Feedback from our readers is always welcome. Let us know what you think about this book-what you liked or disliked. Reader feedback is important for us as it helps us develop titles that you will really get the most out of. To send us general feedback, simply e-mail `feedback@packtpub.com`, and mention the book's title in the subject of your message. If there is a topic that you have expertise in and you are interested in either writing or contributing to a book, see our author guide at `www.packtpub.com/authors`.

Customer support

Now that you are the proud owner of a Packt book, we have a number of things to help you to get the most from your purchase.

Downloading the example code

You can download the example code files for this book from your account at `http://www.packtpub.com`. If you purchased this book elsewhere, you can visit `http://www.packtpub.com/support` and register to have the files e-mailed directly to you.

You can download the code files by following these steps:

1. Log in or register to our website using your e-mail address and password.
2. Hover the mouse pointer on the **SUPPORT** tab at the top.
3. Click on **Code Downloads & Errata**.
4. Enter the name of the book in the **Search** box.
5. Select the book for which you're looking to download the code files.
6. Choose from the drop-down menu where you purchased this book from.
7. Click on **Code Download**.

Once the file is downloaded, please make sure that you unzip or extract the folder using the latest version of:

- WinRAR / 7-Zip for Windows
- Zipeg / iZip / UnRarX for Mac
- 7-Zip / PeaZip for Linux

The code bundle for the book is also hosted on GitHub at `https://github.com/PacktPubl ishing/Spark-for-Data-Science`. We also have other code bundles from our rich catalog of books and videos available at `https://github.com/PacktPublishing/`. Check them out!

Downloading the color images of this book

We also provide you with a PDF file that has color images of the screenshots/diagrams used in this book. The color images will help you better understand the changes in the output. You can download this file from `http://www.packtpub.com/sites/default/files/downloads/SparkforDataScience_Color Images.pdf`.

Errata

Although we have taken every care to ensure the accuracy of our content, mistakes do happen. If you find a mistake in one of our books-maybe a mistake in the text or the code-we would be grateful if you could report this to us. By doing so, you can save other readers from frustration and help us improve subsequent versions of this book. If you find any errata, please report them by visiting `http://www.packtpub.com/submit-errata`, selecting your book, clicking on the **Errata Submission Form** link, and entering the details of your errata. Once your errata are verified, your submission will be accepted and the errata will be uploaded to our website or added to any list of existing errata under the Errata section of that title.

To view the previously submitted errata, go to `https://www.packtpub.com/books/conten t/support` and enter the name of the book in the search field. The required information will appear under the **Errata** section.

Piracy

Piracy of copyrighted material on the Internet is an ongoing problem across all media. At Packt, we take the protection of our copyright and licenses very seriously. If you come across any illegal copies of our works in any form on the Internet, please provide us with the location address or website name immediately so that we can pursue a remedy.

Please contact us at copyright@packtpub.com with a link to the suspected pirated material.

We appreciate your help in protecting our authors and our ability to bring you valuable content.

Questions

If you have a problem with any aspect of this book, you can contact us at questions@packtpub.com, and we will do our best to address the problem.

1
Big Data and Data Science – An Introduction

Big data is definitely a big deal! It promises a wealth of opportunities by deriving hidden insights in huge data silos and by opening new avenues to excel in business. Leveraging **big data** through advanced analytics techniques has become a no-brainer for organizations to create and maintain their competitive advantage.

This chapter explains what big data is all about, the various challenges with big data analysis and how **Apache Spark** pitches in as the de facto standard to address computational challenges and also serves as a data science platform.

The topics covered in this chapter are as follows:

- Big data overview – what is all the fuss about?
- Challenges with big data analytics – why was it so difficult?
- Evolution of big data analytics – the data analytics trend
- Spark for data analytics – the solution to big data challenges
- The Spark stack – all that makes it up for a complete big data solution

Big data overview

Much has already been spoken and written about what big data is, but there is no specific standard as such to clearly define it. It is actually a relative term to some extent. Whether small or big, your data can be leveraged only if you can analyze it properly. To make some sense out of your data, the right set of analysis techniques is needed and selecting the right tools and techniques is of utmost importance in data analytics. However, when the data itself becomes a part of the problem and the computational challenges need to be addressed prior to performing data analysis, it becomes a big data problem.

A revolution took place in the World Wide Web, also referred to as Web 2.0, which changed the way people used the Internet. Static web pages became interactive websites and started collecting more and more data. Technological advancements in cloud computing, social media, and mobile computing created an explosion of data. Every digital device started emitting data and many other sources started driving the data deluge. The dataflow from every nook and corner generated varieties of voluminous data, at speed! The formation of big data in this fashion was a natural phenomenon, because this is how the World Wide Web had evolved and no explicit efforts were involved in specifics. This is about the past! If you consider the change that is happening now, and is going to happen in future, the volume and speed of data generation is beyond what one can anticipate. I am propelled to make such a statement because every device is getting smarter these days, thanks to the**Internet of Things (IoT)**.

The IT trend was such that the technological advancements also facilitated the data explosion. Data storage had experienced a paradigm shift with the advent of cheaper clusters of online storage pools and the availability of commodity hardware with bare minimal price. Storing data from disparate sources in its native form in a single data lake was rapidly gaining over carefully designed data marts and data warehouses. Usage patterns also shifted from rigid schema-driven, RDBMS-based approaches to schema-less, continuously available **NoSQL** data-store-driven solutions. As a result, the rate of data creation, whether structured, semi-structured, or unstructured, started accelerating like never before.

Organizations are very much convinced that not only can specific business questions be answered by leveraging big data; it also brings in opportunities to cover the uncovered possibilities in businesses and address the uncertainties associated with this. So, apart from the natural data influx, organizations started devising strategies to generate more and more data to maintain their competitive advantages and to be future ready. Here, an example would help to understand this better. Imagine sensors are installed on the machines of a manufacturing plant which are constantly emitting data, and hence the status of the machine parts, and a company is able to predict when the machine is going to fail. It lets the company prevent a failure or damage and avoid unplanned downtime, saving a lot of money.

Challenges with big data analytics

There are broadly two types of formidable challenges in the analysis of big data. The first challenge is the requirement for a massive computation platform, and once it is in place, the second challenge is to analyze and make sense out of huge data at scale.

Computational challenges

With the increase in data, the storage requirement for big data also grew more and more. Data management became a cumbersome task. The latency involved in accessing the disk storage due to the seek time became the major bottleneck even though the processing speed of the processor and the frequency of RAM were up to the mark.

Fetching structured and unstructured data from across the gamut of business applications and data silos, consolidating them, and processing them to find useful business insights was challenging. There were only a few applications that could address any one area, or just a few areas of diversified business requirement. However, integrating those applications to address most of the business requirements in a unified way only increased the complexity.

To address these challenges, people turned to the distributed computing framework with distributed file system, for example, Hadoop and **Hadoop Distributed File System (HDFS)**. This could eliminate the latency due to disk I/O, as the data could be read in parallel across the cluster of machines.

Distributed computing technologies had existed for decades before, but gained more prominence only after the importance of big data was realized in the industry. So, technology platforms such as Hadoop and HDFS or Amazon S3 became the industry standard. On top of Hadoop, many other solutions such as Pig, Hive, Sqoop, and others were developed to address different kinds of industry requirements such as storage, **Extract, Transform, and Load** (ETL), and data integration to make Hadoop a unified platform.

Analytical challenges

Analyzing data to find some hidden insights has always been challenging because of the additional intricacies involved in dealing with huge datasets. The traditional BI and OLAP solutions could not address most of the challenges that arose due to big data. As an example, if there were multiple dimensions to a dataset, say 100, it got really difficult to compare these variables with one another to draw a conclusion because there would be around 100C2 combinations for it. Such cases required statistical techniques such as *correlation* and the like to find the hidden patterns.

Though there were statistical solutions to many problems, it got really difficult for data scientists or analytics professionals to slice and dice the data to find intelligent insights unless they loaded the entire dataset into a **DataFrame** in memory. The major roadblock was that most of the general-purpose algorithms for statistical analysis and machine learning were single-threaded and written at a time when datasets were usually not so huge and could fit in the RAM on a single computer. Those algorithms written in R or Python were no longer very useful in their native form to be deployed on a distributed computing environment because of the limitation of in-memory computation.

To address this challenge, statisticians and computer scientists had to work together to rewrite most of the algorithms that would work well in a distributed computing environment. Consequently, a library called **Mahout** for machine learning algorithms was developed on Hadoop for parallel processing. It had most of the common algorithms that were being used most often in the industry. Similar initiatives were taken for other distributed computing frameworks.

Evolution of big data analytics

The previous section outlined how the computational and data analytics challenges were addressed for big data requirements. It was possible because of the convergence of several related trends such as low-cost commodity hardware, accessibility to big data, and improved data analytics techniques. Hadoop became a cornerstone in many large, distributed data processing infrastructures.

However, people soon started realizing the limitations of Hadoop. Hadoop solutions were best suited for only specific types of big data requirements such as ETL; it gained popularity for such requirements only.

There were scenarios when data engineers or analysts had to perform ad hoc queries on the data sets for interactive data analysis. Every time they ran a query on Hadoop, the data was read from the disk (HDFS-read) and loaded into the memory – which was a costly affair. Effectively, jobs were running at the speed of I/O transfers over the network and cluster of disks, instead of the speed of CPU and RAM.

The following is a pictorial representation of the scenario:

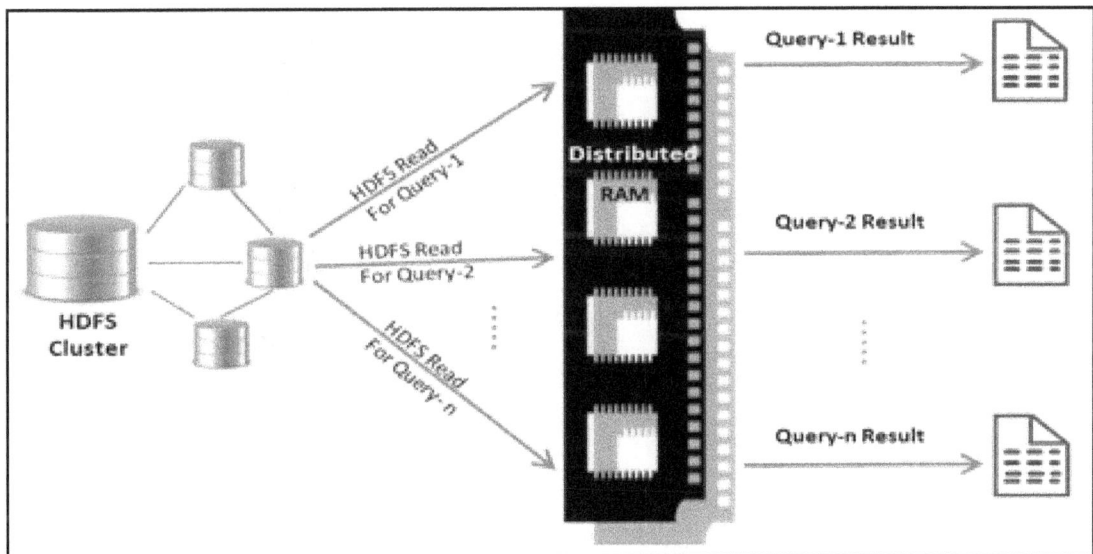

One more case where Hadoop's MapReduce model could not fit in well was with machine learning algorithms that were iterative in nature. Hadoop MapReduce was underperforming, with huge latency in iterative computation. Since MapReduce had a restricted programming model with forbidden communication between Map and Reduce workers, the intermediate results needed to be stored in a stable storage. So, those were pushed on to the HDFS, which in turn writes into the instead of saving in RAM and then loading back in the memory for the subsequent iteration, similarly for the rest of the iterations. The number of disk I/O was dependent on the number of iterations involved in an algorithm and this was topped with the serialization and deserialization overhead while saving and loading the data. Overall, it was computationally expensive and could not get the level of popularity compared to what was expected of it.

The following is a pictorial representation of this scenario:

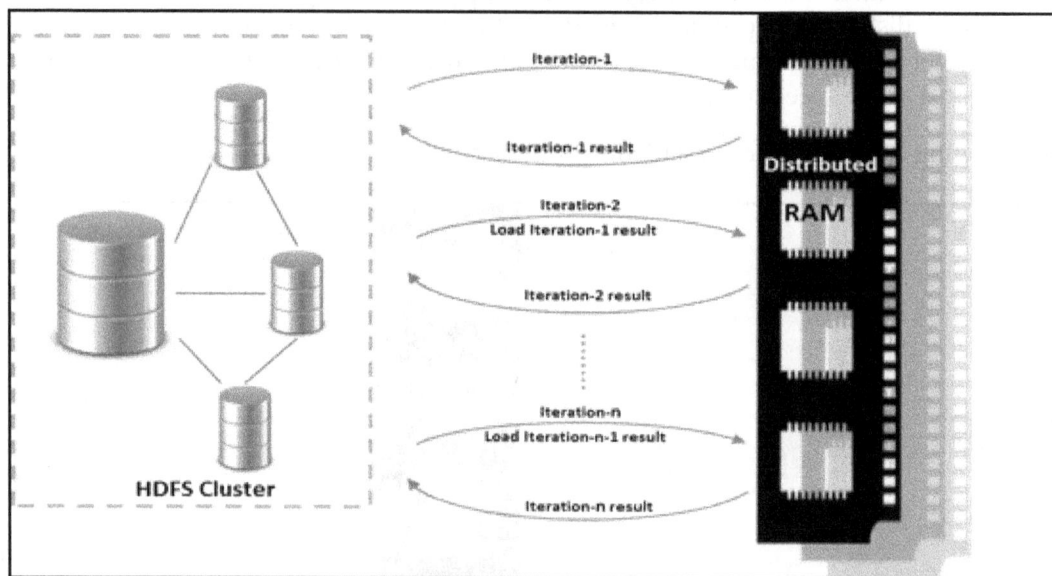

To address this, tailor-made solutions were developed, for example, Google's Pregel, which was an iterative graph processing algorithm and was optimized for inter-process communication and in-memory storage for the intermediate results to make it run faster. Similarly, many other solutions were developed or redesigned that would best suit some of the specific needs that the algorithms used were designed for.

Instead of redesigning all the algorithms, a general-purpose engine was needed that could be leveraged by most of the algorithms for in-memory computation on a distributed computing platform. It was also expected that such a design would result in faster execution of iterative computation and ad hoc data analysis. This is how the Spark project paved its way out at the AMPLab at UC Berkeley.

Spark for data analytics

Soon after the Spark project was successful in the AMP labs, it was made open source in 2010 and transferred to the Apache Software Foundation in 2013. It is currently being led by Databricks.

Spark offers many distinct advantages over other distributed computing platforms, such as:

- A faster execution platform for both iterative machine learning and interactive data analysis
- Single stack for batch processing, SQL queries, real-time stream processing, graph processing, and complex data analytics
- Provides high-level API to develop a diverse range of distributed applications by hiding the complexities of distributed programming
- Seamless support for various data sources such as RDBMS, HBase, Cassandra, Parquet, MongoDB, HDFS, Amazon S3, and so on

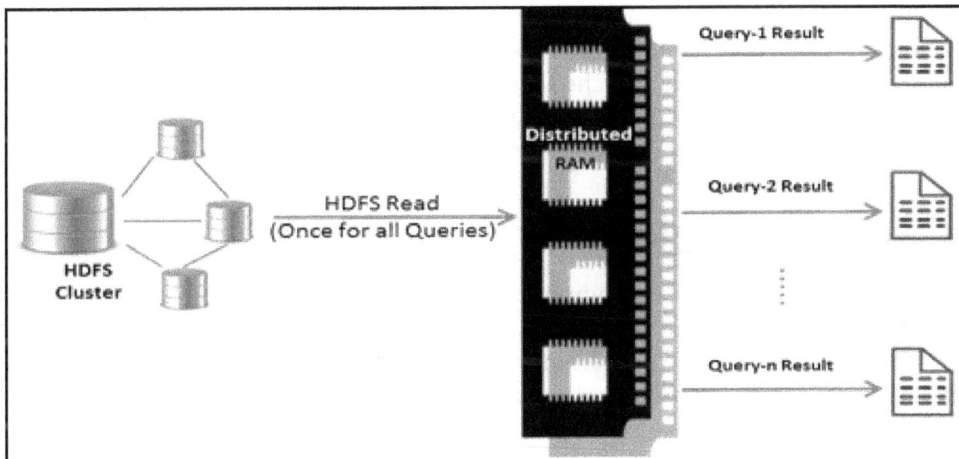

The following is a pictorial representation of in-memory data sharing for iterative algorithms:

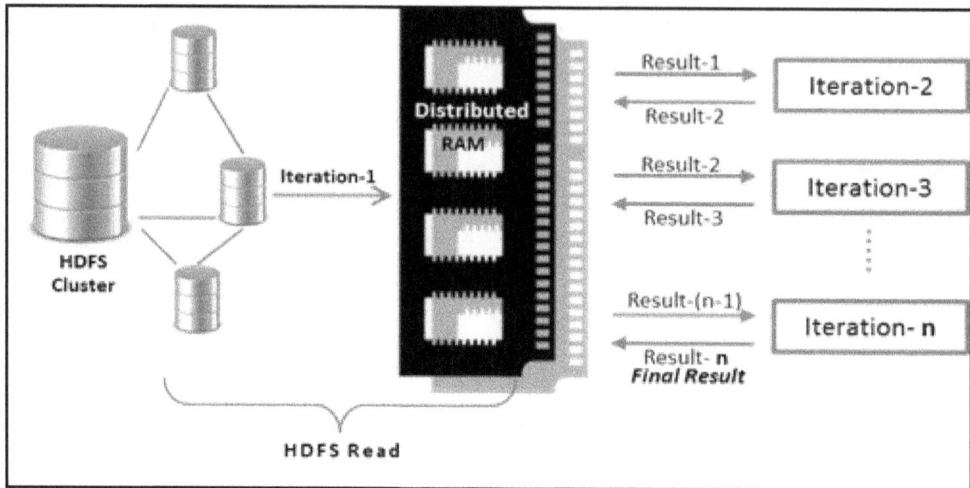

Spark hides the complexities in writing the core MapReduce jobs and provides most of the functionalities through simple function calls. Because of its simplicity, it is able to cater to wider and bigger audience groups such as data scientists, data engineers, statisticians, and R/Python/Scala/Java developers.

The Spark architecture broadly consists of a data storage layer, management framework, and API. It is designed to work on top of an HDFS filesystem, and thereby leverages the existing ecosystem. Deployment could be as a standalone server or on distributed computing frameworks such as Apache Mesos or YARN. An API is provided for Scala, the language in which Spark is written, along with Java, R and Python.

The Spark stack

Spark is a general-purpose cluster computing system that empowers other higher-level components to leverage its core engine. It is interoperable with Apache Hadoop, in the sense that it can read and write data from/to HDFS and can also integrate with other storage systems that are supported by the Hadoop API.

While it allows building other higher-level applications on top of it, it already has a few components built on top that are tightly integrated with its core engine to take advantage of the future enhancements at the core. These applications come bundled with Spark to cover the broader sets of requirements in the industry. Most of the real-world applications need to be integrated across projects to solve specific business problems that usually have a set of requirements. This is eased out with Apache Spark as it allows its higher level components to be seamlessly integrated, such as libraries in a development project.

Also, with Spark's built-in support for Scala, Java, R and Python, a broader range of developers and data engineers are able to leverage the entire Spark stack:

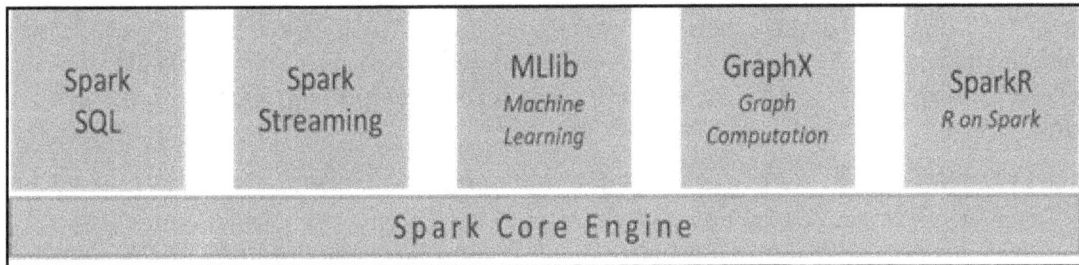

Spark SQL	Spark Streaming	MLlib *Machine* *Learning*	GraphX *Graph* *Computation*	SparkR *R on Spark*
Spark Core Engine				

Spark core

The Spark core, in a way, is similar to the kernel of an operating system. It is the general execution engine, which is fast as well as fault tolerant. The entire Spark ecosystem is built on top of this core engine. It is mainly designed to do job scheduling, task distribution, and monitoring of jobs across worker nodes. It is also responsible for memory management, interacting with various heterogeneous storage systems, and various other operations.

The primary building block of Spark core is the **Resilient Distributed Dataset (RDD)**, which is an immutable, fault-tolerant collection of elements. Spark can create RDDs from a variety of data sources such as HDFS, local filesystems, Amazon S3, other RDDs, NoSQL data stores such as Cassandra, and so on. They are resilient in the sense that they automatically rebuild on failure. RDDs are built through lazy parallel transformations. They may be cached and partitioned, and may or may not be materialized.

The entire Spark core engine may be viewed as a set of simple operations on distributed datasets. All the scheduling and execution of jobs in Spark is done based on the methods associated with each RDD. Also, the methods associated with each RDD define their own ways of distributed in-memory computation.

Spark SQL

This module of Spark is designed to query, analyze, and perform operations on structured data. This is a very important component in the entire Spark stack because of the fact that most of the organizational data is structured, though unstructured data is growing rapidly. Acting as a distributed query engine, it enables Hadoop Hive queries to run up to 100 times faster on it without any modification. Apart from Hive, it also supports Apache Parquet, an efficient columnar storage, JSON, and other structured data formats. Spark SQL enables running SQL queries along with complex programs written in Python, Scala, and Java.

Spark SQL provides a distributed programming abstraction called **DataFrames**, referred to as SchemaRDD before, which had fewer functions associated with it. DataFrames are distributed collections of named columns, analogous to SQL tables or Python's Pandas DataFrames. They can be constructed with a variety of data sources that have schemas with them such as Hive, Parquet, JSON, other RDBMS sources, and also from Spark RDDs.

Spark SQL can be used for ETL processing across different formats and then running ad hoc analysis. Spark SQL comes with an optimizer framework called Catalyst that can transform SQL queries for better efficiency.

Spark streaming

The processing window for the enterprise data is becoming shorter than ever. To address the real-time processing requirement of the industry, this component of Spark was designed, which is fault tolerant as well as scalable. Spark enables real-time data analytics on live streams of data by supporting data analysis, machine learning, and graph processing on them.

It provides an API called **Discretised Stream (DStream)** to manipulate the live streams of data. The live streams of data are sliced up into small batches of, say, x seconds. Spark treats each batch as an RDD and processes them as basic RDD operations. DStreams can be created out of live streams of data from HDFS, Kafka, Flume, or any other source which can stream data on the TCP socket. By applying some higher-level operations on DStreams, other DStreams can be produced.

The final result of Spark streaming can either be written back to the various data stores supported by Spark or can be pushed to any dashboard for visualization.

MLlib

MLlib is the built-in machine learning library in the Spark stack. This was introduced in Spark 0.8. Its goal is to make machine learning scalable and easy. Developers can seamlessly use Spark SQL, Spark Streaming, and GraphX in their programming language of choice, be it Java, Python, or Scala. MLlib provides the necessary functions to perform various statistical analyses such as correlations, sampling, hypothesis testing, and so on. This component also has a broad coverage of applications and algorithms in classification, regression, collaborative filtering, clustering, and decomposition.

The machine learning workflow involves collecting and preprocessing data, building and deploying the model, evaluating the results, and refining the model. In the real world, the preprocessing steps take up significant effort. These are typically multi-stage workflows involving expensive intermediate read/write operations. Often, these processing steps may be performed multiple times over a period of time. A new concept called **ML Pipelines** was introduced to streamline these preprocessing steps. A Pipeline is a sequence of transformations where the output of one stage is the input of another, forming a chain. The ML Pipeline leverages Spark and MLlib and enables developers to define reusable sequences of transformations.

GraphX

GraphX is a thin-layered unified graph analytics framework on Spark. It was designed to be a general-purpose distributed dataflow framework in place of specialized graph processing frameworks. It is fault tolerant and also exploits in-memory computation.

GraphX is an embedded graph processing API for manipulating graphs (for example, social networks) and to do graph parallel computation (for example, Google's Pregel). It combines the advantages of both graph-parallel and data-parallel systems on the Spark stack to unify exploratory data analysis, iterative graph computation, and ETL processing. It extends the RDD abstraction to introduce the **Resilient Distributed Graph** (**RDG**), which is a directed graph with properties associated to each of its vertices and edges.

GraphX includes a decently large collection of graph algorithms, such as PageRank, K-Core, Triangle Count, LDA, and so on.

SparkR

The SparkR project was started to integrate the statistical analysis and machine learning capability of R with the scalability of Spark. It addressed the limitation of R, which was its ability to process as much data as fitted in the memory of a single machine. R programs can now scale in a distributed setting through SparkR.

SparkR is actually an R Package that provides an R shell to leverage Spark's distributed computing engine. With R's rich set of built-in packages for data analytics, data scientists can analyze large datasets interactively at scale.

Summary

In this chapter, we briefly covered what big data is all about. We then discussed the computational and analytical challenges involved in big data analytics. Later, we looked at how the analytics space in the context of big data has evolved over a period of time and what the trend has been. We also covered how Spark addressed most of the big data analytics challenges and became a general-purpose unified analytics platform for data science as well as parallel computation. At the end of this chapter, we just gave you a heads-up on the Spark stack and its components.

In the next chapter, we will learn about the Spark programming model. We will take a deep dive into the basic building block of Spark, which is the RDD. Also, we will learn how to program with the RDD API on Scala and Python.

References

Apache Spark overview:

- `http://spark.apache.org/docs/latest/`
- `https://databricks.com/spark/about`

Apache Spark architecture:

- `http://lintool.github.io/SparkTutorial/slides/day1_context.pdf`

The Spark Programming Model

2

Large-scale data processing using thousands of nodes with built-in fault tolerance has become widespread due to the availability of open source frameworks, with Hadoop being a popular choice. These frameworks are quite successful in executing specific tasks such as **Extract, Transform, and Load** (**ETL**) and storage applications that deal with web-scale data. However, developers were left with a myriad of tools to work with, along with the well-established Hadoop ecosystem. There was a need for a single, general-purpose development platform that caters to batch, streaming, interactive, and iterative requirements. This was the motivation behind Spark.

The previous chapter outlined the big data analytics challenges and how Spark addressed most of them at a very high level. In this chapter, we will examine the design goals and choices involved in the making of Spark to get a clearer understanding of its suitability as a data science platform for big data. We will also cover the core abstraction **Resilient Distributed Dataset** (**RDD**) in depth with examples.

As a prerequisite for this chapter, a basic understanding of Python or Scala along with elementary understanding of Spark is needed. The topics covered in this chapter are as follows:

- The programming paradigm – language support and design benefits
    - Supported programming languages
    - Choosing the right language

- The Spark engine – Spark core components and their implications
  - Driver program
  - Spark shell
  - SparkContext
  - Worker nodes
  - Executors
  - Shared variables
  - Flow of execution
- The RDD API – understanding the RDD fundamentals
  - RDD basics
  - Persistence
- RDD operations – let's get your hands dirty
  - Getting started with the shell
  - Creating RDDs
  - Transformations on normal RDDs
  - Transformations on pair RDDs
  - Actions

The programming paradigm

For Spark to address the big data challenges and serve as a platform for data science and other scalable applications, it was built with well-thought-out design considerations and language support.

There are Spark APIs designed for varieties of application developers to create Spark-based applications using standard API interfaces. Spark provides APIs for Scala, Java, R and Python programming languages, as explained in the following sections.

Supported programming languages

With built-in support for so many languages, Spark can be used interactively through a shell, which is otherwise known as **Read-Evaluate-Print-Loop** (**REPL**), in a way that will feel familiar to developers of any language. The developers can use the language of their choice, leverage existing libraries, and seamlessly interact with Spark and its ecosystem. Let us see the ones supported on Spark and how they fit into the Spark ecosystem.

Scala

Spark itself is written in Scala, a **Java Virtual Machine (JVM)** based functional programming language. The Scala compiler generates byte code that executes on the JVM. So, it can seamlessly integrate with any other JVM-based systems such as HDFS, Cassandra, HBase, and so on. Scala was the language of choice because of its concise programming interface, an interactive shell, and its ability to capture functions and efficiently ship them across the nodes in a cluster. Scala is an extensible (scalable, hence the name), statically typed, efficient multi-paradigm language that supports functional and object-oriented language features.

Apart from the full-blown applications, Scala also supports shell (Spark shell) for interactive data analysis on Spark.

Java

Since Spark is JVM based, it naturally supports Java. This helps existing Java developers to develop data science applications along with other scalable applications. Almost all the built-in library functions are accessible from Java. Coding in Java for data science assignments is comparatively difficult in Spark, but someone very hands-on with Java might find it easy.

This Java API only lacks a shell-based interface for interactive data analysis on Spark.

Python

Python is supported on Spark through PySpark, which is built on top of Spark's Java API (using Py4J). From now on, we will be using the term **PySpark** to refer to the Python environment on Spark. Python was already very popular amongst developers for data wrangling, data munging, and other data science related tasks. Support for Python on Spark became even more popular as Spark could address the scalable computation challenge.

Through Python's interactive shell on Spark (PySpark), interactive data analysis at scale is possible.

R

R is supported on Spark through SparkR, an R package through which Spark's scalability is accessible through R. SparkR empowered R to address its limitation of single-threaded runtime, because of which computation was limited only to a single node.

Since R was originally designed only for statistical analysis and machine learning, it was already enriched with most of the packages. Data scientists can now work on huge data at scale with a minimal learning curve. R is still a default choice for many data scientists.

Choosing the right language

Apart from the developer's language preference, at times there are other constraints that may draw attention. The following aspects could supplement your development experience while choosing one language over the other:

- An interactive shell comes in handy when developing complex logic. All languages supported by Spark except Java have an interactive shell.
- R is the lingua franca of data scientists. It is definitely more suitable for pure data analytics because of its richer set of libraries. R support was added in Spark 1.4.0 so that Spark reaches out to data scientists working on R.
- Java has a broader base of developers. Java 8 has included lambda expressions and hence the functional programming aspect. Nevertheless, Java tends to be verbose.
- Python is gradually gaining more popularity in the data science space. The availability of Pandas and other data processing libraries, and its simple and expressive nature, make Python a strong candidate. Python gives more flexibility than R in scenarios such as data aggregation from different sources, data cleaning, natural language processing, and so on.
- Scala is perhaps the best choice for real-time analytics because this is the closest to Spark. The initial learning curve for developers coming from other languages should not be a deterrent for serious production systems. The latest inclusions to Spark are usually first available in Scala. Its static typing and sophisticated type inference improve efficiency as well as compile-time checks. Scala can draw from Java's libraries as Scala's own library base is still at an early stage, but catching up.

The Spark engine

To program with Spark, a basic understanding of Spark components is needed. In this section, some of the important Spark components along with their execution mechanism will be explained so that developers and data scientists can write programs and build applications.

Before getting into the details, we suggest you take a look at the following diagram so that the descriptions of the Spark gears are more comprehensible as you read further:

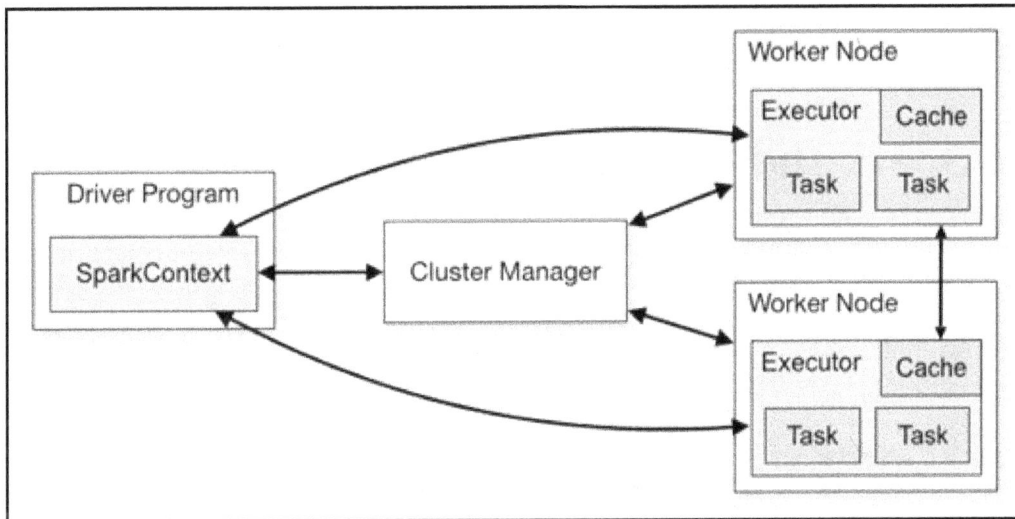

Driver program

The Spark shell is an example of a driver program. A driver program is a process that executes in the JVM and runs the user's *main* function on it. It has a SparkContext object which is a connection to the underlying cluster manager. A Spark application is initiated when the driver starts and it completes when the driver stops. The driver, through an instance of SparkContext, coordinates all processes within a Spark application.

Primarily, an RDD lineage **Directed Acyclic Graph** (**DAG**) is built on the driver side with data sources (which may be RDDs) and transformations. This DAG is submitted to the DAG scheduler when an *action* method is encountered. The DAG scheduler then splits the DAG into logical units of work (for example, map or reduce) called stages. Each stage, in turn, is a set of tasks, and each task is assigned to an executor (worker) by the task scheduler. Jobs may be executed in FIFO order or round robin, depending on the configuration.

> Inside a single Spark application, multiple parallel jobs can run simultaneously if they were submitted from separate threads.

The Spark shell

The Spark shell is none other than the interface provided by Scala and Python. It looks very similar to any other interactive shell. It has a SparkContext object (created by default for you) that lets you leverage the distributed cluster. An interactive shell is quite useful for exploratory or ad hoc analysis. You can develop your complex scripts step by step through the shell without going through the compile-build-execute cycle.

SparkContext

SparkContext is the entry point to the Spark core engine. This object is required to create and manipulate RDDs and create shared variables on a cluster. The SparkContext object connects to a cluster manager, which is responsible for resource allocation. Spark comes with its own standalone cluster manager. Since the cluster manager is a pluggable component in Spark, it can be managed through external cluster managers such as Apache Mesos or YARN.

When you start a Spark shell, a SparkContext object is created by default for you. You can also create it by passing a SparkConf object that is used to set various Spark configuration parameters as key value pairs. Please note that there can be only one SparkContext object in a JVM.

Worker nodes

Worker nodes are the nodes that run the application code in a cluster, obeying the driver program. The real work is actually executed by the worker nodes. Each machine in the cluster may have one or more worker instances (default one). A worker node executes one or more executors that belong to one or more Spark applications. It consists of a *block manager* component, which is responsible for managing data blocks. The blocks can be cached RDD data, intermediate shuffled data, or broadcast data. When the available RAM is not sufficient, it automatically moves some data blocks to disk. Data replication across nodes is another responsibility of block manager.

Executors

Each application has a set of executor processes. Executors reside on worker nodes and communicate directly with the driver once the connection is made by the cluster manager. All executors are managed by SparkContext. An executor is a single JVM instance that serves a single Spark application. An executor is responsible for managing computation through tasks, storage, and caching on each worker node. It can run multiple tasks concurrently.

Shared variables

Normally, the code is shipped to partitions along with separate copies of variables. These variables cannot be used to propagate results (for example, intermediate work counts) back to the driver program. Shared variables are used for this purpose. There are two kinds of shared variables, **broadcast variables** and **accumulators**.

Broadcast variables enable the programmers to retain a read-only copy cached on each node rather than shipping a copy of it with tasks. If large, read-only data is used in multiple operations, it can be designated as broadcast variables and shipped only once to all worker nodes. The data broadcast in this way is cached in serialized form and is deserialized before running each task. Subsequent operations can access these variables along with the local variables moved along with the code. Creating broadcast variables is not necessary in all cases, except the ones where tasks across multiple stages need the same read-only copy of the data.

Accumulators are variables that are always incremented, such as counters or cumulative sums. Spark natively supports accumulators of numeric types, but allows programmers to add support for new types. Please note that the worker nodes cannot read the value of accumulators; they can only modify their values.

Flow of execution

A Spark application consists of a set of processes with one *driver* program and multiple *worker* (*executor*) programs. The driver program contains the application's *main* function and a SparkContext object, which represents a connection to the Spark cluster. Coordination between driver and the other processes happens through the SparkContext object.

A typical Spark client program performs the following steps:

1. When a program is run on a Spark shell, it is called the driver program with the user's `main` method in it. It gets executed in the JVM of the system where you are running the driver program.

2. The first step is to create a SparkContext object with the required configuration parameters. When you run the PySpark or Spark shell, it is instantiated by default, but for other applications, you have to create it explicitly. SparkContext is actually the gateway to Spark.

3. The next step is to define one or more RDDs, either by loading a file or programmatically by passing an array of items, referred to parallel collection

4. Then more RDDs can be defined by a sequence of transformations, which are tracked and managed by a **lineage graph**. These RDD transformations may be viewed as piped UNIX commands where the output of one command becomes the input to the next command and so on. Each resulting RDD of a *transformation* step has a pointer to its parent RDD and also has a function for calculating its data. The RDD is acted on only after encountering an *action* statement. So, the *transformations* are lazy operations used to define new RDDs and *actions* launch a computation to return a value to the program or write data to external storage. We will discuss this aspect a little more in the following sections.

5. At this stage, Spark creates an execution graph where nodes represent the RDDs and edges represent the transformation steps. Spark breaks the job into multiple tasks to run on separate machines. This is how Spark sends the **compute** to the data across the nodes in a cluster, rather than getting all the data together and computing it.

The RDD API

The RDD is a read-only, partitioned, fault-tolerant collection of records. From a design perspective, there was a need for a single data structure abstraction that hides the complexity of dealing with a wide variety of data sources, be it HDFS, filesystems, RDBMS, NOSQL data structures, or any other data source. The user should be able to define the RDD from any of these sources. The goal was to support a wide array of operations and let users compose them in any order.

RDD basics

Each dataset is represented as an object in Spark's programming interface called RDD. Spark provides two ways for creating RDDs. One way is to parallelize an existing collection. The other way is to reference a dataset in an external storage system such as a filesystem.

An RDD is composed of one or more data sources, maybe after performing a series of transformations including several operators. Every RDD or RDD partition knows how to recreate itself in case of failure. It has the log of transformations, or a *lineage* that is required to recreate itself from stable storage or another RDD. Thus, any program using Spark can be assured of built-in fault tolerance, regardless of the underlying data source and the type of RDD.

There are two kinds of methods available on RDDs: transformations, and actions. Transformations are the methods that are used to create RDDs. Actions are the methods that utilize RDDs. RDDs are usually partitioned. Users may choose to persist RDDs that may be reused in their programs.

RDDs are immutable (read-only) data structures, so any transformation results in the creation of a new RDD. The transformations are applied lazily, only when any action is applied on them, and not when an RDD is defined. An RDD is recomputed every time it is used in an action unless the user explicitly persists the RDD in memory. Saving in memory saves a lot of time. If the memory is not sufficient to accommodate the RDD fully, the remaining portion of that RDD will be stored (spilled) on the hard disk automatically. One advantage of lazy transformations is that it is possible to optimize the transformation steps. For example, if the action is to return the first line, Spark computes only a single partition and skips the rest.

An RDD may be viewed as a set of partitions (splits) with a list of dependencies on parent RDDs and a function to compute a partition given its parents. Sometimes, each partition of a parent RDD is used by a single child RDD. This is called *narrow dependency*. Narrow dependency is desirable because when a parent RDD partition is lost, only a single child partition needs to be recomputed. On the other hand, computing a single child RDD partition that involves operations such as *group-by-keys* depends on several parent RDD partitions. Data from each parent RDD partition in turn is required in creating data in several child RDD partitions. Such a dependency is called *wide dependency*. In the case of narrow dependency, it is possible to keep both parent and child RDD partitions on a single node (co-partition). But this is not possible in the case of wide dependency because parent data is scattered across several partitions. In such cases, data should be *shuffled* across partitions. Data shuffling is a resource-intensive operation that should be avoided to the extent possible. Another issue with wide dependency is that all child RDD partitions need to be recomputed even when a single parent RDD partition is lost.

Persistence

RDDs are computed on the fly every time they are acted upon through an action method. The developer has the ability to override this default behavior and instruct to *persist* or *cache* a dataset in memory across partitions. If this dataset is required to participate in several actions, then persisting saves a significant amount of time, CPU cycles, disk I/O, and network bandwidth. The fault-tolerance mechanism is applicable to the cached partitions too. When any partition is lost due to node failure, it is recomputed using a lineage graph. If the available memory is insufficient, Spark gracefully spills the persisted partitions on to the disk. The developer may remove unwanted RDDs using *unpersist*. Nevertheless, Spark automatically monitors the cache and removes old partitions using **Least Recently Used (LRU)** algorithms.

> Cache() is the same as persist() or persist (MEMORY_ONLY). While the persist() method can have many other arguments for different levels of persistence, such as only memory, memory and disk, only disk, and so on, the cache() method is designed only for persistence in the memory.

RDD operations

Spark programming usually starts by choosing a suitable interface that you are comfortable with. If you intend to do interactive data analysis, then a shell prompt would be the obvious choice. However, choosing a Python shell (PySpark) or Scala shell (Spark-Shell) depends on your proficiency with these languages to some extent. If you are building a full-blown scalable application then proficiency matters a great deal, so you should develop the application in your language of choice between Scala, Java, and Python, and submit it to Spark. We will discuss this aspect in more detail later in the book.

Creating RDDs

In this section, we will use both a Python shell (PySpark) and a Scala shell (Spark-Shell) to create an RDD. Both of these shells have a predefined, interpreter-aware SparkContext that is assigned to a variable `sc`.

Let us get started with some simple code examples. Note that the code assumes the current working directory is Spark's home directory. The following code snippet initiates the Spark interactive shell, reads a file from the local filesystem, and prints the first line from that file:

Python:

```
> bin/pyspark  // Start pyspark shell
>>> _          // For simplicity sake, no Log messages are shown here

>>> type(sc)     //Check the type of Predefined SparkContext object
<class 'pyspark.context.SparkContext'>

//Pass the file path to create an RDD from the local file system
>>> fileRDD = sc.textFile('RELEASE')

>>> type(fileRDD)  //Check the type of fileRDD object
<class 'pyspark.rdd.RDD'>

>>>fileRDD.first()   //action method. Evaluates RDD DAG and also returns
the first item in the RDD along with the time taken
took 0.279229 s
u'Spark Change Log'
```

Scala:

```
> bin/Spark-Shell  // Start Spark-shell
Scala> _        // For simplicity sake, no Log messages are shown here

Scala> sc    //Check the type of Predefined SparkContext object
res1: org.apache.spark.SparkContext =
org.apache.spark.SparkContext@70884875

//Pass the file path to create an RDD from the local file system

Scala> val fileRDD = sc.textFile("RELEASE")

Scala> fileRDD  //Check the type of fileRDD object
res2: org.apache.spark.rdd.RDD[String] = ../ RELEASE
MapPartitionsRDD[1] at textFile at <console>:21

Scala>fileRDD.first()   //action method. Evaluates RDD DAG and also returns
the first item in the RDD along with the time taken
0.040965 s
res6: String = Spark Change Log
```

In both the preceding examples, the first line has invoked the interactive shell. The SparkContext variable `sc` is already defined as expected. We have created an RDD by the name `fileRDD` that points to a file `RELEASE`. This statement is just a transformation and will not be executed until an action is encountered. You can try giving a nonexistent filename but you will not get any error until you execute the next statement, which happens to be an *action* statement.

We have completed the whole cycle of initiating a Spark application (shell), creating an RDD, and consuming it. Since RDDs are recomputed every time an action is executed, `fileRDD` is not persisted in the memory or hard disk. This allows Spark to optimize the sequence of steps and execute intelligently. In fact, in the previous example, the optimizer would have just read one partition of the input file because `first()` does not require a complete file scan.

Recall that there are two ways to create an RDD: one way is to create a pointer to a data source and the other is to parallelize an existing collection. The previous examples covered one way, by loading a file from a storage system. We will now see the second way, which is parallelizing an existing collection. RDD creation by passing in-memory collections is simple but may not work very well for large collections, because the input collection should fit completely in the driver node's memory.

The following example creates an RDD by passing a Python/Scala list with the `parallelize` function:

Python:

```
// Pass a Python collection to create an RDD
>>> numRDD = sc.parallelize([1,2,3,4],2)
>>> type(numRDD)
<class 'pyspark.rdd.RDD'>
>>> numRDD
ParallelCollectionRDD[1] at parallelize at PythonRDD.scala:396
>>> numRDD.first()
1
>>> numRDD.map(lambda(x) : x*x).collect()
[1,4,9,16]
>>> numRDD.map(lambda(x) : x * x).reduce(lambda a,b: a+b)
30
```

> **TIP**
>
> A lambda function is an unnamed function, typically used as function arguments to other functions. A Python lambda function can be a single expression only. If your logic requires multiple steps, create a separate function and use it in the lambda expression.

Scala:

```
// Pass a Scala collection to create an RDD
Scala> val numRDD = sc.parallelize(List(1,2,3,4),2)
numRDD: org.apache.spark.rdd.RDD[Int] = ParallelCollectionRDD[8] at
parallelize at <console>:21

Scala> numRDD
res15: org.apache.spark.rdd.RDD[Int] = ParallelCollectionRDD[8] at
parallelize at <console>:21

Scala> numRDD.first()
res16: Int = 1

Scala> numRDD.map(x => x*x).collect()
res2: Array[Int] = Array(1, 4, 9, 16)

Scala> numRDD.map(x => x * x).reduce(_+_)
res20: Int = 30
```

As we saw in the previous example, we were able to pass a Scala/Python collection to create an RDD and we also had the liberty to specify the number of partitions to cut those collections into. Spark runs one task for each partition of the cluster, so it has to be carefully decided to optimize the computation effort. Though Spark sets the number of partitions automatically based on the cluster, we have the liberty to set it manually by passing it as a second argument to the `parallelize` function (for example, `sc.parallelize(data, 3)`). The following is a diagrammatic representation of an RDD which is created with a dataset with, say, 14 records (or tuples) and is partitioned into 3, distributed across 3 nodes:

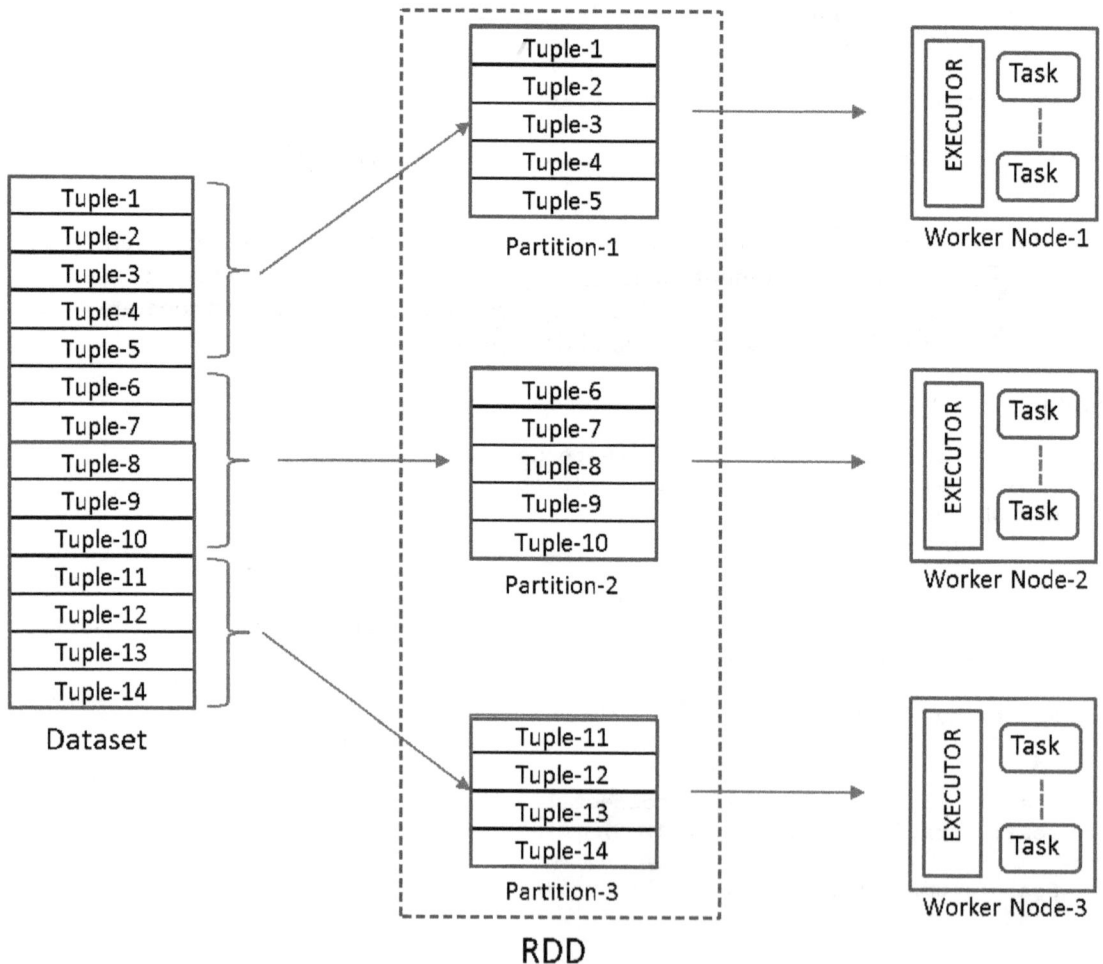

Writing a Spark program usually consists of transformations and actions. Transformations are lazy operations that define how to build an RDD. Most of the transformations accept a single function argument. All these methods convert one data source to another. Every time you perform a transformation on any RDD, a new RDD will be generated, even if it is a small change as shown in the following diagram:

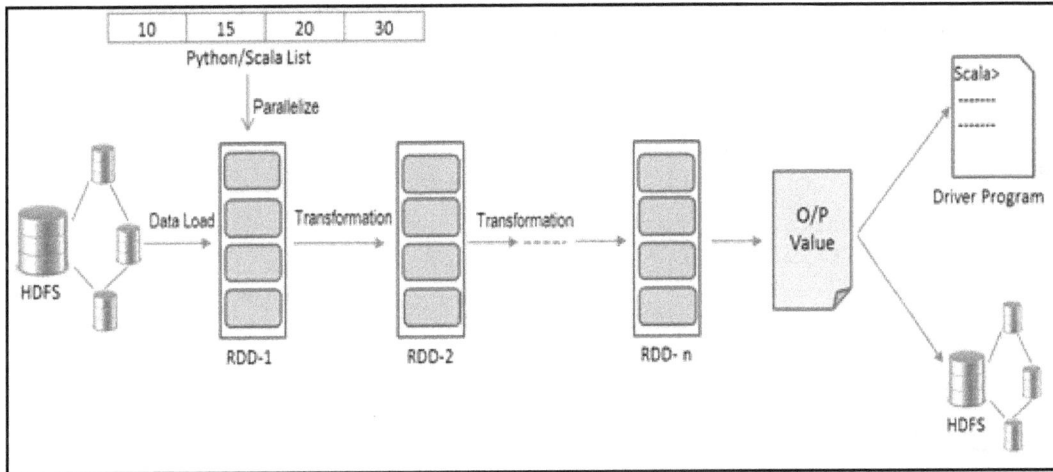

This is because the RDDs are immutable (read-only) abstractions by design. The resulting output from an action can either be written back to the storage system or it can be returned to the driver program for local computation if needed to produce the final output.

So far, we have seen some simple transformations that define RDDs and some actions to process them and generate some output. Let us go on a quick tour of some handy transformations and actions followed by transformations on pair RDDs.

Transformations on normal RDDs

The Spark API includes a rich set of transformation operators, and developers can compose them in arbitrary ways. Try out the following examples on the interactive shell to gain a better understanding of these operations.

The filter operation

The `filter` operation returns an RDD with only those elements that satisfy a `filter` condition, similar to the WHERE condition in SQL.

Python:

```
a = sc.parallelize([1,2,3,4,5,6], 3)
b = a.filter(lambda x: x % 3 == 0)
b.collect()
[3,6]
```

Scala:

```
val a = sc.parallelize(1 to 10, 3)
val b = a.filter(_ % 3 == 0)
b.collect

res0: Array[Int] = Array(3, 6, 9)
```

The distinct operation

The distinct ([numTasks]) operation returns an RDD with a new dataset after eliminating duplicates:

Python:

```
c = sc.parallelize(["John", "Jack", "Mike", "Jack"], 2)
c.distinct().collect()

['Mike', 'John', 'Jack']
```

Scala:

```
val c = sc.parallelize(List("John", "Jack", "Mike", "Jack"), 2)
c.distinct.collect
res6: Array[String] = Array(Mike, John, Jack)

val a = sc.parallelize(List(11,12,13,14,15,16,17,18,19,20))
a.distinct(2).partitions.length    //create 2 tasks on two partitions of
the same RDD for parallel execution

res16: Int = 2
```

The intersection operation

The intersection operation takes another dataset as input. It returns a dataset that contains common elements:

Python:

```
x = sc.parallelize([1,2,3,4,5,6,7,8,9,10])
y = sc.parallelize([5,6,7,8,9,10,11,12,13,14,15])
z = x.intersection(y)
z.collect()

[8, 9, 10, 5, 6, 7]
```

Scala:

```
val x = sc.parallelize(1 to 10)
val y = sc.parallelize(5 to 15)
val z = x.intersection(y)
z.collect

res74: Array[Int] = Array(8, 9, 5, 6, 10, 7)
```

The union operation

The union operation takes another dataset as input. It returns a dataset that contains elements of itself and the input dataset supplied to it. If there are common values in both sets, then they will appear as duplicate values in the resulting set after union:

Python:

```
a = sc.parallelize([3,4,5,6,7], 1)
b = sc.parallelize([7,8,9], 1)
c = a.union(b)
c.collect()

[3, 4, 5, 6, 7, 7, 8, 9]
```

Scala:

```
val a = sc.parallelize(3 to 7, 1)
val b = sc.parallelize(7 to 9, 1)
val c = a.union(b)       // An alternative way is (a ++ b).collect

res0: Array[Int] = Array(3, 4, 5, 6, 7, 7, 8, 9)
```

The map operation

The map operation returns a distributed dataset formed by executing an input function on each of the elements in the input dataset:

Python:

```
a = sc.parallelize(["animal", "human", "bird", "rat"], 3)
b = a.map(lambda x: len(x))
c = a.zip(b)
c.collect()

[('animal', 6), ('human', 5), ('bird', 4), ('rat', 3)]
```

Scala:

```
val a = sc.parallelize(List("animal", "human", "bird", "rat"), 3)
val b = a.map(_.length)
val c = a.zip(b)
c.collect

res0: Array[(String, Int)] = Array((animal,6), (human,5), (bird,4),
(rat,3))
```

The flatMap operation

The flatMap operation is similar to the map operation. While map returns one element per input element, flatMap returns a list of zero or more elements for each input element:

Python:

```
a = sc.parallelize([1,2,3,4,5], 4)
a.flatMap(lambda x: range(1,x+1)).collect()
    // Range(1,3) returns 1,2 (excludes the higher boundary element)
[1, 1, 2, 1, 2, 3, 1, 2, 3, 4, 1, 2, 3, 4, 5]

sc.parallelize([5, 10, 20], 2).flatMap(lambda x:[x, x, x]).collect()
[5, 5, 5, 10, 10, 10, 20, 20, 20]
```

Scala:

```
val a = sc.parallelize(1 to 5, 4)
a.flatMap(1 to _).collect
res47: Array[Int] = Array(1, 1, 2, 1, 2, 3, 1, 2, 3, 4, 1, 2, 3, 4, 5)

//One more example
sc.parallelize(List(5, 10, 20), 2).flatMap(x => List(x, x, x)).collect
res85: Array[Int] = Array(5, 5, 5, 10, 10, 10, 20, 20, 20)
```

The keys operation

The keys operation returns an RDD with the key of each tuple:

Python:

```
a = sc.parallelize(["black", "blue", "white", "green", "grey"], 2)
b = a.map(lambda x:(len(x), x))
c = b.keys()
c.collect()

[5, 4, 5, 5, 4]
```

Scala:

```
val a = sc.parallelize(List("black", "blue", "white", "green", "grey"), 2)
val b = a.map(x => (x.length, x))
b.keys.collect

res2: Array[Int] = Array(5, 4, 5, 5, 4)
```

The cartesian operation

The cartesian operation takes another dataset as argument and returns the Cartesian product of both datasets. This can be an expensive operation, returning a dataset of size m x n where m and n are the sizes of input datasets:

Python:

```
x = sc.parallelize([1,2,3])
y = sc.parallelize([10,11,12])
x.cartesian(y).collect()

[(1, 10), (1, 11), (1, 12), (2, 10), (2, 11), (2, 12), (3, 10), (3, 11),
(3, 12)]
```

Scala:

```
val x = sc.parallelize(List(1,2,3))
val y = sc.parallelize(List(10,11,12))
x.cartesian(y).collect

res0: Array[(Int, Int)] = Array((1,10), (1,11), (1,12), (2,10), (2,11),
(2,12), (3,10), (3,11), (3,12))
```

Transformations on pair RDDs

Some Spark operations are available only on RDDs of key value pairs. Note that most of these operations, except counting operations, usually involve shuffling, because the data related to a key may not always reside on a single partition.

The groupByKey operation

Similar to the SQL groupBy operation, this groups input data based on the key and you can use aggregateKey or reduceByKey to perform aggregate operations:

Python:

```
a = sc.parallelize(["black", "blue", "white", "green", "grey"], 2)
b = a.groupBy(lambda x: len(x)).collect()
sorted([(x,sorted(y)) for (x,y) in b])

[(4, ['blue', 'grey']), (5, ['black', 'white', 'green'])]
```

Scala:

```
val a = sc.parallelize(List("black", "blue", "white", "green", "grey"), 2)
val b = a.keyBy(_.length)
b.groupByKey.collect

res11: Array[(Int, Iterable[String])] = Array((4,CompactBuffer(blue,
grey)), (5,CompactBuffer(black, white, green)))
```

The join operation

The join operation takes another dataset as input. Both datasets should be of the key value pairs type. The resulting dataset is yet another key value dataset having keys and values from both datasets:

Python:

```
a = sc.parallelize(["blue", "green", "orange"], 3)
b = a.keyBy(lambda x: len(x))
c = sc.parallelize(["black", "white", "grey"], 3)
d = c.keyBy(lambda x: len(x))
b.join(d).collect()
[(4, ('blue', 'grey')), (5, ('green', 'black')), (5, ('green', 'white'))]

//leftOuterJoin
b.leftOuterJoin(d).collect()
[(6, ('orange', None)), (4, ('blue', 'grey')), (5, ('green', 'black')), (5,
('green', 'white'))]

//rightOuterJoin
b.rightOuterJoin(d).collect()
[(4, ('blue', 'grey')), (5, ('green', 'black')), (5, ('green', 'white'))]

//fullOuterJoin
b.fullOuterJoin(d).collect()
[(6, ('orange', None)), (4, ('blue', 'grey')), (5, ('green', 'black')), (5,
('green', 'white'))]
```

Scala:

```
val a = sc.parallelize(List("blue", "green", "orange"), 3)
val b = a.keyBy(_.length)
val c = sc.parallelize(List("black", "white", "grey"), 3)
val d = c.keyBy(_.length)
b.join(d).collect
res38: Array[(Int, (String, String))] = Array((4,(blue,grey)),
(5,(green,black)), (5,(green,white)))

//leftOuterJoin
b.leftOuterJoin(d).collect
res1: Array[(Int, (String, Option[String]))] = Array((6,(orange,None)),
(4,(blue,Some(grey))), (5,(green,Some(black))), (5,(green,Some(white))))

//rightOuterJoin
b.rightOuterJoin(d).collect
res1: Array[(Int, (Option[String], String))] = Array((4,(Some(blue),grey)),
(5,(Some(green),black)), (5,(Some(green),white)))

//fullOuterJoin
b.fullOuterJoin(d).collect
res1: Array[(Int, (Option[String], Option[String]))] =
Array((6,(Some(orange),None)), (4,(Some(blue),Some(grey))),
(5,(Some(green),Some(black))), (5,(Some(green),Some(white))))
```

The reduceByKey operation

The reduceByKey operation merges the values for each key using an associative reduce function. This will also perform the merging locally on each mapper before sending results to a reducer and producing hash-partitioned output:

Python:

```
a = sc.parallelize(["black", "blue", "white", "green", "grey"], 2)
b = a.map(lambda x: (len(x), x))
b.reduceByKey(lambda x,y: x + y).collect()
[(4, 'bluegrey'), (5, 'blackwhitegreen')]

a = sc.parallelize(["black", "blue", "white", "orange"], 2)
b = a.map(lambda x: (len(x), x))
b.reduceByKey(lambda x,y: x + y).collect()
[(4, 'blue'), (6, 'orange'), (5, 'blackwhite')]
```

Scala:

```
val a = sc.parallelize(List("black", "blue", "white", "green", "grey"), 2)
val b = a.map(x => (x.length, x))
b.reduceByKey(_ + _).collect
res86: Array[(Int, String)] = Array((4,bluegrey), (5,blackwhitegreen))

val a = sc.parallelize(List("black", "blue", "white", "orange"), 2)
val b = a.map(x => (x.length, x))
b.reduceByKey(_ + _).collect
res87: Array[(Int, String)] = Array((4,blue), (6,orange), (5,blackwhite))
```

The aggregate operation

The aggregrate operation returns an RDD with the keys of each tuple:

Python:

```
z = sc.parallelize([1,2,7,4,30,6], 2)
z.aggregate(0,(lambda x, y: max(x, y)),(lambda x, y: x + y))
37
z = sc.parallelize(["a","b","c","d"],2)
z.aggregate("",(lambda x, y: x + y),(lambda x, y: x + y))
'abcd'
z.aggregate("s",(lambda x, y: x + y),(lambda x, y: x + y))
'ssabsscds'
z = sc.parallelize(["12","234","345","56789"],2)
z.aggregate("",(lambda x, y: str(max(len(str(x)), len(str(y))))),(lambda x,
y: str(y) + str(x)))
'53'
z.aggregate("",(lambda x, y: str(min(len(str(x)), len(str(y))))),(lambda x,
y: str(y) + str(x)))
'11'
z = sc.parallelize(["12","234","345",""],2)
z.aggregate("",(lambda x, y: str(min(len(str(x)), len(str(y))))),(lambda x,
y: str(y) + str(x)))
'01'
```

Scala:

```scala
val z = sc.parallelize(List(1,2,7,4,30,6), 2)
z.aggregate(0)(math.max(_, _), _ + _)
res40: Int = 37

val z = sc.parallelize(List("a","b","c","d"),2)
z.aggregate("")(_ + _, _+_)
res115: String = abcd

z.aggregate("x")(_ + _, _+_)
res116: String = xxabxcd

val z = sc.parallelize(List("12","234","345","56789"),2)
z.aggregate("")((x,y) => math.max(x.length, y.length).toString, (x,y) => x
+ y)
res141: String = 53

z.aggregate("")((x,y) => math.min(x.length, y.length).toString, (x,y) => x
+ y)
res142: String = 11

val z = sc.parallelize(List("12","234","345",""),2)
z.aggregate("")((x,y) => math.min(x.length, y.length).toString, (x,y) => x
+ y)
res143: String = 01
```

> Note that in the preceding aggregate examples, the resultant strings (for example, abcd, xxabxcd, 53, 01) you get need not match the output shown here exactly. It depends on the order in which the individual tasks return their output.

Actions

Once an RDD has been created, the various transformations get executed only when an *action* is performed on it. The result of an action can either be data written back to the storage system or returned to the driver program that initiated this for further computation locally to produce the final result.

We have already covered some of the action functions in the previous examples of transformations. The following are a few more, but there are a lot more that you have to explore.

The collect() function

The collect() function returns all the results of an RDD operation as an array to the driver program. This is usually useful for operations that produce sufficiently small datasets. Ideally, the result should easily fit in the memory of the system that's hosting the driver program.

The count() function

This returns the number of elements in a dataset or the resulting output of an RDD operation.

The take(n) function

The take(n) function returns the first (n) elements of a dataset or the resulting output of an RDD operation.

The first() function

The first() function returns the first element of the dataset or the resulting output of an RDD operation. It works similarly to the take(1) function.

The takeSample() function

The takeSample(withReplacement, num, [seed]) function returns an array with a random sample of elements from a dataset. It has three arguments as follows:

- withReplacement/withoutReplacement: This indicates sampling with or without replacement (while taking multiple samples, it indicates whether to replace the old sample back to the set and then take a fresh sample or sample without replacing). For withReplacement, argument should be True and False otherwise.
- num: This indicates the number of elements in the sample.
- Seed: This is a random number generator seed (optional).

The countByKey() function

The `countByKey()` function is available only on RDDs of type key value. It returns a table of (`K`, `Int`) pairs with the count of each key.

The following are some example code snippets on Python and Scala:

Python:

```
>>> sc.parallelize([2, 3, 4]).count()
3

>>> sc.parallelize([2, 3, 4]).collect()
[2, 3, 4]

>>> sc.parallelize([2, 3, 4]).first()
2

>>> sc.parallelize([2, 3, 4]).take(2)
[2, 3]
```

Scala:

```
Scala> sc.parallelize(List(2, 3, 4)).count()
res0: Long = 3

Scala> sc.parallelize(List(2, 3, 4)).collect()
res1: Array[Int] = Array(2, 3, 4)

Scala> sc.parallelize(List(2, 3, 4)).first()
res2: Int = 2

Scala> sc.parallelize(List(2, 3, 4)).take(2)
res3: Array[Int] = Array(2, 3)
```

Summary

In this chapter, we touched upon the supported programming languages, their advantages and when to choose one language over the other. We discussed the design of the Spark engine along with its core components and their execution mechanism. We saw how Spark sends the data to be computed across many cluster nodes. We then discussed some RDD concepts. We learnt how to create RDDs and perform transformations and actions on them through both Scala and Python. We also discussed some advanced operations on RDDs.

In the next chapter, we will learn about DataFrames in detail and how they justify their suitability for all sorts of data science requirements.

References

Scala language:

- `http://www.scala-lang.org`

Apache Spark architecture:

- `http://lintool.github.io/SparkTutorial/slides/day1_context.pdf`

The Spark programming guide is the primary resource for concepts; refer to the language-specific API documents for a complete list of operations available:

- `http://spark.apache.org/docs/latest/programming-guide.html`

Resilient Distributed Datasets: A Fault-Tolerant Abstraction for In-Memory Cluster Computing by Matei Zaharia and others is the original source for RDD basics:

- https://people.csail.mit.edu/matei/papers/2012/nsdi_spark.pdf
- http://www.eecs.berkeley.edu/Pubs/TechRpts/2014/EECS-2014-12.pdf

Spark Summit, the official event series of Apache Spark, has a wealth of the latest information. Check out past events' presentations and videos:

- https://spark-summit.org/2016/

3
Introduction to DataFrames

To solve any real-world big data analytics problem, access to an efficient and scalable computing system is definitely mandatory. However, if the computing power is not accessible to the target users in a way that's easy and familiar to them, it will barely make any sense. Interactive data analysis gets easier with datasets that can be represented as named columns, which was not the case with plain RDDs. So, the need for a schema-based approach to represent data in a standardized way was the inspiration behind DataFrames.

The previous chapter outlined some design aspects of Spark. We learnt how Spark enabled distributed data processing on distributed collections of data (RDDs) through in-memory computation. It covered most of the points that revealed Spark as a fast, efficient, and scalable computing platform. In this chapter, we will see how Spark introduced the DataFrame API to make data scientists feel at home to carry out their usual data analysis activities with ease.

This topic is going to serve as a foundation for many upcoming chapters and we strongly recommend you to understand the concepts covered in here very well. As a prerequisite for this chapter, a basic understanding of SQL and Spark is needed. The topics covered in this chapter are as follows:

- Why DataFrames?
- Spark SQL
    - Catalyst optimizer
- DataFrame API
    - DataFrame basics
    - RDD versus DataFrame

- Creating DataFrames
    - From RDDs
    - From JSON
    - From JDBC sources
    - From other data sources
- Manipulating DataFrames

Why DataFrames?

Apart from massive, scalable computing capability, big data applications also need a mix of a few more features, such as support for a relational system for interactive data analysis (simple SQL style), heterogeneous data sources, and different storage formats along with different processing techniques.

Though Spark provided a functional programming API to manipulate distributed collections of data, it ended up with tuples (_1, _2, ...). Coding to operate on tuples was a little complicated and messy, and was slow at times. So, a standardized layer was needed, with the following characteristics:

- Named columns with a schema (higher-level abstraction than tuples) so that manipulating and tracking them would be easy
- Functionality to consolidate data from various data sources such as Hive, Parquet, SQL Server, PostgreSQL, JSON, and also Spark's native RDDs, and unify them to a common format
- Ability to take advantage of built-in schemas in special file formats such as Avro, CSV, JSON, and so on.
- Support for simple relational as well as complex logical operations
- Elimination of the need to define column objects based on domain-specific tasks for the ML algorithms to work on, and to serve as a common data layer for all algorithms in MLlib
- A language-independent entity that can be passed between functions of different languages

To address the above requirements, the DataFrame API was built as one more level of abstraction on top of Spark SQL.

Spark SQL

Executing SQL queries for basic business needs is very common and almost every business does it using some kind of database. So Spark SQL also supports the execution of SQL queries written using either a basic SQL syntax or HiveQL. Spark SQL can also be used to read data from an existing Hive installation. Apart from these plain SQL operations, Spark SQL also addresses some tough problems. Designing complex logic through relational queries was cumbersome and almost impossible at times. So, Spark SQL was designed to integrate the capabilities of relational processing and functional programming so that complex logics can be implemented, optimized, and scaled on a distributed computing setup. There are basically three ways to interact with Spark SQL, including SQL, the DataFrame API, and the Dataset API. The Dataset API is an experimental layer added in Spark 1.6 at the time of writing this book so we will limit our discussions to DataFrames only.

Spark SQL exposes DataFrames as a higher-level API and takes care of all the complexities involved and also performs all the background tasks. Through the declarative syntax, users can focus on what the program should accomplish and not bother about the control flow, which will be taken care of by the Catalyst optimizer, built inside Spark SQL.

The Catalyst optimizer

The Catalyst optimizer is the fulcrum of Spark SQL and DataFrame. It is built with the functional programming constructs of Scala and has the following features:

- Schema inference from various data formats:
    - Spark has built-in support for JSON schema inference. Users can just create a table out of any JSON file by registering it as a table and simply query it with SQL syntaxes.
    - RDDs that are Scala objects; the type information is extracted from Scala's type system, that is, **case classes**, if they contain case classes.
    - RDDs that are Python objects; the type information is extracted with a different approach. Since Python is not statically typed and follows a dynamic type system, the RDD can contain multiple types. So, Spark SQL samples the dataset and infers the schema using an algorithm similar to JSON schema inference.
    - In future, built-in support for CSV, XML, and other formats will be provided.

- Built-in support for a wide range of data sources and query federation for efficient data import:
    - Spark has a built-in mechanism to fetch data from some external data sources (for example, JSON, JDBC, Parquet, MySQL, Hive, PostgreSQL, HDFS, S3, and so on) through query federation. It can accurately model the sourced data by using out-of-the-box SQL data types and other complex data types such as Struct, Union, Array, and so on.
    - It also allows users to source data using the **Data Source API** from the data sources that are not supported out of the box (for example, CSV, Avro HBase, Cassandra, and so on).
    - Spark uses predicate pushdown (pushes filtering or aggregation into external storage systems) to optimize data sourcing from external systems and combine them to form the data pipeline.
- Control and optimization of code generation:
    - Optimization actually happens very late in the entire execution pipeline.
    - Catalyst is designed to optimize all phases of query execution: analysis, logical optimization, physical planning, and code generation to compile parts of queries to Java bytecode.

The DataFrame API

Excel spreadsheets like data representation, or output from a database projection (select statement's output), the data representation closest to human being had always been a set of uniform columns with multiple rows. Such a two-dimensional data structure that usually has labelled rows and columns is called a DataFrame in some realms, such as R DataFrames and Python's Pandas DataFrames. In a DataFrame, typically, a single column has the same kind of data, and rows describe data points about that column that mean something together, be it data about a person, a purchase, or a baseball game outcome. You can think of it as a matrix, or a spreadsheet, or an RDBMS table.

DataFrames in R and Pandas are very handy in slicing, reshaping, and analyzing data - essential operations in any data wrangling and data analysis workflow. This inspired the development of a similar concept on Spark, called DataFrames.

DataFrame basics

The DataFrame API was first introduced in Spark 1.3.0, released in March 2015. It is a programming abstraction of Spark SQL for structured and semi-structured data processing. It enables developers to harness the power of the DataFrames, data structure through Python, Java, Scala, and R. Like RDDs, a Spark DataFrame is a distributed collection of records organized into named columns, similar to an RDBMS table or the DataFrames of R or Pandas. Unlike RDDs, however, they keep track of schemas and facilitate relational operations as well as procedural operations such as `map`. Internally, DataFrames store data in columnar format, but construct row objects on the fly when required by the procedural functions.

The DataFrame API brings two features with it:

- Built-in support for a variety of data formats such as Parquet, Hive, and JSON. Nonetheless, through Spark SQL's external data sources API, DataFrames can access a wide array of third-party data sources such as databases and NoSQL stores.
- A more robust and feature-rich DSL with functions designed for common tasks such as:
  - Metadata
  - Sampling
  - Relational data processing – project, filter, aggregation, join
  - UDFs

The DataFrame API builds on the Spark SQL query optimizer to automatically execute code efficiently on a cluster of machines.

RDDs versus DataFrames

RDDs and DataFrames are two different types of fault-tolerant and distributed data abstractions provided by Spark. They are similar to an extent but greatly differ when it comes to implementation. Developers need to have a clear understanding of their differences to be able to match their requirements to the right abstraction.

Similarities

The following are the similarities between RDDs and DataFrames:

- Both are fault-tolerant, partitioned data abstractions in Spark
- Both can handle disparate data sources
- Both are lazily evaluated (execution happens when an output operation is performed on them), thereby having the ability to take the most optimized execution plan
- Both APIs are available in all four languages: Scala, Python, Java, and R

Differences

The following are the differences between RDDs and DataFrames:

- DataFrames are a higher-level abstraction than RDDs.
- The definition of RDD implies defining a **Directed Acyclic Graph (DAG)** whereas defining a DataFrame leads to the creation of an **Abstract Syntax Tree (AST)**. An AST will be utilized and optimized by the Spark SQL catalyst engine.
- RDD is a general data structure abstraction whereas a DataFrame is a specialized data structure to deal with two-dimensional, table-like data.

The DataFrame API is actually SchemaRDD-renamed. The renaming was to signify that it is no longer inherited from RDD and to comfort data scientists with a familiar name and concept.

Creating DataFrames

Spark DataFrame creation is similar to RDD creation. To get access to the DataFrame API, you need SQLContext or HiveContext as an entry point. In this section, we are going to demonstrate how to create DataFrames from various data sources, starting from basic code examples with in-memory collections:

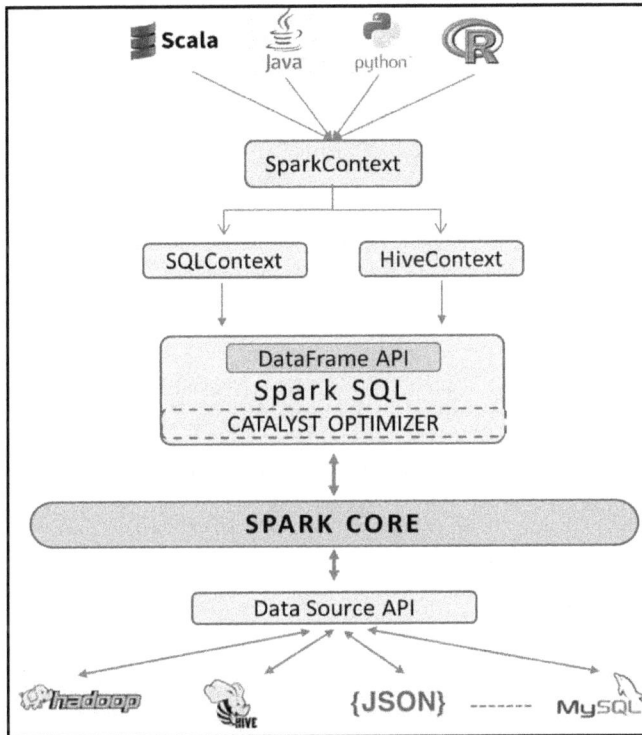

Creating DataFrames from RDDs

The following code creates an RDD from a list of colors followed by a collection of tuples containing the color name and its length. It creates a DataFrame using the `toDF` method to convert the RDD into a DataFrame. The `toDF` method takes a list of column labels as an optional argument:

Python:

```
    //Create a list of colours
>>> colors = ['white','green','yellow','red','brown','pink']
//Distribute a local collection to form an RDD
//Apply map function on that RDD to get another RDD containing colour,
length tuples
>>> color_df = sc.parallelize(colors)
        .map(lambda x:(x,len(x))).toDF(["color","length"])

>>> color_df
DataFrame[color: string, length: bigint]

>>> color_df.dtypes        //Note the implicit type inference
[('color', 'string'), ('length', 'bigint')]

>>> color_df.show()  //Final output as expected. Order need not be the same
as shown
+------+------+
| color|length|
+------+------+
| white|     5|
| green|     5|
|yellow|     6|
|   red|     3|
| brown|     5|
|  pink|     4|
+------+------+
```

Scala:

```
//Create a list of colours
Scala> val colors = List("white","green","yellow","red","brown","pink")
//Distribute a local collection to form an RDD
//Apply map function on that RDD to get another RDD containing colour,
length tuples
Scala> val color_df = sc.parallelize(colors)
        .map(x => (x,x.length)).toDF("color","length")

Scala> color_df
```

```
res0: org.apache.spark.sql.DataFrame = [color: string, length: int]

Scala> color_df.dtypes   //Note the implicit type inference
res1: Array[(String, String)] = Array((color,StringType),
(length,IntegerType))

Scala> color_df.show()//Final output as expected. Order need not be the
same as shown
+------+------+
| color|length|
+------+------+
| white|     5|
| green|     5|
|yellow|     6|
|   red|     3|
| brown|     5|
|  pink|     4|
+------+------+
```

As you can see from the preceding example, the creation of a DataFrame is similar to that of an RDD from a developer's perspective. We created an RDD here and then transformed that to tuples which are then sent to the toDF method. Note that toDF takes a list of tuples instead of scalar elements. You need to pass tuples even to create single-column DataFrames. Each tuple is akin to a row. You can optionally label the columns; otherwise, Spark creates obscure names such as _1, _2. Type inference of the columns happens implicitly.

If you already have the data as RDDs, Spark SQL supports two different methods for converting existing RDDs into DataFrames:

- The first method uses reflection to infer the schema of an RDD that contains specific types of object, which means you are aware of the schema.
- The second method is through a programmatic interface that lets you construct a schema and then apply it to an existing RDD. While this method is more verbose, it allows you to construct DataFrames when the column types are not known until runtime.

Creating DataFrames from JSON

JavaScript Object Notation, or JSON, is a language-independent, self-describing, lightweight data-exchange format. JSON has become a popular data exchange format and has become ubiquitous. In addition to JavaScript and RESTful interfaces, databases such as MySQL have accepted JSON as a data type and MongoDB stores all data as JSON documents in binary form. Conversion of data to and from JSON is essential for any modern data analysis workflow. The Spark DataFrame API lets developers convert JSON objects into DataFrames and vice versa. Let's have a close look at the following examples for a better understanding:

Python:

```
//Pass the source json data file path
>>> df = sqlContext.read.json("./authors.json")
>>> df.show() //json parsed; Column names and data    types inferred
implicitly
+----------+---------+
|first_name|last_name|
+----------+---------+
|      Mark|    Twain|
|   Charles|  Dickens|
|    Thomas|    Hardy|
+----------+---------+
```

Scala:

```
//Pass the source json data file path
Scala> val df = sqlContext.read.json("./authors.json")
Scala> df.show()  //json parsed; Column names and    data types inferred
implicitly
+----------+---------+
|first_name|last_name|
+----------+---------+
|      Mark|    Twain|
|   Charles|  Dickens|
|    Thomas|    Hardy|
+----------+---------+
```

Spark infers schemas automatically from the keys and creates a DataFrame accordingly.

Creating DataFrames from databases using JDBC

Spark allows developers to create DataFrames from other databases using JDBC, provided you ensure that the JDBC driver for the intended database is accessible. A JDBC driver is a software component that allows a Java application to interact with a database. Different databases require different drivers. Usually, database providers such as MySQL supply these driver components to access their databases. You have to ensure that you have the right driver for the database you want to work with.

The following example assumes that you already have a MySQL database running at the given URL, a table called people in the database called test with some data in it, and valid credentials to log in. There is an additional step of relaunching the REPL shell with the appropriate JAR file:

> If you do not already have the JAR file in your system, download it from the MySQL site at the following link:
> https://dev.mysql.com/downloads/connector/j/.

Python:

```
//Launch shell with driver-class-path as a command line argument
pyspark --driver-class-path /usr/share/   java/mysql-connector-java.jar
   //Pass the connection parameters
>>> peopleDF = sqlContext.read.format('jdbc').options(
                    url = 'jdbc:mysql://localhost',
                    dbtable = 'test.people',
                    user = 'root',
                    password = 'mysql').load()
   //Retrieve table data as a DataFrame
>>> peopleDF.show()
+----------+---------+------+----------+----------+---------+
|first_name|last_name|gender|       dob|occupation|person_id|
+----------+---------+------+----------+----------+---------+
|    Thomas|    Hardy|     M|1840-06-02|    Writer|      101|
|     Emily|   Bronte|     F|1818-07-30|    Writer|      102|
| Charlotte|   Bronte|     F|1816-04-21|    Writer|      103|
|   Charles|  Dickens|     M|1812-02-07|    Writer|      104|
+----------+---------+------+----------+----------+---------+
```

Scala:

```
//Launch shell with driver-class-path as a command line argument
spark-shell --driver-class-path /usr/share/   java/mysql-connector-java.jar
   //Pass the connection parameters
scala> val peopleDF = sqlContext.read.format("jdbc").options(
          Map("url" -> "jdbc:mysql://localhost",
              "dbtable" -> "test.people",
              "user" -> "root",
              "password" -> "mysql")).load()
peopleDF: org.apache.spark.sql.DataFrame = [first_name: string, last_name:
string, gender: string, dob: date, occupation: string, person_id: int]
//Retrieve table data as a DataFrame
scala> peopleDF.show()
+----------+---------+------+----------+----------+---------+
|first_name|last_name|gender|       dob|occupation|person_id|
+----------+---------+------+----------+----------+---------+
|    Thomas|    Hardy|     M|1840-06-02|    Writer|      101|
|     Emily|   Bronte|     F|1818-07-30|    Writer|      102|
| Charlotte|   Bronte|     F|1816-04-21|    Writer|      103|
|   Charles|  Dickens|     M|1812-02-07|    Writer|      104|
+----------+---------+------+----------+----------+---------+
```

Creating DataFrames from Apache Parquet

Apache Parquet is an efficient, compressed columnar data representation available to any project in the Hadoop ecosystem. Columnar data representations store data by column, as opposed to the traditional approach of storing data row by row. Use cases that require frequent querying of two to three columns from several columns benefit greatly from such an arrangement because columns are stored contiguously on the disk and you do not have to read unwanted columns in row-oriented storage. Another advantage is in compression. Data in a single column belongs to a single type. The values tend to be similar, and sometimes identical. These qualities greatly enhance compression and encoding efficiency. Parquet allows compression schemes to be specified on a per-column level and allows adding more encodings as they are invented and implemented.

Apache Spark provides support for both reading and writing Parquet files that automatically preserves the schema of the original data. The following example writes the people data loaded into a DataFrame in the previous example into Parquet format and then re-reads it into an RDD:

Python:

```
//Write DataFrame contents into Parquet format
>>> peopleDF.write.parquet('writers.parquet')
//Read Parquet data into another DataFrame
>>> writersDF = sqlContext.read.parquet('writers.parquet')
writersDF: org.apache.spark.sql.DataFrame = [first_name:    string,
last_name: string, gender: string, dob:    date, occupation: string,
person_id: int]
```

Scala:

```
//Write DataFrame contents into Parquet format
scala> peopleDF.write.parquet("writers.parquet")
//Read Parquet data into another DataFrame
scala> val writersDF = sqlContext.read.parquet("writers.parquet")
writersDF: org.apache.spark.sql.DataFrame = [first_name:    string,
last_name: string, gender: string, dob:    date, occupation: string,
person_id: int]
```

Creating DataFrames from other data sources

Spark provides built-in support for multiple data sources such as JSON, JDBC, HDFS, Parquet, MYSQL, Amazon S3, and so on. In addition, it provides a Data Source API that provides a pluggable mechanism for accessing structured data through Spark SQL. There are several libraries built on top of this pluggable component, for example, CSV, Avro, Cassandra, and MongoDB, to name a few. These libraries are not part of the Spark code base. These are built for individual data sources and hosted on a community site, Spark packages.

DataFrame operations

In the previous section of this chapter, we learnt many different ways of creating DataFrames. In this section, we will focus on various operations that can be performed on DataFrames. Developers chain multiple operations to filter, transform, aggregate, and sort data in the DataFrames. The underlying Catalyst optimizer ensures efficient execution of these operations. These functions you find here are similar to those you commonly find in SQL operations on tables:

Python:

```
//Create a local collection of colors first
>>> colors = ['white','green','yellow','red','brown','pink']
//Distribute the local collection to form an RDD
//Apply map function on that RDD to get another RDD containing colour,
length tuples and convert that RDD to a DataFrame
>>> color_df = sc.parallelize(colors)
        .map(lambda x:(x,len(x))).toDF(['color','length'])
//Check the object type
>>> color_df
DataFrame[color: string, length: bigint]
//Check the schema
>>> color_df.dtypes
[('color', 'string'), ('length', 'bigint')]

//Check row count
>>> color_df.count()
6
//Look at the table contents. You can limit displayed rows by passing
parameter to show
color_df.show()
+------+------+
| color|length|
+------+------+
| white|     5|
| green|     5|
|yellow|     6|
|   red|     3|
| brown|     5|
|  pink|     4|
+------+------+

//List out column names
>>> color_df.columns
[u'color', u'length']

//Drop a column. The source DataFrame color_df remains the same. //Spark
```

returns a new DataFrame which is being passed to show
```
>>> color_df.drop('length').show()
+------+
| color|
+------+
| white|
| green|
|yellow|
|   red|
| brown|
|  pink|
+------+
//Convert to JSON format
>>> color_df.toJSON().first()
u'{"color":"white","length":5}'
//filter operation is similar to WHERE clause in SQL
//You specify conditions to select only desired columns and rows
//Output of filter operation is another DataFrame object that is usually
passed on to some more operations
//The following example selects the colors having a length of four or five
only and label the column as "mid_length"
filter
------
>>> color_df.filter(color_df.length.between(4,5))
      .select(color_df.color.alias("mid_length")).show()
+----------+
|mid_length|
+----------+
|     white|
|     green|
|     brown|
|      pink|
+----------+

//This example uses multiple filter criteria
>>> color_df.filter(color_df.length > 4)
     .filter(color_df[0]!="white").show()
+------+------+
| color|length|
+------+------+
| green|     5|
|yellow|     6|
| brown|     5|
+------+------+

//Sort the data on one or more columns
sort
----
```

```
//A simple single column sorting in default (ascending) order
>>> color_df.sort("color").show()
+------+------+
| color|length|
+------+------+
| brown|     5|
| green|     5|
|  pink|     4|
|   red|     3|
| white|     5|
|yellow|     6|
+------+------+
//First filter colors of length more than 4 and then sort on multiple
columns
//The Filtered rows are sorted first on the column length in default
ascending order. Rows with same length are sorted on color in descending
order
>>> color_df.filter(color_df['length']>=4).sort("length",
'color',ascending=False).show()
+------+------+
| color|length|
+------+------+
|yellow|     6|
| white|     5|
| green|     5|
| brown|     5|
|  pink|     4|
+------+------+

//You can use orderBy instead, which is an alias to sort
>>> color_df.orderBy('length','color').take(4)
[Row(color=u'red', length=3), Row(color=u'pink', length=4),
Row(color=u'brown', length=5), Row(color=u'green', length=5)]

//Alternative syntax, for single or multiple columns.
>>> color_df.sort(color_df.length.desc(),   color_df.color.asc()).show()
+------+------+
| color|length|
+------+------+
|yellow|     6|
| brown|     5|
| green|     5|
| white|     5|
|  pink|     4|
|   red|     3|
+------+------+
//All the examples until now have been acting on one row at a time,
filtering or transforming or reordering.
```

```
//The following example deals with regrouping the data
//These operations require "wide dependency" and often involve shuffling.
groupBy
-------
>>> color_df.groupBy('length').count().show()
+------+-----+
|length|count|
+------+-----+
|     3|    1|
|     4|    1|
|     5|    3|
|     6|    1|
+------+-----+
//Data often contains missing information or null values. We may want to
drop such rows or replace with some filler information. dropna is provided
for dropping such rows
//The following json file has names of famous authors. Firstname data is
missing in one row.
dropna
------
>>> df1 = sqlContext.read.json('./authors_missing.json')
>>> df1.show()
+----------+---------+
|first_name|last_name|
+----------+---------+
|      Mark|    Twain|
|   Charles|  Dickens|
|      null|    Hardy|
+----------+---------+

//Let us drop the row with incomplete information
>>> df2 = df1.dropna()
>>> df2.show()  //Unwanted row is dropped
+----------+---------+
|first_name|last_name|
+----------+---------+
|      Mark|    Twain|
|   Charles|  Dickens|
+----------+---------+
```

Scala:

```
//Create a local collection of colors first
Scala> val colors = List("white","green","yellow","red","brown","pink")
//Distribute a local collection to form an RDD
//Apply map function on that RDD to get another RDD containing color,
length tuples and convert that RDD to a DataFrame
Scala> val color_df = sc.parallelize(colors)
```

```
            .map(x => (x,x.length)).toDF("color","length")
//Check the object type
Scala> color_df
res0: org.apache.spark.sql.DataFrame = [color: string, length: int]
//Check the schema
Scala> color_df.dtypes
res1: Array[(String, String)] = Array((color,StringType),
(length,IntegerType))
//Check row count
Scala> color_df.count()
res4: Long = 6
//Look at the table contents. You can limit displayed rows by passing
parameter to show
color_df.show()
+------+------+
| color|length|
+------+------+
| white|     5|
| green|     5|
|yellow|     6|
|   red|     3|
| brown|     5|
|  pink|     4|
+------+------+
//List out column names
Scala> color_df.columns
res5: Array[String] = Array(color, length)
//Drop a column. The source DataFrame color_df remains the same.
//Spark returns a new DataFrame which is being passed to show
Scala> color_df.drop("length").show()
+------+
| color|
+------+
| white|
| green|
|yellow|
|   red|
| brown|
|  pink|
+------+
//Convert to JSON format
color_df.toJSON.first()
res9: String = {"color":"white","length":5}


//filter operation is similar to WHERE clause in SQL
//You specify conditions to select only desired columns and rows
//Output of filter operation is another DataFrame object that is usually
```

passed on to some more operations
```
//The following example selects the colors having a length of four or five
only and label the column as "mid_length"
filter
------
Scala> color_df.filter(color_df("length").between(4,5))
        .select(color_df("color").alias("mid_length")).show()
+----------+
|mid_length|
+----------+
|     white|
|     green|
|     brown|
|      pink|
+----------+


//This example uses multiple filter criteria. Notice the not equal to
operator having double equal to symbols
Scala> color_df.filter(color_df("length") > 4).filter(color_df(
"color")!=="white").show()
+------+------+
| color|length|
+------+------+
| green|     5|
|yellow|     6|
| brown|     5|
+------+------+
//Sort the data on one or more columns
sort
----
//A simple single column sorting in default (ascending) order
Scala> color_df..sort("color").show()
+------+------+
| color|length|
+------+------+
| brown|     5|
| green|     5|
|  pink|     4|
|   red|     3|
| white|     5|
|yellow|     6|
+------+------+
//First filter colors of length more than 4 and then sort on multiple
columns
//The filtered rows are sorted first on the column length in default
ascending order. Rows with same length are sorted on color in descending
order
```

```
Scala> color_df.filter(color_df("length")>=4).sort($"length",
$"color".desc).show()
+------+------+
| color|length|
+------+------+
|  pink|     4|
| white|     5|
| green|     5|
| brown|     5|
|yellow|     6|
+------+------+
//You can use orderBy instead, which is an alias to sort.
scala> color_df.orderBy("length","color").take(4)
res19: Array[org.apache.spark.sql.Row] = Array([red,3], [pink,4],
[brown,5], [green,5])
//Alternative syntax, for single or multiple columns
scala> color_df.sort(color_df("length").desc, color_df("color").asc).show()
+------+------+
| color|length|
+------+------+
|yellow|     6|
| brown|     5|
| green|     5|
| white|     5|
|  pink|     4|
|   red|     3|
+------+------+
//All the examples until now have been acting on one row at a time,
filtering or transforming or reordering.
//The following example deals with regrouping the data.
//These operations require "wide dependency" and often involve shuffling.
groupBy
-------
Scala> color_df.groupBy("length").count().show()
+------+-----+
|length|count|
+------+-----+
|     3|    1|
|     4|    1|
|     5|    3|
|     6|    1|
+------+-----+
//Data often contains missing information or null values.
//The following json file has names of famous authors. Firstname data is
missing in one row.
dropna
------
Scala> val df1 = sqlContext.read.json("./authors_missing.json")
```

```
Scala> df1.show()
+----------+---------+
|first_name|last_name|
+----------+---------+
|      Mark|    Twain|
|   Charles|  Dickens|
|      null|    Hardy|
+----------+---------+
//Let us drop the row with incomplete information
Scala> val df2 = df1.na.drop()
Scala> df2.show()  //Unwanted row is dropped
+----------+---------+
|first_name|last_name|
+----------+---------+
|      Mark|    Twain|
|   Charles|  Dickens|
+----------+---------+
```

Under the hood

You already know by now that the DataFrame API is empowered by Spark SQL and that the Spark SQL's Catalyst optimizer plays a crucial role in optimizing the performance.

Though the query is executed lazily, it uses the *catalog* component of Catalyst to identify whether the column names used in the program or expressions exist in the table being used and the data types are proper, and also takes many other such precautionary actions. The advantage to this approach is that, instead of waiting till program execution, an error pops up as soon as the user types an invalid expression.

Summary

In this chapter, we explained the motivation behind the development of the DataFrame API in Spark and how development in Spark has become easier than ever. We briefly covered the design aspect of the DataFrame API and how it is built on top of Spark SQL. We discussed various ways of creating DataFrames from different data sources such as RDDs, JSON, Parquet, and JDBC. At the end of this chapter, we just gave you a heads-up on how to perform operations on DataFrames. We will discuss DataFrame operations in the context of data science and machine learning in more detail in the upcoming chapters.

In the next chapter, we will learn how Spark supports unified data access and discuss on Dataset and Structured Stream components in details.

References

DataFrame reference on the SQL programming guide of Apache Spark official resource:

- `https://spark.apache.org/docs/latest/sql-programming-guide.html#crea ting-dataframes`

Databricks: Introducing DataFrames in Apache Spark for Large Scale Data Science:

- https://databricks.com/blog/2015/02/17/introducing-dataframes-in-spark-for-large -scale-data-science.html

Databricks: From Pandas to Apache Spark's DataFrame:

- https://databricks.com/blog/2015/08/12/from-pandas-to-apache-sparks-dataframe. html

API reference guide on Scala for Spark DataFrames:

- `https://spark.apache.org/docs/latest/api/scala/index.html#org.apache .spark.sql.DataFrame`

A Cloudera blogpost on Parquet – an efficient general-purpose columnar file format for Apache Hadoop:

- http://blog.cloudera.com/blog/2013/03/introducing-parquet-columnar-storage-for -apache-hadoop/

4
Unified Data Access

Data integration from disparate data sources had always been a daunting feat. The three V's of big data and ever-shrinking processing time frames have made the task even more challenging. Delivering a clear view of well-curated data in near real time is extremely important for business. However, real-time curated data along with the ability to perform different operations such as ETL, ad hoc querying, and machine learning in a unified fashion is what is emerging as a key business differentiator.

Apache Spark was created to offer a single general-purpose engine that can process data from a variety of data sources and support large-scale data processing for various different operations. Spark enables developers to combine SQL, Streaming, graphs, and machine learning algorithms in a single workflow!

In the previous chapters, we discussed **Resilient Distributed Datasets** (**RDDs**) as well as DataFrames. In `Chapter 3`, *Introduction to DataFrames*, we introduced Spark SQL and the Catalyst optimizer. This chapter builds on this foundation and delves deeper into these topics to help you realize the real essence of unified data access. We'll introduce new constructs such as Datasets and Structured Streaming. Specifically, we'll discuss the following:

- Data abstractions in Apache Spark
- Datasets
    - Working with Datasets
    - Dataset API limitations
- Spark SQL
    - SQL operations
    - Under the hood

- Structured Streaming
    - Spark streaming programming model
    - Under the hood
    - Comparison with other streaming engines
- Continuous applications
- Summary

Data abstractions in Apache Spark

The MapReduce framework and its popular open source implementation Hadoop enjoyed widespread adoption in the past decade. However, iterative algorithms and interactive ad-hoc querying are not well supported. Any data sharing between jobs or stages within an algorithm is always through disk writes and reads as against in-memory data sharing. So, the logical next step would be to have a mechanism that facilitates reuse of intermediate results across multiple jobs. RDD is a general-purpose data abstraction that was developed to address this requirement.

RDD is the core abstraction in Apache Spark. It is an immutable, fault-tolerant distributed collection of statically typed objects that are usually stored in-memory. RDD API offer simple operations such as map, reduce, and filter that can be composed in arbitrary ways.

DataFrame abstraction is built on top of RDD and it adds "named" columns. So, a Spark DataFrame has rows of named columns similar to relational database tables and DataFrames in R and Python (pandas). This familiar higher level abstraction makes the development effort much easier because it lets you perceive data like an SQL table or an Excel file. Moreover, the Catalyst optimizer, under the hood, compiles the operations and generates JVM bytecode for efficient execution. However, the named columns approach gives rise to a new problem. Static type information is no longer available to the compiler, and hence we lose the advantage of compile-time type safety.

Dataset API was introduced to combine the best traits from both RDDs and DataFrames plus some more features of its own. Datasets provide row and column data abstraction similar to the DataFrames, but with a structure defined on top of them. This structure may be defined by a case class in Scala or a class in Java. They provide type safety and lambda functions like RDDs. So, they support both typed methods such as `map` and `groupByKey` as well as untyped methods such as `select` and `groupBy`. In addition to the Catalyst optimizer, Datasets leverage in-memory encoding provided by the Tungsten execution engine, which improves performance even further.

The data abstractions introduced so far form the core abstractions. There are some more specialized data abstractions that work on top of these abstractions. Streaming APIs are introduced to process real-time streaming data from various sources such as Flume and Kafka. These APIs work together to provide data engineers a unified, continuous DataFrame abstraction that can be used for interactive and batch queries. Another example of specialized data abstraction is a GraphFrame. This enables developers to analyze social networks and any other graphs alongside Excel-like two-dimensional data.

Now with the basics of the available data abstractions in mind, let's understand what we exactly mean by a unified data access platform:

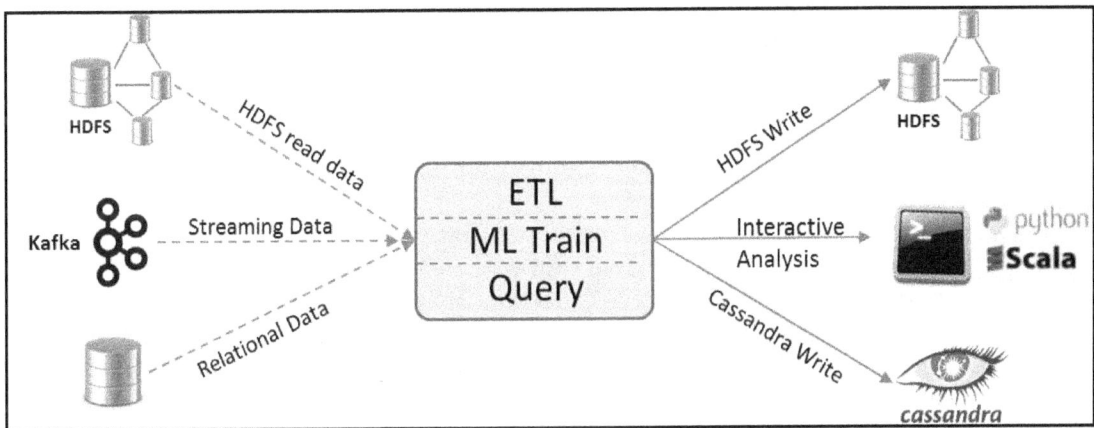

The intention behind this unified platform is that it not only lets you combine the static and streaming data together, but also allows various different kinds of operations on the data in a unified way! From the developer's perspective, a Dataset is the core abstraction to work with, and Spark SQL is the main interface to the Spark functionality. A two-dimensional data structure coupled with a SQL declarative programming interface had been a familiar way of dealing with data, thereby shortening the learning curve for the data engineers. So, understanding the unified platform translates to understanding Datasets and Spark SQL.

Datasets

Apache Spark **Datasets** are an extension of the DataFrame API that provide a type-safe object-oriented programming interface. This API was first introduced in the 1.6 release. Spark 2.0 version brought out unification of DataFrame and Dataset APIs. DataFrame becomes a generic, untyped Dataset; or a Dataset is a DataFrame with an added structure. The term "structure" in this context refers to a pattern or an organization of underlying data, more like a table schema in RDBMS parlance. The structure imposes a limit on what can be expressed or contained in the underlying data. This in turn enables better optimizations in memory organization as well as physical execution. Compile-time type checking leads to catching errors earlier than during runtime. For example, a type mismatch in a SQL comparison does not get caught until runtime, whereas it would be caught during compile time itself if it were expressed as a sequence of operations on Datasets. However, the inherent dynamic nature of Python and R implies that there is no compile-time type safety, and hence the concept Datasets does not apply to those languages. The unification of Datasets and DataFrames applies to Scala and Java API only.

At the core of Dataset abstraction are the **encoders**. These encoders translate between JVM objects and Spark's internal Tungsten binary format. This internal representation bypasses JVM's memory management and garbage collection. Spark has its own C-style memory access that is specifically written to address the kind of workflows it supports. The resultant internal representations take less memory and have efficient memory management. Compact memory representation leads to reduced network load during shuffle operations. The encoders generate compact byte code that directly operates on serialized objects without de-serializing, thereby enhancing performance. Knowing the schema early on results in a more optimal layout in memory when caching Datasets.

Working with Datasets

In this section, we will create Datasets and perform transformations and actions, much like DataFrames and RDDs.

Example 1-creating a Dataset from a simple collection:

Scala:

```
//Create a Dataset from a simple collection
scala> val ds1 = List.range(1,5).toDS()
ds1: org.apache.spark.sql.Dataset[Int] = [value: int]
//Perform an action
scala> ds1.collect()
res3: Array[Int] = Array(1, 2, 3, 4)

//Create from an RDD
scala> val colors = List("red","orange","blue","green","yellow")
scala> val color_ds = sc.parallelize(colors).map(x =>
    (x,x.length)).toDS()
//Add a case class
case class Color(var color: String, var len: Int)
val color_ds = sc.parallelize(colors).map(x =>
    Color(x,x.length)).toDS()
```

As shown in the last example in the preceding code, `case class` adds structure information. Spark uses this structure to create the best data layout and encoding. The following code shows us the structure and the plan for execution:

Scala:

```
//Examine the structure
scala> color_ds.dtypes
res26: Array[(String, String)] = Array((color,StringType),
(len,IntegerType))
scala> color_ds.schema
res25: org.apache.spark.sql.types.StructType =
StructType(StructField(color,StringType,true),
StructField(len,IntegerType,false))
//Examine the execution plan
scala> color_ds.explain()
== Physical Plan ==
Scan ExistingRDD[color#57,len#58]
```

The preceding example shows the structure and the implementation physical plan as anticipated. If you want to get a more detailed execution plan, you have to pass explain (true), which prints extended information, including the logical plan as well.

We have examined Dataset creation from simple collections and RDDs. We have already discussed that DataFrames are just untyped Datasets. The following examples show conversion between Datasets and DataFrames.

Example 2-converting the Dataset to a DataFrame

Scala:

```
//Convert the dataset to a DataFrame
scala> val color_df = color_ds.toDF()
color_df: org.apache.spark.sql.DataFrame = [color: string, len: int]

scala> color_df.show()
+------+---+
| color|len|
+------+---+
|   red|  3|
|orange|  6|
|  blue|  4|
| green|  5|
|yellow|  6|
+------+---+
```

This example looks very much like the examples we have seen in Chapter 3, *Introduction to DataFrames*. These conversions become very handy in the real world. Consider adding a structure (aka case class) to imperfect data. You may first read that data into a DataFrame, perform cleansing, and then convert it to a Dataset. Another use case could be that you want to expose only a subset (rows and columns) of the data based on some runtime information, such as user_id. You could read the data into a DataFrame, register it as a temporary table, apply conditions, and expose the subset as a Dataset. The following example creates a DataFrame first and then converts it into Dataset. Note that the DataFrame column names must match the case class.

Example 3-convert a DataFrame to a Dataset

```
//Construct a DataFrame first
scala> val color_df = sc.parallelize(colors).map(x =>
            (x,x.length)).toDF("color","len")
color_df: org.apache.spark.sql.DataFrame = [color: string, len: int]
//Convert the DataFrame to a Dataset with a given structure
scala> val ds_from_df = color_df.as[Color]
ds_from_df: org.apache.spark.sql.Dataset[Color] = [color: string, len: int]
//Check the execution plan
scala> ds_from_df.explain
== Physical Plan ==
WholeStageCodegen
```

```
:   +- Project [_1#102 AS color#105,_2#103 AS len#106]
:      +- INPUT
+- Scan ExistingRDD[_1#102,_2#103]
```

The explain command response shows WholeStageCodegen, which fuses multiple operations into a single Java function call. This enhances performance due to reduction in multiple virtual function calls. Code generation had been around in Spark engine since 1.1, but at that time it was limited to expression evaluation and a small number of operations such as filter. In contrast, whole stage code generation from Tungsten generates code for the entire query plan.

Creating Datasets from JSON

Datasets can be created from JSON files, similar to DataFrames. Note that a JSON file may contain several records, but each record has to be on one line. If your source JSON has newlines, you have to programmatically remove them. The JSON records may have arrays and may be nested. They need not have uniform schema. The following example file has JSON records with one record having an additional tag and an array of data.

Example 4-creating a Dataset from JSON

Scala:

```
//Set filepath
scala> val file_path = <Your path>
file_path: String = ./authors.json
//Create case class to match schema
scala> case class Auth(first_name: String, last_name: String,books:
Array[String])
defined class Auth

//Create dataset from json using case class
//Note that the json document should have one record per line
scala> val auth = spark.read.json(file_path).as[Auth]
auth: org.apache.spark.sql.Dataset[Auth] = [books: array<string>,
firstName: string ... 1 more field]

//Look at the data
scala> auth.show()
+--------------------+----------+---------+
|               books|first_name|last_name|
+--------------------+----------+---------+
|                null|      Mark|    Twain|
|                null|   Charles|  Dickens|
|[Jude the Obscure...|    Thomas|    Hardy|
```

```
+--------------------+----------+---------+

//Try explode to see array contents on separate lines

scala> auth.select(explode($"books") as "book",
          $"first_name",$"last_name").show(2,false)
+-----------------------+----------+---------+
|book                   |first_name|last_name|
+-----------------------+----------+---------+
|Jude the Obscure       |Thomas    |Hardy    |
|The Return of the Native|Thomas   |Hardy    |
+-----------------------+----------+---------+
```

Datasets API's limitations

Even though the Datasets API is created using the best of both RDDs and DataFrames, it still has some limitations as of its current stage of development:

- While querying the dataset, the selected fields should be given specific data types as in the case class, or else the output will become a DataFrame. An example is `auth.select(col("first_name").as[String])`.
- Python and R are inherently dynamic in nature, and hence typed Datasets do not fit in.

Spark SQL

Spark SQL is a Spark module for structured data processing that was introduced in Spark 1.0. This module is a tightly integrated relational engine that inert-operates with the core Spark API. It enables data engineers to write applications that load structured data from disparate sources and join them as a unified, and possibly continuous, Excel-like data frames; and then they can implement complex ETL workflows and advanced analytics.

The Spark 2.0 release brought in significant unification of APIs and expanded the SQL capabilities, including support for subqueries. The Dataset API and DataFrames API are now unified, with DataFrames being a "kind" of Datasets. The unified APIs build the foundation for Spark's future, spanning across all libraries. Developers can impose "structure" onto their data and can work with high-level declarative APIs, thereby improving performance as well as their productivity. The performance gains come as a result of the underlying optimization layer. DataFrames, Datasets, and SQL share the same optimization and execution pipeline.

SQL operations

SQL operations are most widely used constructs for data manipulation. Some of most used operations are, selecting all or some of the columns, filtering based on one or more conditions, sorting and grouping operations, and computing summary functions such as `average` on GroupedData. The `JOIN` operations on multiple data sources and `set` operations such as `union`, `intersect` and `minus` are some other operations that are widely performed. Furthermore, data frames are registered as temporary tables and passed traditional SQL statements to perform the aforementioned operations. **User-Defined Functions (UDF)** are defined and used with and without registration. We'll be focusing on window operations, which have been just introduced in Spark 2.0. They address sliding window operations. For example, if you want to report the average peak temperature every day in the past seven days, then you are operating on a sliding window of seven days until today. Here is an example that computes average sales per month for the past three months. The data file contains 24 observations showing monthly sales for two products, P1 and P2.

Example 5-window example with moving average computation

Scala:

```
scala> import org.apache.spark.sql.expressions.Window
import org.apache.spark.sql.expressions.Window
//Create a DataFrame containing monthly sales data for two products
scala> val monthlySales =
spark.read.options(Map({"header"->"true"},{"inferSchema" -> "true"})).
                        csv("<Your Path>/MonthlySales.csv")
monthlySales: org.apache.spark.sql.DataFrame = [Product: string, Month: int
... 1 more field]

//Prepare WindowSpec to create a 3 month sliding window for a product
//Negative subscript denotes rows above current row
scala> val w =
Window.partitionBy(monthlySales("Product")).orderBy(monthlySales("Month")).
rangeBetween(-2,0)
w: org.apache.spark.sql.expressions.WindowSpec =
org.apache.spark.sql.expressions.WindowSpec@3cc2f15

//Define compute on the sliding window, a moving average in this case
scala> val f = avg(monthlySales("Sales")).over(w)
f: org.apache.spark.sql.Column = avg(Sales) OVER (PARTITION BY Product
ORDER BY Month ASC RANGE BETWEEN 2 PRECEDING AND CURRENT ROW)
//Apply the sliding window and compute. Examine the results
scala> monthlySales.select($"Product",$"Sales",$"Month",
bround(f,2).alias("MovingAvg")).
                        orderBy($"Product",$"Month").show(6)
+-------+-----+-----+---------+
```

```
|Product|Sales|Month|MovingAvg|
+-------+-----+-----+---------+
|    P1 |  66 |   1 |    66.0 |
|    P1 |  24 |   2 |    45.0 |
|    P1 |  54 |   3 |    48.0 |
|    P1 |   0 |   4 |    26.0 |
|    P1 |  56 |   5 |   36.67 |
|    P1 |  34 |   6 |    30.0 |
+-------+-----+-----+---------+
```

Python:

```
>>> from pyspark.sql import Window
>>> import pyspark.sql.functions as func
//Create a DataFrame containing monthly sales data for two products
>> file_path = <Your path>/MonthlySales.csv"
>>> monthlySales = spark.read.csv(file_path,header=True,
inferSchema=True)
//Prepare WindowSpec to create a 3 month sliding window for a product
//Negative subscript denotes rows above current row
>>> w =
Window.partitionBy(monthlySales["Product"]).orderBy(monthlySales["Month"]).
rangeBetween(-2,0)
>>> w
<pyspark.sql.window.WindowSpec object at 0x7fdc33774a50>
>>>
//Define compute on the sliding window, a moving average in this case
>>> f = func.avg(monthlySales["Sales"]).over(w)
>>> f
Column<avg(Sales) OVER (PARTITION BY Product ORDER BY Month ASC RANGE
BETWEEN 2 PRECEDING AND CURRENT ROW)>
>>>
//Apply the sliding window and compute. Examine the results
>>>
monthlySales.select(monthlySales.Product,monthlySales.Sales,monthlySales.Mo
nth,
                         func.bround(f,2).alias("MovingAvg")).orderBy(
                         monthlySales.Product,monthlySales.Month).show(6)
+-------+-----+-----+---------+
|Product|Sales|Month|MovingAvg|
+-------+-----+-----+---------+
|    P1 |  66 |   1 |    66.0 |
|    P1 |  24 |   2 |    45.0 |
|    P1 |  54 |   3 |    48.0 |
|    P1 |   0 |   4 |    26.0 |
|    P1 |  56 |   5 |   36.67 |
|    P1 |  34 |   6 |    30.0 |
+-------+-----+-----+---------+
```

Under the hood

When a developer is writing programs using RDD API, efficient execution for the workload on hand is his/her responsibility. The data types and computations are not available for Spark. In contrast, when a developer is using DataFrames and Spark SQL, the underlying engine has information about the schema and operations. In this case, the developer can write less code while the optimizer does all the hard work.

The Catalyst optimizer contains libraries for representing trees and applying rules to transform the trees. These tree transformations are applied to create the most optimized logical and physical execution plans. In the final phase, it generates Java bytecode using a special feature of the Scala language called **quasiquotes**. The optimizer also enables external developers to extend the optimizer by adding data-source-specific rules that result in pushing operations to external systems, or support for new data types.

The Catalyst optimizer arrives at the most optimized plan to execute the operations on hand. The actual execution and related improvements are provided by the Tungsten engine. The goal of Tungsten is to improve the memory and CPU efficiency of Spark backend execution. The following are some salient features of this engine:

- Reducing the memory footprint and eliminating garbage collection overheads by bypassing (off-heap) Java memory management.
- Code generation fuses across multiple operators and too many virtual function calls are avoided. The generated code looks like hand-optimized code.
- Memory layout is in columnar, in-memory parquet format because that enables vectorized processing and is also closer to usual data access operations.
- In-memory encoding using encoders. Encoders use runtime code generation to build custom byte code for faster and compact serialization and deserialization. Many operations can be performed in-place without deserialization because they are already in Tungsten binary format.

Structured Streaming

Streaming is a seemingly broad topic! If you take a closer look at the real-world problems, businesses do not just want a streaming engine to make decisions in real time. There has always been a need to integrate both batch stack and streaming stack, and integrate with external storage systems and applications. Also, the solution should be such that it should adapt to dynamic changes in business logic to address new and changing business requirements.

Apache Spark 2.0 has the first version of the higher level stream processing API called the **Structured Streaming** engine. This scalable and fault-tolerant engine leans on the Spark SQL API to simplify the development of real-time, continuous big data applications. It is probably the first successful attempt in unifying the batch and streaming computation.

At a technical level, Structured Streaming leans on the Spark SQL API, which extends DataFrames/Datasets, which we already discussed in the previous sections. Spark 2.0 lets you perform radically different activities in a unified way, such as:

- Building ML models and applying them on streaming data
- Combining streaming data with other static data
- Performing ad hoc, interactive, and batch queries
- Changing queries at runtime
- Aggregating data streams and serving using Spark SQL JDBC

Unlike other streaming engines, Spark lets you combine real-time **Streaming Data** with**Static data** and lets you perform the preceding operations.

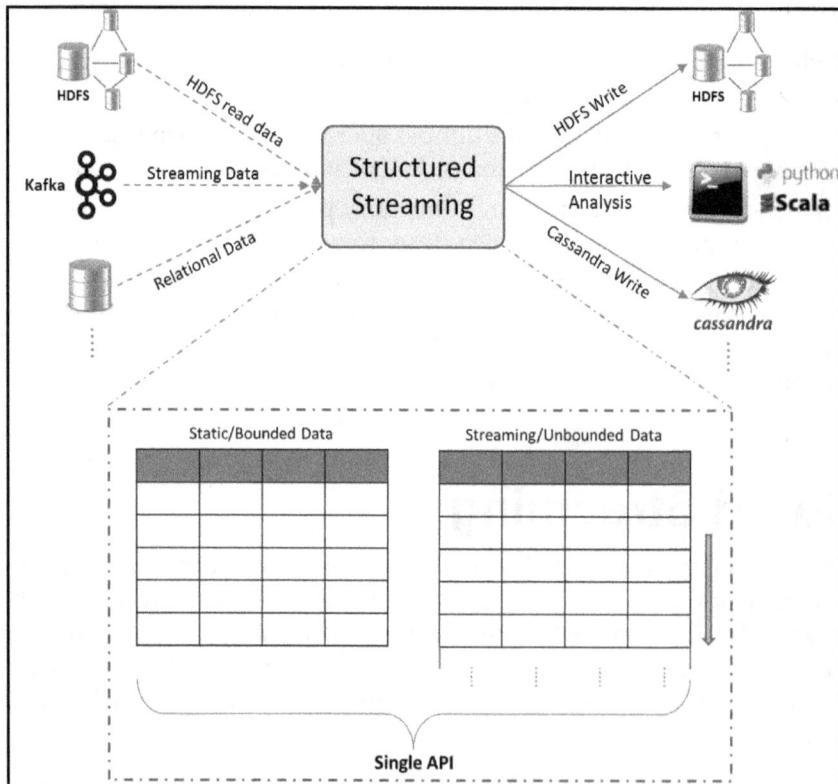

Fundamentally, Structured Streaming is empowered by Spark SQL's Catalyst optimizer. So, it frees up the developers from worrying about the underlying plumbing of making queries more efficient while dealing with static or real-time streams of data.

As of this writing, Structured Streaming of Spark 2.0 is focused on ETL, and later versions will have more operators and libraries.

Let us look at a simple example. The following example listens to **System Activity Report (sar)** on Linux on a local machine and computes the average free memory. System Activity Report gives system activity statistics and the current example collects memory usage, reported 20 times at a 2-second interval. The Spark stream reads this streaming output and computes average memory. We use a handy networking utility **netcat (nc)** to redirect the sar output onto a given port. The options l and k specify that nc should listen for an incoming connection and it has to keep listening for another connection even after its current connection is completed.

Scala:

Example 6-Streaming example

```
//Run the following command from one terminal window
sar -r 2 20 | nc -lk 9999

//In spark-shell window, do the following
//Read stream
scala> val myStream = spark.readStream.format("socket").
                      option("host","localhost").
                      option("port",9999).load()
myStream: org.apache.spark.sql.DataFrame = [value: string]

//Filter out unwanted lines and then extract free memory part as a float
//Drop missing values, if any
scala> val myDF = myStream.filter($"value".contains("IST")).
select(substring($"value",15,9).cast("float").as("memFree")).
          na.drop().select($"memFree")
myDF: org.apache.spark.sql.DataFrame = [memFree: float]

//Define an aggregate function
scala> val avgMemFree = myDF.select(avg("memFree"))
avgMemFree: org.apache.spark.sql.DataFrame = [avg(memFree): double]

//Create StreamingQuery handle that writes on to the console
scala> val query = avgMemFree.writeStream.
        outputMode("complete").
        format("console").
        start()
```

```
query: org.apache.spark.sql.streaming.StreamingQuery = Streaming Query -
query-0 [state = ACTIVE]

Batch: 0
-------------------------------------------
+-----------------+
|      avg(memFree)|
+-----------------+
|4116531.380952381|
+-----------------+
....
```

Python:

```
//Run the following command from one terminal window
 sar -r 2 20 | nc -lk 9999
//In another window, open pyspark shell and do the following
>>> import pyspark.sql.functions as func
//Read stream
>>> myStream = spark.readStream.format("socket"). \
                     option("host","localhost"). \
                     option("port",9999).load()
myStream: org.apache.spark.sql.DataFrame = [value: string]
//Filter out unwanted lines and then extract free memory part as a
float
//Drop missing values, if any
>>> myDF = myStream.filter("value rlike 'IST'"). \
          select(func.substring("value",15,9).cast("float"). \
          alias("memFree")).na.drop().select("memFree")
//Define an aggregate function
>>> avgMemFree = myDF.select(func.avg("memFree"))
//Create StreamingQuery handle that writes on to the console
>>> query = avgMemFree.writeStream. \
          outputMode("complete"). \
          format("console"). \
          start()
Batch: 0
-------------------------------------------
+-----------+
|avg(memFree)|
+-----------+
|   4042749.2|
+-----------+
.....
```

The preceding example defined a continuous data frame (also known as stream) to listen to a particular port, perform some transformations, and aggregations and show continuous output.

The Spark streaming programming model

As demonstrated earlier in this chapter, there is just a single API to take care of both static and streaming data. The idea is to treat the real-time data stream as a table that is continuously being appended, as shown in the following figure:

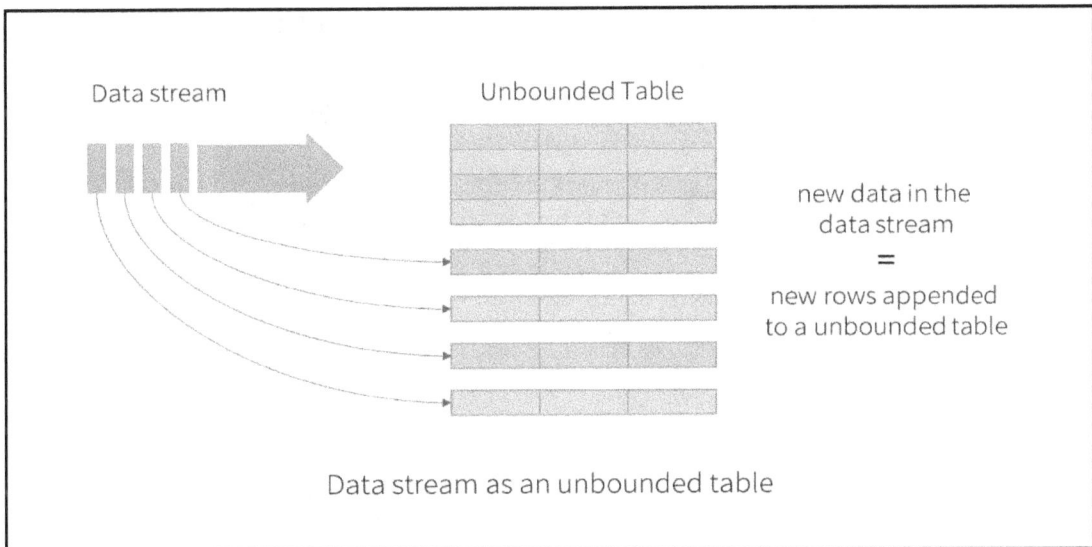

Data stream as an unbounded table

So whether for static or streaming data, you just fire up the batch-like queries as you would do on static data tables, and Spark runs it as an incremental query on the unbounded input table, as shown in the following figure:

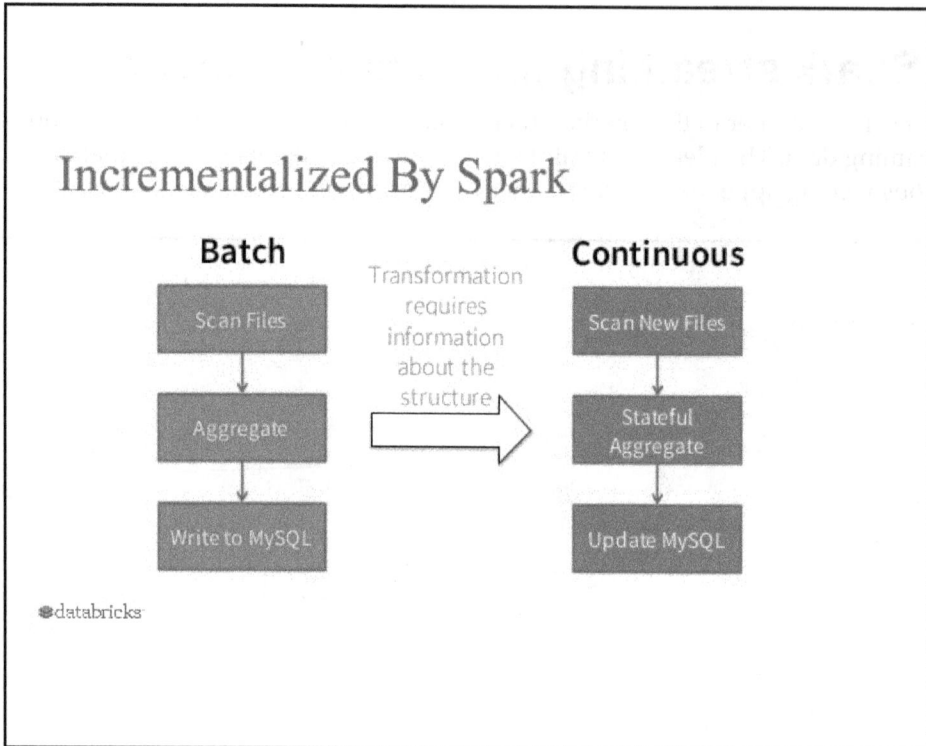

So, the developers define a query on the input table, in the same way for both static-bounded as well as dynamic-unbounded table. Let us understand the various technical jargons for this whole process to understand how it works:

- **Input:** Data from sources as an append-only table
- **Trigger:** When to check the input for new data
- **Query:** What operation to perform on the data, such as filter, group, and so on
- **Result:** The resultant table at every trigger interval
- **Output:** Choose what part of the result to write to the data sink after every trigger

Let's now look at how the Spark SQL planner treats the whole process:

Structured Streaming Processing Model
Users express queries using a batch API; Spark incrementalizes them to run on streams

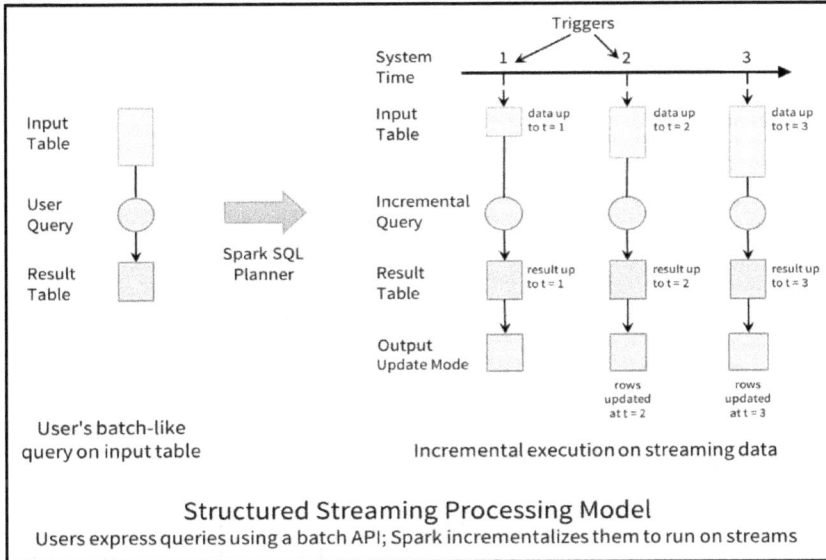

The preceding screenshot is very simply explained in the structured programming guide at the official Apache Spark site, as indicated in the *References* section.

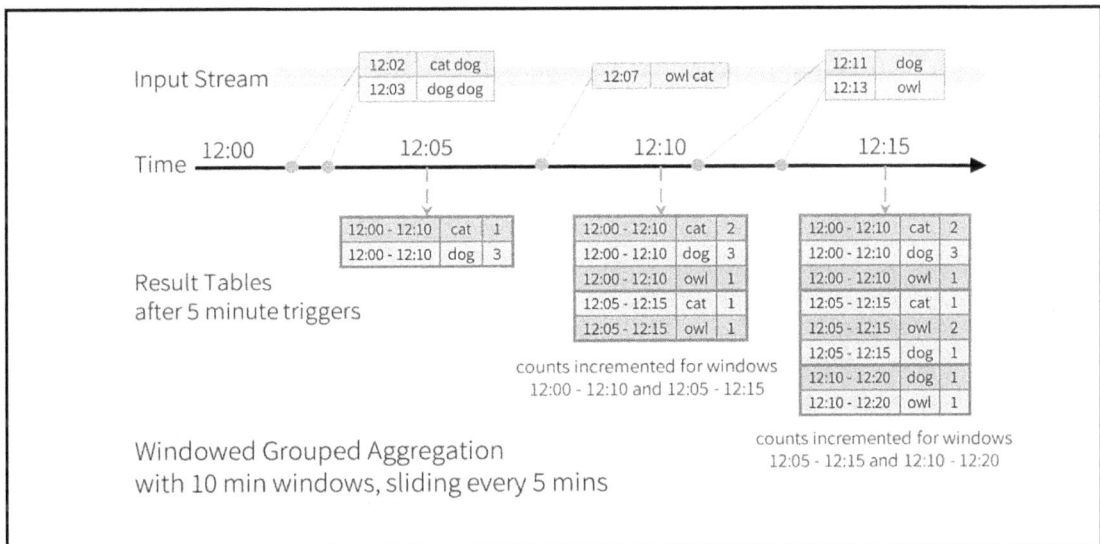

At this point, we need to know about the supported output models. Every time the result table is updated, the changes need to be written to an external system, such as HDFS, S3, or any other database. We usually prefer to write output incrementally. For this purpose, Structured Streaming provides three output modes:

- **Append:** In the external storage, only the new rows appended to the result table since the last trigger will be written. This is applicable only on queries where existing rows in the result table cannot change (for example, a map on an input stream).
- **Complete:** In the external storage, the entire updated result table will be written as is.
- **Update:** In the external storage, only the rows that were updated in the result table since the last trigger will be changed. This mode works for output sinks that can be updated in place, such as a MySQL table.

In our example, we used complete mode, which was straightaway writing to the console. You may want to write into some external file such as Parquet to get a better understanding.

Under the hood

If you look at the "behind the screen" execution mechanism of the operations performed on **DataFrames/Datasets**, it would appear as the following figure suggests:

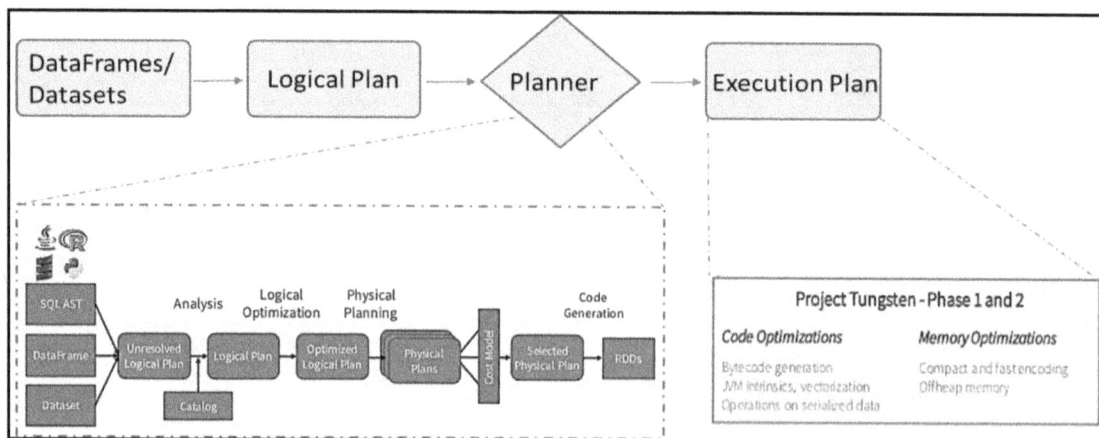

Please note here that the **Planner** knows apriori how to convert a streaming **Logical Plan** to a continuous series of **Incremental Execution Plans**. This can be represented by the following figure:

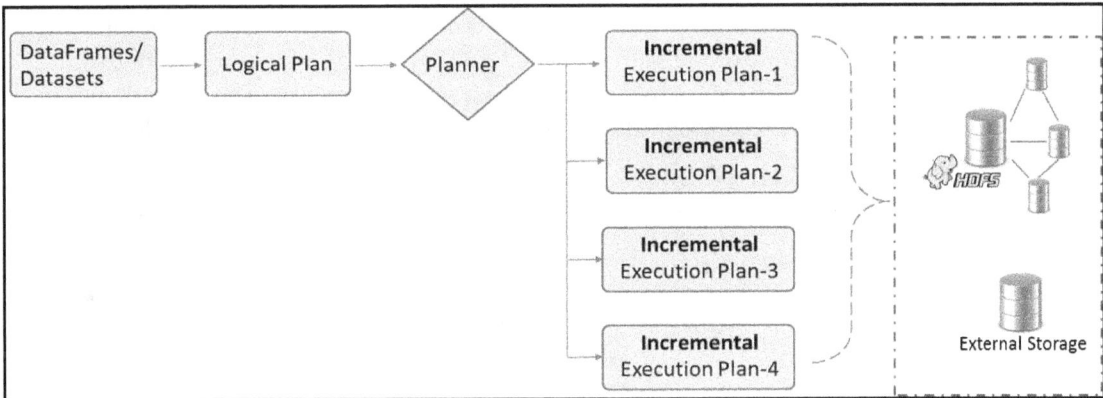

The **Planner** can poll the data sources for new data to be able to plan the execution in an optimized way.

Comparison with other streaming engines

We have discussed many unique features of Structured Streaming. Let us now have a comparative view with other available streaming engines:

Property	Structured Streaming	Spark Streaming	Apache Storm	Apache Flink	Kafka Streams	Google Dataflow
Streaming API	incrementalize batch queries	integrates with batch	separate from batch	separate from batch	separate from batch	integrates with batch
Prefix Integrity Guarantee	✔	✔	✘	✘	✘	✘
Internal Processing	exactly once	exactly once	at least once	exactly once	at least once	exactly once
Transactional Sources/Sinks	✔	some	some	some	✘	✘
Interactive Queries	✔	✔	✘	✘	✘	✘
Joins with Static Data	✔	✔	✘	✘	✘	✘

Courtesy: Databricks

Continuous applications

We discussed how unified data access is empowered by Spark. It lets you process data in a myriad of ways to build end-to-end continuous applications by enabling various analytic workloads, such as ETL processing, ad hoc queries, online machine learning modeling, or to generate necessary reports... all of this in a unified way by letting you work on both static as well as streaming data using a high-level, SQL-like API. In this way, Structured Streaming has substantially simplified the development and maintenance of real-time, continuous applications.

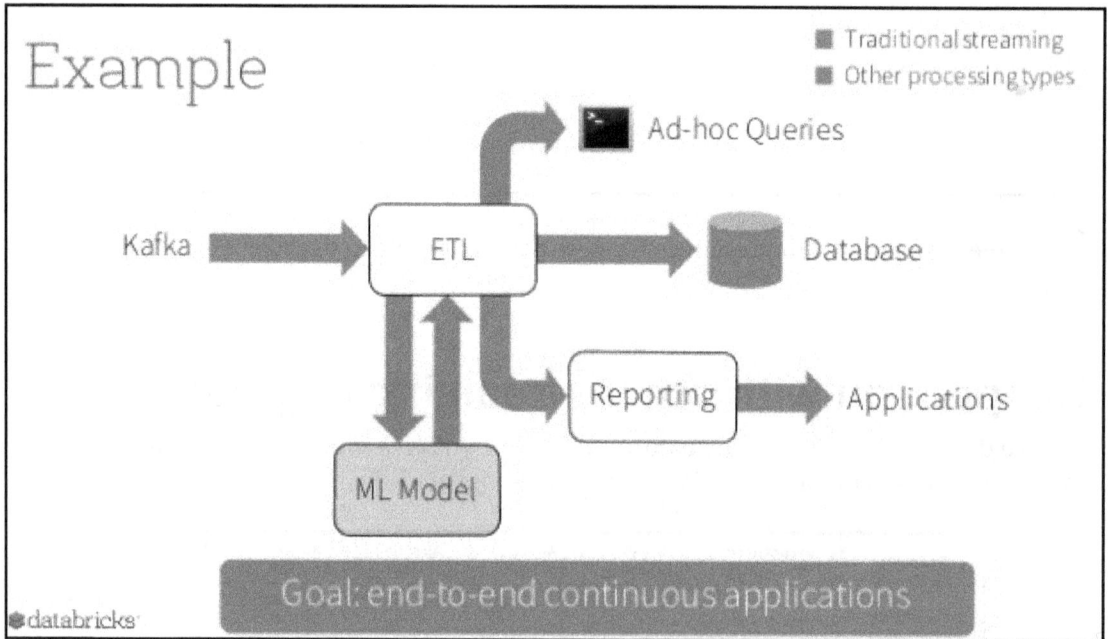

Courtesy: Databricks

Summary

In this chapter, we discussed what is really meant by unified data access and how Spark serves this purpose. We took a closer look at the Datasets API and how real-time streaming is empowered through it. We learned the advantages of Datasets and also their limitations. We also looked at the fundamentals behind continuous applications.

In the following chapter, we will look at the various ways in which we can leverage the Spark platform for data analysis operations at scale.

References

- http://people.csail.mit.edu/matei/papers/2015/sigmod_spark_sql.pdf: Spark SQL: Relational Data Processing in Spark
- https://databricks.com/blog/2016/07/14/a-tale-of-three-apache-spark-apis-rdds-dataframes-and-datasets.html: A Tale of Three Apache Spark APIs: RDDs, DataFrames, and Datasets – When to use them and why
- https://databricks.com/blog/2016/01/04/introducing-apache-spark-datasets.html: Introducing Apache Spark Datasets
- https://databricks.com/blog/2015/04/13/deep-dive-into-spark-sqls-catalyst-optimizer.html: Deep Dive into Spark SQL's Catalyst Optimizer
- https://databricks.com/blog/2016/05/23/apache-spark-as-a-compiler-joining-a-billion-rows-per-second-on-a-laptop.html: Apache Spark as a Compiler: Joining a Billion Rows per Second on a Laptop
- https://databricks.com/blog/2015/04/28/project-tungsten-bringing-spark-closer-to-bare-metal.html: Bringing Spark closer to baremetal
- https://databricks.com/blog/2016/07/28/structured-streaming-in-apache-spark.html: Structured Streaming API details
- https://spark.apache.org/docs/latest/structured-streaming-programming-guide.html: Spark Structured Streaming Programming Guide
- https://spark-summit.org/east-2016/events/structuring-spark-dataframes-datasets-and-streaming/: Structuring Apache Spark SQL, DataFrames, Datasets, and Streaming by Michael Armbrust
- https://databricks.com/blog/2016/06/22/apache-spark-key-terms-explained.html: Apache Spark Key terms explained

5
Data Analysis on Spark

The field of data analytics at scale has been evolving like never before. Various libraries and tools were developed for data analysis with a rich set of algorithms. On a parallel line, distributed computing techniques were evolving with time, to process huge datasets at scale. These two traits had to converge, and that was the primary intention behind the development of Spark.

The previous two chapters outlined the technology aspects of data science. It covered some fundamentals on the DataFrame API, Datasets, streaming data and how it facilitated data representation through DataFrames that R and Python users were familiar with. After introducing this API, we saw how operating on datasets became easier than ever. We also looked at how Spark SQL played a background role in supporting the DataFrame API with its robust features and optimization techniques. In this chapter, we are going to cover the scientific aspect of big data analysis and learn various data analytics techniques that can be executed on Spark.

As a prerequisite for this chapter, a basic understanding of the DataFrame API and statistics fundamentals is good to have. However, we have tried to make the content as simple as possible and covered some important fundamentals in detail so that anyone can get started with statistical analysis on Spark. The topics covered in this chapter are as follows:

- Data analytics life cycle
- Data acquisition
- Data preparation
    - Data consolidation
    - Data cleansing
    - Data transformation

- Basics of statistics
  - Sampling
  - Data distributions
- Descriptive statistics
  - Measures of location
  - Measures of spread
  - Summary statistics
  - Graphical techniques
- Inferential statistics
  - Discrete probability distributions
  - Continuous probability distributions
  - Standard error
  - Confidence level
  - Margin of error and confidence interval
  - Variability in population
  - Estimating sample size
  - Hypothesis testing
  - Chi-square test
  - F-test
  - Correlations

Data analytics life cycle

For most real-world projects, there is some defined sequence of steps to be followed. However, there are no universally agreed upon definitions or boundaries for data analytics and data science. Generally, the term "data analytics" encompasses the techniques and processes involved in examining data, discovering useful insights, and communicating them. The term "data science" can be best treated as an interdisciplinary field drawing from *statistics*, *computer science*, and *mathematics*. Both terms deal with processing raw data to derive knowledge or insights, usually in an iterative fashion, and some people use them interchangeably.

Based on diverse business requirements, there are different ways of approaching problems but there is no unique standard process that fits in well with all possible scenarios. A typical process workflow can be summarized as a cycle of formulating a question, exploring, hypothesizing, validating the hypothesis, analyzing the results, and starting all over again. This is depicted in the following figure with the thick arrows. From a data perspective, the workflow consists of data acquisition, preprocessing, exploring the data, modeling, and communicating the results. This is shown in the figure as circles. Analysis and visualization happen at every stage, right from data collection to results communication. The data analytics workflow encompasses all the activities shown in both views:

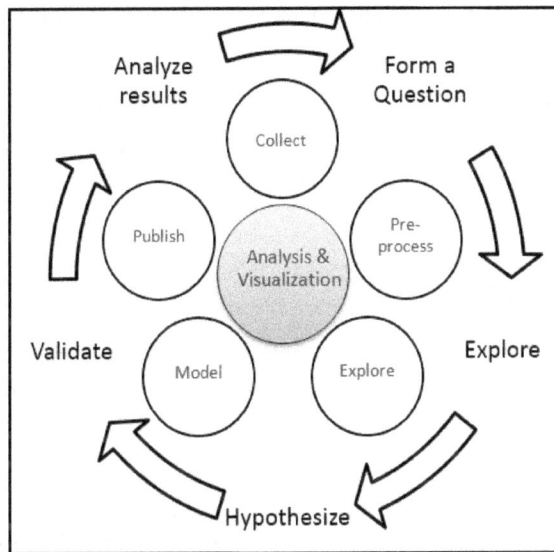

The most important thing in the entire life cycle is the question at hand. Data that might contain an answer (relevant data!) to that question comes next. Depending on the question, the first task is to collect the right data from one or more data sources as needed. Organizations often maintain**data lakes**, which are humongous repositories of data in their original format.

The next step is to clean/transform the data to the desired format. Data cleansing is also called data munging, data wrangling, or data dredging. This involves activities such as missing value treatment and outlier treatment upon assessing the quality of the data at hand. You may also have to aggregate/plot the data for better understanding. This process of formulating the final data matrix to work with is touted as the most time-consuming step. This also happens to be an underestimated component that is considered to be part of preprocessing, along with other activities such as feature extraction and data transformation.

The crux of data science, that is, training models and extracting patterns, comes next, which requires heavy use of statistics and machine learning. The final step is publishing the results.

The remaining sections in this chapter delve deeper into each of these steps and how they can be implemented using Spark. Some basics of statistics are also included so as to enable the reader to follow the code snippets with ease.

Data acquisition

Data acquisition, or data collection, is the very first step in any data science project. Usually, you won't find the complete set of required data in one place as it is distributed across **line-of-business (LOB)** applications and systems.

The majority of this section has already been covered in the previous chapter, which outlined how to source data from different data sources and store the data in DataFrames for easier analysis. There is a built-in mechanism in Spark to fetch data from some of the common data sources and the *Data Source API* is provided for the ones not supported out of the box on Spark.

To get a better understanding of the data acquisition and preparation phases, let us assume a scenario and try to address all the steps involved with example code snippets. The scenario is such that employee data is present across native RDDs, JSON files, and on a SQL server. So, let's see how we can get those to Spark DataFrames:

Python

```
// From RDD: Create an RDD and convert to DataFrame
>>> employees = sc.parallelize([(1, "John", 25), (2, "Ray", 35), (3,
"Mike", 24), (4, "Jane", 28), (5, "Kevin", 26), (6, "Vincent", 35), (7,
"James", 38), (8, "Shane", 32), (9, "Larry", 29), (10, "Kimberly", 29),
(11, "Alex", 28), (12, "Garry", 25), (13, "Max",
31)]).toDF(["emp_id","name","age"])
>>>
```

```
// From JSON: reading a JSON file
>>> salary = sqlContext.read.json("./salary.json")
>>> designation = sqlContext.read.json("./designation.json")
```

Scala

```scala
// From RDD: Create an RDD and convert to DataFrame
scala> val employees = sc.parallelize(List((1, "John", 25), (2, "Ray", 35),
(3, "Mike", 24), (4, "Jane", 28), (5, "Kevin", 26), (6, "Vincent", 35), (7,
"James", 38), (8, "Shane", 32), (9, "Larry", 29), (10, "Kimberly", 29),
(11, "Alex", 28), (12, "Garry", 25), (13, "Max",
31))).toDF("emp_id","name","age")
employees: org.apache.spark.sql.DataFrame = [emp_id: int, name: string ...
1 more field]
scala> // From JSON: reading a JSON file
scala> val salary = spark.read.json("./salary.json")
salary: org.apache.spark.sql.DataFrame = [e_id: bigint, salary: bigint]
scala> val designation = spark.read.json("./designation.json")
designation: org.apache.spark.sql.DataFrame = [id: bigint, role: string]
```

Data preparation

Data quality has always been a pervasive problem in the industry. The presence of incorrect or inconsistent data can produce misleading results of your analysis. Implementing better algorithm or building better models will not help much if the data is not cleansed and prepared well, as per the requirement. There is an industry jargon called **data engineering** that refers to data sourcing and preparation. This is typically done by data scientists and in a few organizations, there is a dedicated team for this purpose. However, while preparing data, a scientific perspective is often needed to do it right. As an example, you may not just do *mean substitution* to treat missing values and look into data distribution to find more appropriate values to substitute. Another such example is that you may not just look at a box plot or scatter plot to look for outliers, as there could be multivariate outliers which are not visible if you plot a single variable. There are different approaches, such as **Gaussian Mixture Models** (**GMMs**) and **Expectation Maximization** (**EM**) algorithms that use **Mahalanobis distance** to look for multivariate outliers.

The data preparation phase is an extremely important phase, not only for the algorithms to work properly, but also for you to develop a better understanding of your data so that you can take the right approach while implementing an algorithm.

Once the data has been acquired from different sources, the next step is to consolidate them all so that the data as a whole can be cleaned, formatted, and transformed to the format needed for your analysis. Please note that you might have to take samples of data from the sources, depending on the scenario, and then prepare the data for further analysis. Various sampling techniques that can be used are discussed later in this chapter.

Data consolidation

In this section, we will take a look at how to combine data acquired from various data sources:

Python

```
// Creating the final data matrix using the join operation
>>> final_data = employees.join(salary, employees.emp_id ==
salary.e_id).join(designation, employees.emp_id ==
designation.id).select("emp_id", "name", "age", "role", "salary")
>>> final_data.show(5)
+------+-----+---+---------+------+
|emp_id| name|age|     role|salary|
+------+-----+---+---------+------+
|     1| John| 25|Associate| 10000|
|     2|  Ray| 35|  Manager| 12000|
|     3| Mike| 24|  Manager| 12000|
|     4| Jane| 28|Associate|  null|
|     5|Kevin| 26|  Manager|   120|
+------+-----+---+---------+------+
only showing top 5 rows
```

Scala

```
// Creating the final data matrix using the join operation
scala> val final_data = employees.join(salary, $"emp_id" ===
$"e_id").join(designation, $"emp_id" === $"id").select("emp_id", "name",
"age", "role", "salary")
final_data: org.apache.spark.sql.DataFrame = [emp_id: int, name: string ...
3 more fields]
```

After integrating data from those sources, the final dataset (in this case it is `final_data`) should be of the following format (just example data):

emp_id	name	age	role	salary
1	John	25	Associate	10,000 $
2	Ray	35	Manager	12,000 $
3	Mike	24	Manager	12,000 $
4	Jane	28	Associate	null
5	Kevin	26	Manager	12,000 $
6	Vincent	35	Senior Manager	22,000 $
7	James	38	Senior Manager	20,000 $
8	Shane	32	Manager	12,000 $
9	Larry	29	Manager	10,000 $
10	Kimberly	29	Associate	8,000 $
11	Alex	28	Manager	12,000 $
12	Garry	25	Manager	12.000 $
13	Max	31	Manager	12,000 $

Data cleansing

Once you have the data consolidated in one place, it is extremely important that you spend enough time and effort in cleaning it before analyzing it. This is an iterative process because you have to validate the actions you have taken on the data and continue till you are satisfied with the data quality. It is advisable that you spend time analyzing the causes of anomalies you detect in the data.

Some level of impurity in data usually exists in any dataset. There can be various kinds of issues with data, but we are going to address a few common cases, such as missing values, duplicate values, transforming, or formatting (adding or removing digits from a number, splitting a column into two, merging two columns into one).

Missing value treatment

There are various ways of handling missing values. One way is dropping rows containing missing values. We may want to drop a row even if a single column has missing value, or may have different strategies for different columns. We may want to retain the row as long as the total number of missing values in that row are under a threshold. Another approach may be to replace nulls with a constant value, say the mean value in case of numeric variables.

In this section, we will not be providing some examples in both Scala and Python and will try to cover various scenarios to give you a broader perspective.

Python

```
// Dropping rows with missing value(s)
>>> clean_data = final_data.na.drop()
>>>
// Replacing missing value by mean
>>> import math
>>> from pyspark.sql import functions as F
>>> mean_salary =
math.floor(salary.select(F.mean('salary')).collect()[0][0])
>>> clean_data = final_data.na.fill({'salary' : mean_salary})
>>>
//Another example for missing value treatment
>>> authors = [['Thomas','Hardy','June 2, 1840'],
        ['Charles','Dickens','7 February 1812'],
         ['Mark','Twain',None],
         ['Jane','Austen','16 December 1775'],
        ['Emily',None,None]]
>>> df1 = sc.parallelize(authors).toDF(
        ["FirstName","LastName","Dob"])
>>> df1.show()
+---------+--------+----------------+
|FirstName|LastName|             Dob|
+---------+--------+----------------+
|   Thomas|   Hardy|    June 2, 1840|
|  Charles| Dickens| 7 February 1812|
|     Mark|   Twain|            null|
|     Jane|  Austen|16 December 1775|
|    Emily|    null|            null|
+---------+--------+----------------+

// Drop rows with missing values
>>> df1.na.drop().show()
+---------+--------+----------------+
|FirstName|LastName|             Dob|
```

```
+---------+--------+----------------+
|   Thomas|   Hardy|     June 2, 1840|
|  Charles| Dickens| 7 February 1812|
|     Jane|  Austen|16 December 1775|
+---------+--------+----------------+
```

```
// Drop rows with at least 2 missing values
>>> df1.na.drop(thresh=2).show()
+---------+--------+----------------+
|FirstName|LastName|             Dob|
+---------+--------+----------------+
|   Thomas|   Hardy|     June 2, 1840|
|  Charles| Dickens| 7 February 1812|
|     Mark|   Twain|            null|
|     Jane|  Austen|16 December 1775|
+---------+--------+----------------+
```

```
// Fill all missing values with a given string
>>> df1.na.fill('Unknown').show()
+---------+--------+----------------+
|FirstName|LastName|             Dob|
+---------+--------+----------------+
|   Thomas|   Hardy|     June 2, 1840|
|  Charles| Dickens| 7 February 1812|
|     Mark|   Twain|         Unknown|
|     Jane|  Austen|16 December 1775|
|    Emily| Unknown|         Unknown|
+---------+--------+----------------+
```

```
// Fill missing values in each column with a given string
>>> df1.na.fill({'LastName':'--','Dob':'Unknown'}).show()
+---------+--------+----------------+
|FirstName|LastName|             Dob|
+---------+--------+----------------+
|   Thomas|   Hardy|     June 2, 1840|
|  Charles| Dickens| 7 February 1812|
|     Mark|   Twain|         Unknown|
|     Jane|  Austen|16 December 1775|
|    Emily|      --|         Unknown|
+---------+--------+----------------+
```

Scala

```
//Missing value treatment
// Dropping rows with missing value(s)
scala> var clean_data = final_data.na.drop() //Note the var declaration
instead of val
clean_data: org.apache.spark.sql.DataFrame = [emp_id: int, name: string ...
```

```
3 more fields]
scala>

// Replacing missing value by mean
scal> val mean_salary = final_data.select(floor(avg("salary"))).
          first()(0).toString.toDouble
mean_salary: Double = 20843.0
scal> clean_data = final_data.na.fill(Map("salary" -> mean_salary))

//Reassigning clean_data
clean_data: org.apache.spark.sql.DataFrame = [emp_id: int, name: string ...
3 more fields]
scala>

//Another example for missing value treatment
scala> case class Author (FirstName: String, LastName: String, Dob: String)
defined class Author
scala> val authors = Seq(
        Author("Thomas","Hardy","June 2, 1840"),
        Author("Charles","Dickens","7 February 1812"),
        Author("Mark","Twain",null),
        Author("Emily",null,null))
authors: Seq[Author] = List(Author(Thomas,Hardy,June 2, 1840),
   Author(Charles,Dickens,7 February 1812), Author(Mark,Twain,null),
   Author(Emily,null,null))
scala> val ds1 = sc.parallelize(authors).toDS()
ds1: org.apache.spark.sql.Dataset[Author] = [FirstName: string, LastName:
string ... 1 more field]
scala> ds1.show()
+---------+--------+---------------+
|FirstName|LastName|            Dob|
+---------+--------+---------------+
|   Thomas|   Hardy|   June 2, 1840|
|  Charles| Dickens|7 February 1812|
|     Mark|   Twain|           null|
|    Emily|    null|           null|
+---------+--------+---------------+
scala>

// Drop rows with missing values
scala> ds1.na.drop().show()
+---------+--------+---------------+
|FirstName|LastName|            Dob|
+---------+--------+---------------+
|   Thomas|   Hardy|   June 2, 1840|
|  Charles| Dickens|7 February 1812|
+---------+--------+---------------+
scala>
```

```
//Drop rows with at least 2 missing values
//Note that there is no direct scala function to drop rows with at least n
missing values
//However, you can drop rows containing under specified non nulls
//Use that function to achieve the same result
scala> ds1.na.drop(minNonNulls = df1.columns.length - 1).show()
//Fill all missing values with a given string
scala> ds1.na.fill("Unknown").show()
+---------+--------+---------------+
|FirstName|LastName|            Dob|
+---------+--------+---------------+
|   Thomas|   Hardy|   June 2, 1840|
|  Charles| Dickens|7 February 1812|
|     Mark|   Twain|        Unknown|
|    Emily| Unknown|        Unknown|
+---------+--------+---------------+
scala>

//Fill missing values in each column with a given string
scala> ds1.na.fill(Map("LastName"->"--",
                 "Dob"->"Unknown")).show()
+---------+--------+---------------+
|FirstName|LastName|            Dob|
+---------+--------+---------------+
|   Thomas|   Hardy|   June 2, 1840|
|  Charles| Dickens|7 February 1812|
|     Mark|   Twain|        Unknown|
|    Emily|      --|        Unknown|
+---------+--------+---------------+
```

Outlier treatment

Understanding what an outlier is also important to treat it well. To put it simply, an outlier is a data point that does not share the same characteristics as the rest of the data points. Example: if you have a dataset of schoolchildren and there are a few age values in the range of 30-40 then they could be outliers. Let us look into a different example now: if you have a dataset where a variable can have data points only in two ranges, say, in the 10-20 or 80-90 range, then the data points (say, 40 or 55) with values in between these two ranges could also be outliers. In this example, 40 or 55 do not belong to the 10-20 range, nor do they belong to the 80-90 range, and are outliers.

Also, there can be univariate outliers and there can be multivariate outliers as well. We will focus on univariate outliers in this book for simplicity's sake as Spark MLlib may not have all the algorithms needed at the time of writing this book.

In order to treat the outliers, you have to first see if there are outliers. There are different ways, such as summary statistics and plotting techniques, to find the outliers. You can use the built-in library functions such as `matplotlib` of Python to visualize your data. You can do so by connecting to Spark through a notebook (for example, Jupyter) so that the visuals can be generated, which may not be possible on a command shell.

Once you find outliers, you can either delete the rows containing outliers or impute the mean values in place of outliers or do something more relevant, as applicable to your case. Let us have a look at the mean substitution method here:

Python

```
// Identify outliers and replace them with mean
//The following example reuses the clean_data dataset and mean_salary
computed in previous examples
>>> mean_salary
20843.0
>>>
//Compute deviation for each row
>>> devs = final_data.select(((final_data.salary - mean_salary) **
2).alias("deviation"))

//Compute standard deviation
>>> stddev = math.floor(math.sqrt(devs.groupBy().
        avg("deviation").first()[0]))

//check standard deviation value
>>> round(stddev,2)
30351.0
>>>
//Replace outliers beyond 2 standard deviations with the mean salary
>>> no_outlier = final_data.select(final_data.emp_id, final_data.name,
final_data.age, final_data.salary, final_data.role,
F.when(final_data.salary.between(mean_salary-(2*stddev),
mean_salary+(2*stddev)),
final_data.salary).otherwise(mean_salary).alias("updated_salary"))
>>>
//Observe modified values
>>> no_outlier.filter(no_outlier.salary !=
no_outlier.updated_salary).show()
+------+----+---+------+-------+--------------+
|emp_id|name|age|salary|   role|updated_salary|
+------+----+---+------+-------+--------------+
|    13| Max| 31|120000|Manager|       20843.0|
+------+----+---+------+-------+--------------+
>>>
```

Scala

```
// Identify outliers and replace them with mean
//The following example reuses the clean_data dataset and mean_salary
computed in previous examples
//Compute deviation for each row
scala> val devs = clean_data.select(((clean_data("salary") - mean_salary) *
        (clean_data("salary") - mean_salary)).alias("deviation"))
devs: org.apache.spark.sql.DataFrame = [deviation: double]

//Compute standard deviation
scala> val stddev = devs.select(sqrt(avg("deviation"))).
            first().getDouble(0)
stddev: Double = 29160.932595617614

//If you want to round the stddev value, use BigDecimal as shown
scala> scala.math.BigDecimal(stddev).setScale(2,
            BigDecimal.RoundingMode.HALF_UP)
res14: scala.math.BigDecimal = 29160.93
scala>

//Replace outliers beyond 2 standard deviations with the mean salary
scala> val outlierfunc = udf((value: Long, mean: Double) => {if (value >
mean+(2*stddev)
            || value < mean-(2*stddev)) mean else value})

//Use the UDF to compute updated_salary
//Note the usage of lit() to wrap a literal as a column
scala> val no_outlier = clean_data.withColumn("updated_salary",
            outlierfunc(col("salary"),lit(mean_salary)))

//Observe modified values
scala> no_outlier.filter(no_outlier("salary") =!=  //Not !=
            no_outlier("updated_salary")).show()
+------+----+---+-------+------+--------------+
|emp_id|name|age|   role|salary|updated_salary|
+------+----+---+-------+------+--------------+
|    13| Max| 31|Manager|120000|       20843.0|
+------+----+---+-------+------+--------------+
```

Duplicate values treatment

There are different ways of treating the duplicate records in a dataset. We will demonstrate those in the following code snippets:

Python

```
// Deleting the duplicate rows
>>> authors = [['Thomas','Hardy','June 2,1840'],
    ['Thomas','Hardy','June 2,1840'],
    ['Thomas','H',None],
    ['Jane','Austen','16 December 1775'],
    ['Emily',None,None]]
>>> df1 = sc.parallelize(authors).toDF(
    ["FirstName","LastName","Dob"])
>>> df1.show()
+---------+--------+----------------+
|FirstName|LastName|             Dob|
+---------+--------+----------------+
|   Thomas|   Hardy|    June 2, 1840|
|   Thomas|   Hardy|    June 2, 1840|
|   Thomas|       H|            null|
|     Jane|  Austen|16 December 1775|
|    Emily|    null|            null|
+---------+--------+----------------+

// Drop duplicated rows
>>> df1.dropDuplicates().show()
+---------+--------+----------------+
|FirstName|LastName|             Dob|
+---------+--------+----------------+
|    Emily|    null|            null|
|     Jane|  Austen|16 December 1775|
|   Thomas|       H|            null|
|   Thomas|   Hardy|    June 2, 1840|
+---------+--------+----------------+

// Drop duplicates based on a sub set of columns
>>> df1.dropDuplicates(subset=["FirstName"]).show()
+---------+--------+----------------+
|FirstName|LastName|             Dob|
+---------+--------+----------------+
|    Emily|    null|            null|
|   Thomas|   Hardy|    June 2, 1840|
|     Jane|  Austen|16 December 1775|
+---------+--------+----------------+
>>>
```

Scala:

```
//Duplicate values treatment
// Reusing the Author case class
// Deleting the duplicate rows
scala> val authors = Seq(
            Author("Thomas","Hardy","June 2,1840"),
            Author("Thomas","Hardy","June 2,1840"),
            Author("Thomas","H",null),
            Author("Jane","Austen","16 December 1775"),
            Author("Emily",null,null))
authors: Seq[Author] = List(Author(Thomas,Hardy,June 2,1840),
Author(Thomas,Hardy,June 2,1840), Author(Thomas,H,null),
Author(Jane,Austen,16 December 1775), Author(Emily,null,null))
scala> val ds1 = sc.parallelize(authors).toDS()
ds1: org.apache.spark.sql.Dataset[Author] = [FirstName: string, LastName:
string ... 1 more field]
scala> ds1.show()
+---------+--------+----------------+
|FirstName|LastName|             Dob|
+---------+--------+----------------+
|   Thomas|   Hardy|     June 2,1840|
|   Thomas|   Hardy|     June 2,1840|
|   Thomas|       H|            null|
|     Jane|  Austen|16 December 1775|
|    Emily|    null|            null|
+---------+--------+----------------+
scala>

// Drop duplicated rows
scala> ds1.dropDuplicates().show()
+---------+--------+----------------
+
|FirstName|LastName|             Dob|
+---------+--------+----------------+
|     Jane|  Austen|16 December 1775|
|    Emily|    null|            null|
|   Thomas|   Hardy|     June 2,1840|
|   Thomas|       H|            null|
+---------+--------+----------------+
scala>

// Drop duplicates based on a sub set of columns
scala> ds1.dropDuplicates("FirstName").show()
+---------+--------+----------------+

|FirstName|LastName|             Dob|
+---------+--------+----------------+
```

```
|    Emily|    null|               null|
|     Jane|  Austen|16 December 1775|
|   Thomas|   Hardy|      June 2,1840|
+---------+--------+----------------+
```

Data transformation

There can be various kinds of data transformation needs and every case is mostly unique. We are going to cover some basic types of transformations, as follows:

- Merging two columns into one
- Adding characters/numbers to the existing ones
- Deleting or replacing characters/numbers from the existing ones
- Changing date formats

Python

```
// Merging columns
//Create a udf to concatenate two column values
>>> import pyspark.sql.functions
>>> concat_func = pyspark.sql.functions.udf(lambda name, age: name + "_" +
str(age))

//Apply the udf to create merged column
>>> concat_df = final_data.withColumn("name_age",
concat_func(final_data.name, final_data.age))
>>> concat_df.show(4)
+------+----+---+---------+------+--------+
|emp_id|name|age|     role|salary|name_age|
+------+----+---+---------+------+--------+
|     1|John| 25|Associate| 10000| John_25|
|     2| Ray| 35|  Manager| 12000|  Ray_35|
|     3|Mike| 24|  Manager| 12000| Mike_24|
|     4|Jane| 28|Associate|  null| Jane_28|
+------+----+---+---------+------+--------+
only showing top 4 rows
// Adding constant to data
>>> data_new = concat_df.withColumn("age_incremented",concat_df.age + 10)
>>> data_new.show(4)
+------+----+---+---------+------+--------+---------------+
|emp_id|name|age|     role|salary|name_age|age_incremented|
+------+----+---+---------+------+--------+---------------+
|     1|John| 25|Associate| 10000| John_25|             35|
|     2| Ray| 35|  Manager| 12000|  Ray_35|             45|
|     3|Mike| 24|  Manager| 12000| Mike_24|             34|
```

```
|    4|Jane| 28|Associate|  null| Jane_28|          38|
+------+----+---+---------+------+--------+--------------+
only showing top 4 rows
>>>


//Replace values in a column
>>> df1.replace('Emily','Charlotte','FirstName').show()
+---------+--------+----------------+
|FirstName|LastName|             Dob|
+---------+--------+----------------+
|   Thomas|   Hardy|    June 2, 1840|
|  Charles| Dickens| 7 February 1812|
|     Mark|   Twain|            null|
|     Jane|  Austen|16 December 1775|
|Charlotte|    null|            null|
+---------+--------+----------------+


// If the column name argument is omitted in replace, then replacement is
applicable to all columns
//Append new columns based on existing values in a column
//Give 'LastName' instead of 'Initial' if you want to overwrite
>>> df1.withColumn('Initial',df1.LastName.substr(1,1)).show()
+---------+--------+----------------+-------+
|FirstName|LastName|             Dob|Initial|
+---------+--------+----------------+-------+
|   Thomas|   Hardy|    June 2, 1840|      H|
|  Charles| Dickens| 7 February 1812|      D|
|     Mark|   Twain|            null|      T|
|     Jane|  Austen|16 December 1775|      A|
|    Emily|    null|            null|   null|
+---------+--------+----------------+-------+
```

Scala:

```
// Merging columns
//Create a udf to concatenate two column values
scala> val concatfunc = udf((name: String, age: Integer) =>
                         {name + "_" + age})
concatfunc: org.apache.spark.sql.expressions.UserDefinedFunction =
UserDefinedFunction(<function2>,StringType,Some(List(StringType,
IntegerType)))
scala>


//Apply the udf to create merged column
scala> val concat_df = final_data.withColumn("name_age",
                       concatfunc($"name", $"age"))
concat_df: org.apache.spark.sql.DataFrame =
        [emp_id: int, name: string ... 4 more fields]
```

```
scala> concat_df.show(4)
+------+----+---+---------+------+--------+
|emp_id|name|age|     role|salary|name_age|
+------+----+---+---------+------+--------+
|     1|John| 25|Associate| 10000| John_25|
|     2| Ray| 35|  Manager| 12000|  Ray_35|
|     3|Mike| 24|  Manager| 12000| Mike_24|
|     4|Jane| 28|Associate|  null| Jane_28|
+------+----+---+---------+------+--------+
only showing top 4 rows
scala>

// Adding constant to data
scala> val addconst = udf((age: Integer) => {age + 10})
addconst: org.apache.spark.sql.expressions.UserDefinedFunction =
      UserDefinedFunction(<function1>,IntegerType,Some(List(IntegerType)))
scala> val data_new = concat_df.withColumn("age_incremented",
                    addconst(col("age")))
data_new: org.apache.spark.sql.DataFrame =
      [emp_id: int, name: string ... 5 more fields]
scala> data_new.show(4)
+------+----+---+---------+------+--------+---------------+
|emp_id|name|age|     role|salary|name_age|age_incremented|
+------+----+---+---------+------+--------+---------------+
|     1|John| 25|Associate| 10000| John_25|             35|
|     2| Ray| 35|  Manager| 12000|  Ray_35|             45|
|     3|Mike| 24|  Manager| 12000| Mike_24|             34|
|     4|Jane| 28|Associate|  null| Jane_28|             38|
+------+----+---+---------+------+--------+---------------+
only showing top 4 rows

// Replace values in a column
//Note: As of Spark 2.0.0, there is no replace on DataFrame/ Dataset does
not work so .na. is a work around
scala> ds1.na.replace("FirstName",Map("Emily" -> "Charlotte")).show()
+---------+--------+---------------+
|FirstName|LastName|            Dob|
+---------+--------+---------------+
|   Thomas|   Hardy|   June 2, 1840|
|  Charles| Dickens|7 February 1812|
|     Mark|   Twain|           null|
|Charlotte|    null|           null|
+---------+--------+---------------+
scala>

// If the column name argument is "*" in replace, then replacement is
applicable to all columns
//Append new columns based on existing values in a column
```

```
//Give "LastName" instead of "Initial" if you want to overwrite
scala> ds1.withColumn("Initial",ds1("LastName").substr(1,1)).show()
+---------+--------+---------------+-------+
|FirstName|LastName|            Dob|Initial|
+---------+--------+---------------+-------+
|   Thomas|   Hardy|   June 2, 1840|      H|
|  Charles| Dickens|7 February 1812|      D|
|     Mark|   Twain|           null|      T|
|    Emily|    null|           null|   null|
+---------+--------+---------------+-------+
```

Now that we are familiar with basic examples, let us put together a somewhat complex example. You might have noticed that the date column in Authors data has different date formats. In some cases, month is followed by day, and vice versa. Such anomalies are common in the real world, wherein data might be collected from different sources. Here, we are looking at a case where the date column has data points with many different date formats. We need to standardize all the different date formats into one format. To do so, we first have to create a **user-defined function (udf)** that can take care of the different formats and convert those to one common format.

```
// Date conversions
//Create udf for date conversion that converts incoming string to YYYY-MM-
DD format
// The function assumes month is full month name and year is always 4
digits
// Separator is always a space or comma
// Month, date and year may come in any order
//Reusing authors data
>>> authors = [['Thomas','Hardy','June 2, 1840'],
        ['Charles','Dickens','7 February 1812'],
        ['Mark','Twain',None],
        ['Jane','Austen','16 December 1775'],
        ['Emily',None,None]]
>>> df1 = sc.parallelize(authors).toDF(
      ["FirstName","LastName","Dob"])
>>>

// Define udf
//Note: You may create this in a script file and execute with
execfile(filename.py)
>>> def toDate(s):
 import re
 year = month = day = ""
 if not s:
  return None
 mn = [0,'January','February','March','April','May',
  'June','July','August','September',
```

```
    'October','November','December']

  //Split the string and remove empty tokens
  l = [tok for tok in re.split(",| ",s) if tok]

//Assign token to year, month or day
 for a in l:
  if a in mn:
   month = "{:0>2d}".format(mn.index(a))
  elif len(a) == 4:
   year = a
  elif len(a) == 1:
   day = '0' + a
  else:
   day = a
 return year + '-' + month + '-' + day
>>>


//Register the udf
>>> from pyspark.sql.functions import udf
>>> from pyspark.sql.types import StringType
>>> toDateUDF = udf(toDate, StringType())

//Apply udf
>>> df1.withColumn("Dob",toDateUDF("Dob")).show()
+---------+--------+----------+
|FirstName|LastName|       Dob|
+---------+--------+----------+
|   Thomas|   Hardy|1840-06-02|
|  Charles| Dickens|1812-02-07|
|     Mark|   Twain|      null|
|     Jane|  Austen|1775-12-16|
|    Emily|    null|      null|
+---------+--------+----------+
>>>
```

Scala

```
//Date conversions
//Create udf for date conversion that converts incoming string to YYYY-MM-
DD format
// The function assumes month is full month name and year is always 4
digits
// Separator is always a space or comma
// Month, date and year may come in any order
//Reusing authors case class and data
>>> val authors = Seq(
        Author("Thomas","Hardy","June 2, 1840"),
```

```
        Author("Charles","Dickens","7 February 1812"),
        Author("Mark","Twain",null),
        Author("Jane","Austen","16 December 1775"),
        Author("Emily",null,null))
authors: Seq[Author] = List(Author(Thomas,Hardy,June 2, 1840),
Author(Charles,Dickens,7 February 1812), Author(Mark,Twain,null),
Author(Jane,Austen,16 December 1775), Author(Emily,null,null))
scala> val ds1 = sc.parallelize(authors).toDS()
ds1: org.apache.spark.sql.Dataset[Author] = [FirstName: string, LastName:
string ... 1 more field]
scala>


// Define udf
//Note: You can type :paste on REPL to paste  multiline code. CTRL + D
signals end of paste mode
def toDateUDF = udf((s: String) => {
    var (year, month, day) = ("","","")
    val mn = List("","January","February","March","April","May",
        "June","July","August","September",
        "October","November","December")
    //Tokenize the date string and remove trailing comma, if any
    if(s != null) {
      for (x <- s.split(" ")) {
        val token = x.stripSuffix(",")
        token match {
        case "" =>
        case x if (mn.contains(token)) =>
            month = "%02d".format(mn.indexOf(token))
        case x if (token.length() == 4) =>
            year = token
        case x =>
            day = token
        }
     }   //End of token processing for
     year + "-" + month + "-" + day=
    } else {
        null
    }
})
toDateUDF: org.apache.spark.sql.expressions.UserDefinedFunction
scala>


//Apply udf and convert date strings to standard form YYYY-MM-DD
scala> ds1.withColumn("Dob",toDateUDF(ds1("Dob"))).show()
+---------+--------+----------+
|FirstName|LastName|       Dob|
+---------+--------+----------+
|   Thomas|   Hardy| 1840-06-2|
```

```
|   Charles|  Dickens|  1812-02-7|
|      Mark|    Twain|       null|
|      Jane|   Austen|1775-12-16|
|     Emily|     null|       null|
+---------+--------+----------+
```

That lines up the date of birth strings neatly. We can keep fine-tuning the udf as we encounter more varieties of date formats.

At this stage, before getting started with data analysis, it is extremely important that you should pause for a moment and re-evaluate the actions you have taken from starting data acquisition to cleaning and transforming it. There have been a lot of cases where tremendous time and effort involved went for a toss and led to project failure because of incorrect data being analyzed and modeled. Such cases became perfect examples of a famous computer adage – **Garbage In, Garbage Out (GIGO)**.

Basics of statistics

The field of statistics is all about using mathematical procedures to summarize the raw facts and figures of a dataset in some meaningful way so that it makes sense to you. This includes, and is not limited to: gathering data, analyzing it, interpreting it, and representing it.

The field of statistics exists mainly because it is usually impossible to collect data for the entire population. So using statistical techniques, we estimate the population parameters using the sample statistics by addressing the uncertainties.

In this section, we will cover some basic statistics and analysis techniques on which we are going to build up our complete understanding of the concepts covered in this book.

The study of statistics can be broadly categorized into two main branches:

- Descriptive statistics
- Inferential statistics

The following diagram depicts these two terms and shows how we estimate the population parameters from samples:

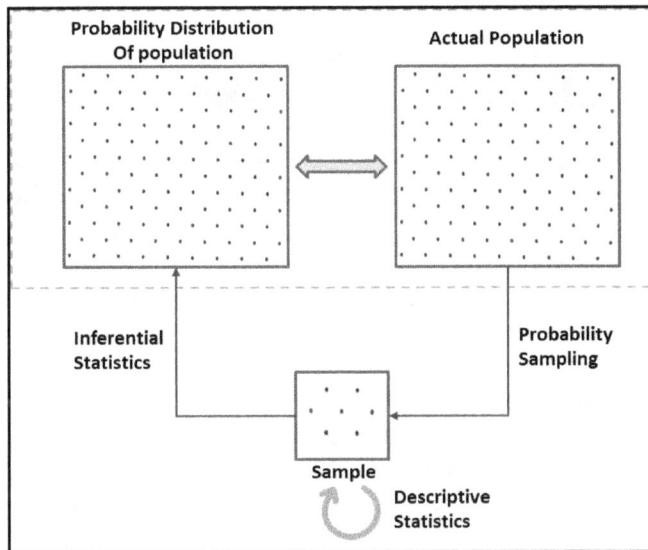

Before we get started on these, it is important to get some familiarity with sampling and distributions.

Sampling

Through sampling techniques, we just take a portion of the population dataset and work on it:

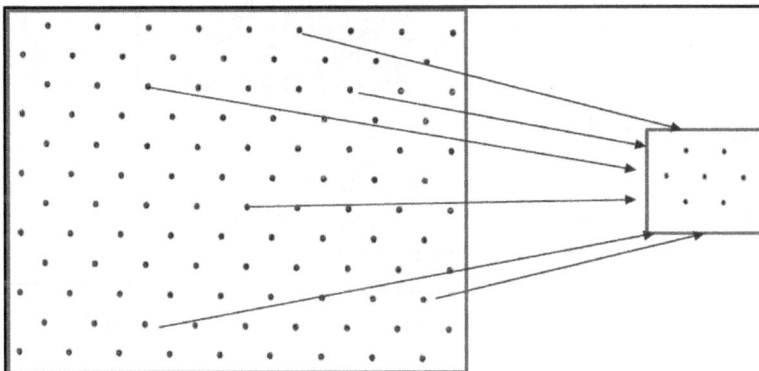

But why do we sample? The following are various reasons for sampling:

- Difficult to get the entire population's data; for example, the heights of the citizens of any country.
- Difficult to process the entire dataset. When we talk about big data computing platforms such as Spark, the scope of this challenge nearly disappears. However, there can be scenarios where you have to treat the entire data at hand as a sample and extrapolate your analysis result to a future time or to a larger population.
- Difficult to plot voluminous data to visualize it. There can be technical limitations to it.
- For validation of your analysis or validation of your predictive models – especially when you are working with small datasets and you have to rely on cross-validation.

For effective sampling, there are two important constraints: one is determining the sample size and the other is the technique to choose for sampling. The sample size greatly influences the estimation of population parameters. We will cover this aspect later in this chapter after covering some of the prerequisite basics. In this section, we will focus on sampling techniques.

There are various probability-based (the probability of each sample being selected is known) and non-probability-based (the probability of each sample being selected is not known) sampling techniques available, but we are going to limit our discussion to probability-based techniques only.

Simple random sample

The **simple random sample** (**SRS**) is the most basic type of probability sampling method, where every element has the same probability of being chosen. This means that every possible sample of *n* elements has an equal chance of selection.

Systematic sampling

Systematic sampling is probably the simplest of all probability-based sampling techniques, where every *kth* element of the population is sampled. So this is otherwise known as interval sampling. It starts with a fixed starting point chosen at random and then an interval is estimated (the *kth* element, where k = *(population size)/(sample size)*). Here, the progression through the elements is circled to start from the beginning when it reaches the end till your sample size is reached.

Stratified sampling

This sampling technique is preferred when the subgroups or subpopulations within the population vary, because other sampling techniques might not help extract a sample that is a good representative of the population. Through stratified sampling, the population is divided into homogeneous subgroups called **strata** and a sample is taken by randomly selecting the subjects from those strata in proportion to the population. So, the stratum size to population size ratio is maintained in the sample as well:

Python

```
/* "Sample" function is defined for DataFrames (not RDDs) which takes three
parameters:
withReplacement - Sample with replacement or not (input: True/False)
fraction - Fraction of rows to generate (input: any number between 0 and 1
as per your requirement of sample size)
seed - Seed for sampling (input: Any random seed)
*/
>>> sample1 = data_new.sample(False, 0.6) //With random seed as no seed
value specified
>>> sample2 = data_new.sample(False, 0.6, 10000) //With specific seed value
of 10000
```

Scala:

```
scala> val sample1 = data_new.sample(false, 0.6) //With random seed as no
seed value specified
sample1: org.apache.spark.sql.Dataset[org.apache.spark.sql.Row] = [emp_id:
int, name: string ... 5 more fields]
scala> val sample2 = data_new.sample(false, 0.6, 10000) //With specific
seed value of 10000
sample2: org.apache.spark.sql.Dataset[org.apache.spark.sql.Row] = [emp_id:
int, name: string ... 5 more fields]
```

> We only looked at sampling on DataFrames; there are MLlib library functions such as `sampleByKey` and `sampleByKeyExact` to do stratified sampling on RDDs of key-value pairs. Check out `spark.util.random` package for Bernoulli , Poisson or Random samplers.

Data distributions

Understanding how your data is distributed is one of the primary tasks you need to perform to turn data into information. Analyzing the distributions of the variables helps detect the outliers, visualize the trends in the data, and can also shape up your understanding for the data at hand. This helps in thinking right and taking the right approaches in solving a business problem. Plotting the distributions makes it visually more intuitive and we will cover this aspect in the *Descriptive statistics* section.

Frequency distributions

Frequency distribution explains which values a variable takes and how often it takes those values. It is usually represented with a table with each possible value with its corresponding number of occurrences.

Let's consider an example where we roll a six-sided die 100 times and observe the following frequencies:

Face Up	Frequency
1	12
2	16
3	21
4	20
5	18
6	13

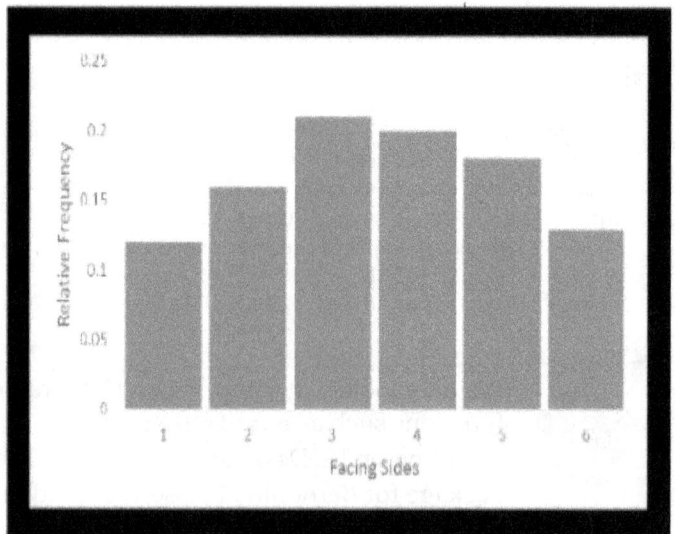

Frequency Table

Similarly, you might observe different distributions on every set of 100 rolls of the die because it would depend on chance.

At times, you might be interested in the proportions of occurrences instead of just occurrences. In the preceding die roll example, we rolled the die 100 times in total, so the proportionate distribution or the **relative frequency distribution** would appear as follows:

Face Up	Relative Frequency
1	0.12
2	0.16
3	0.21
4	0.2
5	0.18
6	0.13

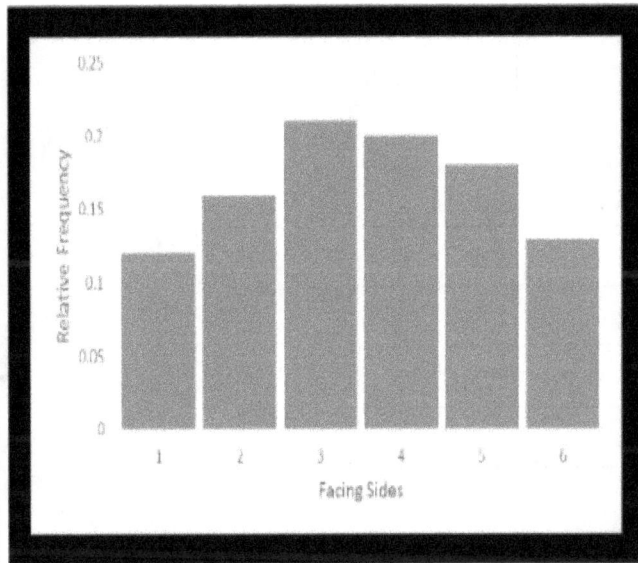

Relative Frequency Table

Probability distributions

In the same example of die rolling, we know that a total probability of 1 is distributed across all faces of the die. This means that a probability of 1/6 (approximately 0.167) is associated with face 1 through face 6. Irrespective of the number of times you roll a die (a fair die!), the same probability of 1/6 would be distributed evenly on all sides of the die. So, if you plot this distribution, it would appear as follows:

Face Up	Probability
1	0.167
2	0.167
3	0.167
4	0.167
5	0.167
6	0.167

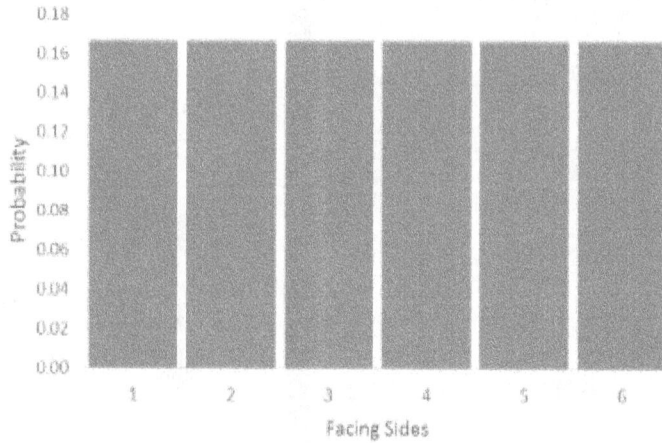

Probability Distribution

We looked at three kinds of distributions here – frequency distributions, relative frequency distribution, and probability distribution.

This probability distribution is actually the distribution of the population. In real-world cases, at times we have prior knowledge of the population distribution (in our example, it is the probability of 0.167 on all six sides of a fair die) and at times we don't. In scenarios where we don't have the population distribution, finding the distribution of the population itself becomes part of your inferential statistics. Also, unlike the fair die example, where the same probability is associated with all the sides, there can be different probabilities associated with the values a variable can take and they can follow a particular type of distribution as well.

Now it's time to reveal the secret! The relation between the relative frequency distribution and the probability distribution is the basis of statistical inference. The relative frequency distributions are also called empirical distributions based on what we observe in the samples we take (here, it is a sample of 100). As discussed earlier, the empirical distributions of every 100 rolls of the die would differ depending on chance. Now, the larger the number of rolls, the closer will be the relative frequency distribution to the probability distribution. So, the relative frequencies of an infinite number of die rolls is the probability distribution, which in turn is the population distribution.

There are various kinds of probability distributions, which are again categorized into two, based on the type of variable – categorical or continuous. We will cover these distributions in detail in the subsequent sections of this chapter. However, we should know what these categories imply! Categorical variables can take on only a few categories; for example, pass/fail, zero/one, cancer/malignant are examples of categorical variables with two categories. Similarly, a categorical variable can have more categories, such as red/green/blue, type1/type2/type3/type4, and so on. Continuous variables can take on any value in a given range and measured on a continuous scale, for example, age, height, salary, and so on. Theoretically, there can be an infinite number of possible values between any two values of a continuous variable. For example, between 5'6" and 6'4" height values (foot and inch scale), there can be many fractional values possible. The same holds true when measured in a centimeter scale as well.

Descriptive statistics

In the previous section, we learnt how distributions are formed. In this section, we will learn how to describe them through descriptive statistics. There are two important components of a distribution that can help describe it, which are its location and its spread.

Measures of location

A measure of location is a single value that describes where the center of the data lies. The three most common measures of location are mean, median, and mode.

Mean

By far the most common and widely used measure of central tendency is the **mean**, which is otherwise known as the average. Whether it is a sample or a population, the mean or average is the summation of all the elements divided by the total number of elements.

Median

The **median** is the middle value of a series of data when sorted in any order so that half of the data is greater than the median and the other half smaller. When there are two middle values (with an even number of data items), the median is the average of those middle two. Medians are better measures of location when the data has outliers (extreme values).

Mode

The **mode** is the most frequent data item. It can be determined for both qualitative and quantitative data.

Python

//Reusing data_new created in duplicated value treatment

```
>>> mean_age = data_new.agg({'age': 'mean'}).first()[0]
>>> age_counts = data_new.groupBy("age").agg({"age":
"count"}).alias("freq")
>>> mode_age = age_counts.sort(age_counts["COUNT(age)"].desc(),
age_counts.age.asc()).first()[0]
>>> print(mean_age, mode_age)
(29.615384615384617, 25)
>>> age_counts.sort("count(age)",ascending=False).show(2)
+---+----------
+
|age|count(age)|
+---+----------+
| 28|         3|
| 29|         2|
+---+----------+
only showing top 2 rows
```

Scala

```
//Reusing data_new created
scala> val mean_age = data_new.select(floor(avg("age"))).first().getLong(0)
mean_age: Long = 29
scala> val mode_age = data_new.groupBy($"age").agg(count($"age")).
            sort($"count(age)".desc, $"age").first().getInt(0)
mode_age: Int = 28
scala> val age_counts = data_new.groupBy("age").agg(count($"age") as
"freq")
age_counts: org.apache.spark.sql.DataFrame = [age: int, freq: bigint]
scala> age_counts.sort($"freq".desc).show(2)
+---+----
```

```
+
|age|freq|
+---+----+
| 35|   2|
| 28|   2|
+---+----+
```

Measures of spread

Measures of spread describe how close or scattered the data is for a particular variable or data item.

Range

The range is the difference between the smallest and largest values of a variable. One disadvantage to it is that it does not take into account every value in the data.

Variance

To find the variability in the dataset, we can subtract each value from the mean, square them up so it gets rid of the negative signs (also scales up the magnitude), and then sum them all and divide by the total number of values:

$$Variance = \sigma^2 = \frac{\Sigma(X - \mu)^2}{N}$$

If the data is more spread out, the variance will be a large number. One disadvantage to it is that it gives undue weight to the outliers.

Standard deviation

Like variance, standard deviation is also a measure of dispersion within the data. Variance had the limitation that the unit of data was also squared along with the data, so it was difficult to relate the variance with the values in the dataset. So, standard deviation is calculated as the square root of the variance:

$$Standard\ Deviation = \sigma = \sqrt{\frac{\Sigma(X - \mu)^2}{N}}$$

Python

```
//Reusing data_new created before
import math
>>> range_salary = data_new.agg({'salary': 'max'}).first()[0] -
data_new.agg({'salary': 'min'}).first()[0]
>>> mean_salary = data_new.agg({'salary': 'mean'}).first()[0]
>>> salary_deviations = data_new.select(((data_new.salary - mean_salary) *
        (data_new.salary - mean_salary)).alias("deviation"))
>>> stddev_salary = math.sqrt(salary_deviations.agg({'deviation' :
'avg'}).first()[0])
>>> variance_salary =
salary_deviations.groupBy().avg("deviation").first()[0]
>>> print(round(range_salary,2), round(mean_salary,2),
        round(variance_salary,2), round(stddev_salary,2))
(119880.0, 20843.33, 921223322.22, 30351.66)
>>>
```

Scala

```
//Reusing data_new created before
scala> val range_salary = data_new.select(max("salary")).first().
        getLong(0) - data_new.select(min("salary")).first().getLong(0)
range_salary: Long = 119880
scala> val mean_salary =
data_new.select(floor(avg("salary"))).first().getLong(0)
mean_salary: Long = 20843
scala> val salary_deviations = data_new.select(((data_new("salary") -
mean_salary)
                    * (data_new("salary") -
mean_salary)).alias("deviation"))
salary_deviations: org.apache.spark.sql.DataFrame = [deviation: bigint]
scala> val variance_salary = { salary_deviations.select(avg("deviation"))
                                .first().getDouble(0) }
variance_salary: Double = 9.212233223333334E8
scala> val stddev_salary = { salary_deviations
                    .select(sqrt(avg("deviation")))
                    .first().getDouble(0) }
stddev_salary: Double = 30351.660948510435
```

Summary statistics

The summary statistics of a dataset is extremely useful information that gives us a quick insight into the data at hand. Using the function `colStats` available in statistics, we can obtain a multivariate statistical summary of `RDD[Vector]` which contains column-wise max, min, mean, variance, number of non-zeros, and the total count. Let us explore this through some code examples:

Python

```
>>> import numpy
>>> from pyspark.mllib.stat import Statistics
// Create an RDD of number vectors
//This example creates an RDD with 5 rows with 5 elements each
>>> observations =
sc.parallelize(numpy.random.random_integers(0,100,(5,5)))
// Compute column summary statistics.
//Note that the results may vary because of random numbers
>>> summary = Statistics.colStats(observations)
>>> print(summary.mean())        // mean value for each column
>>> print(summary.variance())   // column-wise variance
>>> print(summary.numNonzeros())// number of nonzeros in each column
```

Scala

```
scala> import org.apache.spark.mllib.linalg.Vectors
import org.apache.spark.mllib.linalg.Vectors
scala> import org.apache.spark.mllib.stat.{
        MultivariateStatisticalSummary, Statistics}
import org.apache.spark.mllib.stat.{MultivariateStatisticalSummary,
Statistics}
// Create an RDD of number vectors
//This example creates an RDD with 5 rows with 5 elements each
scala> val observations =
sc.parallelize(Seq.fill(5)(Vectors.dense(Array.fill(5)(
                  scala.util.Random.nextDouble))))
observations:
org.apache.spark.rdd.RDD[org.apache.spark.mllib.linalg.Vector] =
ParallelCollectionRDD[43] at parallelize at <console>:27
scala>
// Compute column summary statistics.
//Note that the results may vary because of random numbers
scala> val summary = Statistics.colStats(observations)
summary: org.apache.spark.mllib.stat.MultivariateStatisticalSummary =
org.apache.spark.mllib.stat.MultivariateOnlineSummarizer@36836161
scala> println(summary.mean)  // mean value for each column
[0.5782406967737089,0.5903954680966121,0.4892908815930067,0.456807017992348
```

```
35,0.6611492334819364]
scala> println(summary.variance)      // column-wise variance
[0.11893608153330748,0.07673977181967367,0.023169197889513014,0.08882605965
192601,0.08360159585590332]
scala> println(summary.numNonzeros) // number of nonzeros in each column
[5.0,5.0,5.0,5.0,5.0]
```

> **TIP**
>
> Apache Spark MLlib RDD-based API is in maintenance mode starting
> Spark 2.0. They are expected to deprecated in 2.2+ and removed in Spark
> 3.0.

Graphical techniques

To understand the behavior of your data points, you may have to plot them and see. You
need a platform, however, to visualize your data in terms of *box plots*, *scatter plots*, or
histograms, to name a few. The iPython/Jupyter notebook or any other third-party notebook
supported by Spark can be used for data visualization in your browser itself. Databricks
provides their own notebook. Visualization is covered in its own chapter and this chapter
focuses on the complete life cycle. However, Spark provides histogram data preparation out
of the box so that bucket ranges and frequencies may be transferred to the client machine as
against the complete dataset. The following example shows the same.

Python

```
//Histogram
>>>from random import randint
>>> numRDD = sc.parallelize([randint(0,9) for x in xrange(1,1001)])
// Generate histogram data for given bucket count
>>> numRDD.histogram(5)
([0.0, 1.8, 3.6, 5.4, 7.2, 9], [202, 213, 215, 188, 182])
//Alternatively, specify ranges
>>> numRDD.histogram([0,3,6,10])
([0, 3, 6, 10], [319, 311, 370])
```

Scala:

```
//Histogram
scala> val numRDD = sc.parallelize(Seq.fill(1000)(
                    scala.util.Random.nextInt(10)))
numRDD: org.apache.spark.rdd.RDD[Int] =
    ParallelCollectionRDD[0] at parallelize at <console>:24
// Generate histogram data for given bucket count
scala> numRDD.histogram(5)
res10: (Array[Double], Array[Long]) = (Array(0.0, 1.8, 3.6, 5.4, 7.2,
```

```
9.0),Array(194, 209, 215, 195, 187))
scala>
//Alternatively, specify ranges
scala> numRDD.histogram(Array(0,3.0,6,10))
res13: Array[Long] = Array(293, 325, 382)
```

Inferential statistics

We saw that descriptive statistics were extremely useful in describing and presenting data, but they did not provide a way to use the sample statistics to infer the population parameters or to validate any hypothesis we might have made. So, the techniques of inferential statistics surfaced to address such requirements. Some of the important uses of inferential statistics are:

- Estimation of population parameters
- Hypothesis testing

Please note that a sample can never represent a population perfectly because every time we sample, it naturally incurs sampling errors, hence the need for inferential statistics! Let us spend some time understanding the various types of probability distributions that can help infer the population parameters.

Discrete probability distributions

Discrete probability distributions are used to model data that is discrete in nature, which means that data can only take on certain values, such as integers. Unlike categorical variables, discrete variables can take on only numeric data, especially count data from a set of distinct whole values. Also, the sum of probabilities of all possible values of a random variable is one. The discrete probability distributions are described in terms of probability mass function. There can be various types of discrete probability distributions. The following are a few examples.

Bernoulli distribution

Bernoulli distribution is a type of distribution that describes the trials having only two possible outcomes, such as success/failure, head/tail, the face value of a six-sided die is 4 or not, the message sent was received or not, and so on. Bernoulli distribution can be generalized for any categorical variable with two or more possible outcomes.

Let's take the example of "students' pass rate for an exam" where 0.6 (60 percent) is the probability **P** of the students passing the exam and 0.4 (40 percent) is the probability (**1-P**) for the students to fail in the exam. Let us denote fail as and pass as **1**:

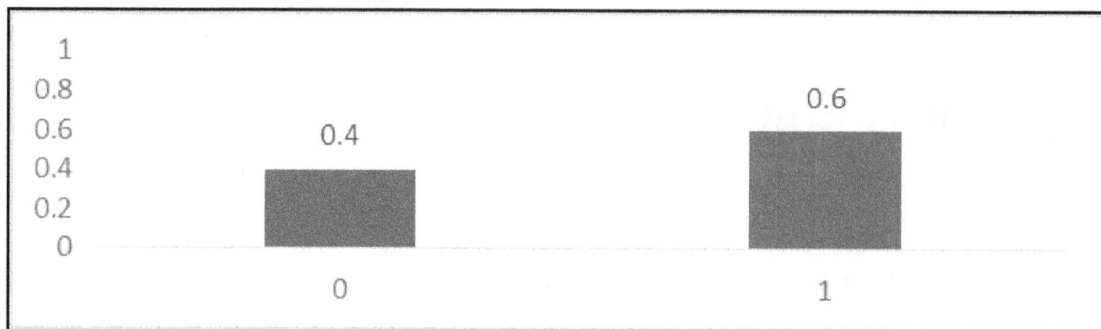

Such distributions cannot answer questions such as the expected pass rate of a student, because the expected value (μ) is going to be some fraction that this distribution cannot take. It can only mean that if you sample 1,000 students, then 600 would pass and 400 would fail.

Binomial distribution

This distribution can describe a series of Bernoulli trials (each with only two possible outcomes). Also, it assumes that the outcome of one trial does not affect the subsequent trials and that the probability of any event occurring is the same on every trial. An example of binomial distribution is tossing a coin five times. Here, the outcome of the first toss does not influence the outcome of the second toss, and the probability associated with each outcome is the same on all tosses.

If n is the number of trials and p is the probability of success in every trial, then the mean (μ) of this binomial distribution would be given by:

$\mu = n * p$

The variance ($\sigma 2x$) would be given by:

$\sigma 2x = n*p*(1-p)$.

In general, a random variable X that follows binomial distribution with parameters n and p, we can write as $X \sim B(n, p)$. For such a distribution, the probability of getting exactly k successes in n trials can be described by the probability mass function as follows:

$$f(k \mid n, p) = P(X = k) = \binom{n}{k} p^k (1 - p)^{n-k}$$

$$\binom{n}{k} = \frac{n!}{k!(n-k)!}$$

here, $k = 0, 1, 2, ..., n$

Sample problem

Let us assume a hypothetical scenario. Suppose 24 percent of companies in a city announced they would provide support to the tsunami-affected areas of the country as part of their CSR activity. In a sample of 20 companies chosen at random, find the probability of the number of companies that have announced they will help tsunami-affected areas:

- Exactly three
- Less than three
- Three or more

Solution:

The sample size = n = 20.

The probability that a company chosen at random has announced it will help = $P = 0.24$.

a) $P(x = 3) = {}^{20}C_3 (0.24)^3 (0.76)^{17} = 0.15$

b) $P(x < 3) = P(0) + P(1) + P(2)$

$= (0.76)^{20} + {}^{20}C_1 (0.24)(0.76)^{19} + {}^{20}C_2 (0.24)^2 (0.76)^{18}$

$= 0.0041 + 0.0261 + 0.0783 = 0.11$

c) $P(x \geq 3) = 1 - P(x \leq 2) = 1 - 0.11 = 0.89$

Note that binomial distribution is widely used in scenarios where you want to model the success rate in a sample of size n drawn from a population of size N, with replacement. If it is done without replacement then the draws will no longer be independent and hence will not follow binomial distribution rightly. However, such scenarios do exist and can be modeled using different types of distributions, such as hypergeometric distributions.

Poisson distribution

Poisson distribution can describe the probability of a given number of independent events that occur with a known average rate in a fixed interval of time or space. Please note that the events should only have binary outcomes such as success or failure, for example, the number of phone calls you receive per day or the number of cars passing a signal per hour. You need to carefully take a closer look at these examples. Please note here that you do not have the opposite half of this information, that is, how many phone calls you did not receive per day or how many cars did not pass that signal. Such data points do not have the other half of the information. On the contrary, if I say that 30 out of 50 students passed in an exam, you can easily infer that 20 students have failed! You have this other half of the information.

If μ is the mean number of events occurring (a known average rate in a fixed interval of time or space) then the probability of k events occurring at the same interval can be described by the probability mass function:

$$P(X = k \mid \mu) = \frac{e^{-\mu}\mu^k}{k!}$$

here, $k = 0, 1, 2, 3...$

The preceding equation describes the Poisson distribution.

For a Poisson distribution, mean and variance are the same. Also, the Poisson distribution tends to be more symmetric as its mean or variance increases.

Sample problem

Suppose you knew that the mean number of calls to a fire station on a weekday is eight. What is the probability that on a given weekday there would be 11 calls? This problem can be solved using the following formula based on the Poisson distribution:

$$P = \frac{e^{-8}8^{11}}{11!} = 0.07$$

Continuous probability distributions

Continuous probability distributions are used to model data that is continuous in nature, which means that data can only take on any value within a specified range. So we deal with probabilities associated with intervals and not with any particular value as it is zero. Continuous probability distributions are the theoretical models of experiments; it is a relative frequency distribution built from an infinite number of observations. This means that when you reduce the interval, the number of observations increases, and as the number of observations increases more and more and approaches infinity, it forms a continuous probability distribution. The total area under the curve is one and to find the probability associated with any particular range, we have to find the area under the curve. Therefore, continuous distributions are normally described in terms of **probability density function (PDF)** which is of the following type:

$P(a \leq X \leq b) = a\int^b f(x)\,dx$

There can be various types of continuous probability distributions. The following sections are a few examples.

Normal distribution

A normal distribution is a simple, straightforward, yet very important continuous probability distribution. It is otherwise known as a Gaussian distribution or **bell curve** because of its appearance when plotted. Also, for a perfect normal distribution, the mean, median, and mode are all the same.

Many naturally occurring phenomena follow a normal distribution (they may follow a different distribution as well!), such as the heights of people, errors in measurement, and so on. However, normal distributions are not suitable to model variables that are highly skewed or are inherently positive (for example, share prices or students' test scores where the difficulty level was minimal). Such variables may be better described by different distributions or by the normal distribution after a data transformation (like logarithmic transformation).

Normal distributions can be described using two descriptors: mean for the location of the center and standard deviation for the spread (height and width). The probability density function that represents a normal distribution is as follows:

$$f(x, \mu, \sigma) = \frac{1}{\sigma\sqrt{2\pi}} e^{-\frac{(x-\mu)^2}{2\sigma^2}}$$

One of the reasons this normal distribution tops the chart for popularity is because of the **Central Limit Theorem** (**CLT**). It states that, regardless of the population distribution, the mean of samples independently drawn from same population distribution is distributed almost normally and this normality increases more and more with the increase in sample size. This behavior is actually the basis of statistical hypothesis testing.

Additionally, every normal distribution, irrespective of its mean and standard deviation, follows an empirical rule (68-95-99.7 rule) which states that about 68 percent of the area under the curve falls within one standard deviation of the mean, 95 percent of the area under the curve falls within two standard deviations of the mean, and around 99.7 percent of the area under the curve falls within three standard deviations of the mean.

Now, to find the probability of an event, you can either use integral calculus or transform the distribution into a standard normal distribution as explained in the next section.

Standard normal distribution

A standard normal distribution is a type of normal distribution with mean and standard deviation 1. Such a distribution is rarely found naturally. It is designed mainly to find the area under the curve of a normal distribution (instead of integrating using calculus) or to normalize the data points.

Suppose a random variable X is normally distributed with mean (μ) and standard deviation (σ), then the random variable Z will have a standard normal distribution with mean and standard deviation 1. The value of Z can be found as:

$$Z = \frac{X - \mu}{\sigma}$$

Since data can be standardized in this manner, the data points can be represented and interpreted as *how many standard deviations away from the mean* they lie in the distribution. It helps in comparing two distributions with different scales.

You can find the applications of a normal distribution in scenarios where one wants to find what percent would fall under a specified range – assuming that the distribution is approximately normal.

Consider the following example:

If the time a shopkeeper operates the shop on a given day follows the normal distribution with $\mu = 8$ hours and $\sigma = 0.5$ hours, what is the probability that he stays at the shop for less than 7.5 hours?

The probability distribution would look as follows:

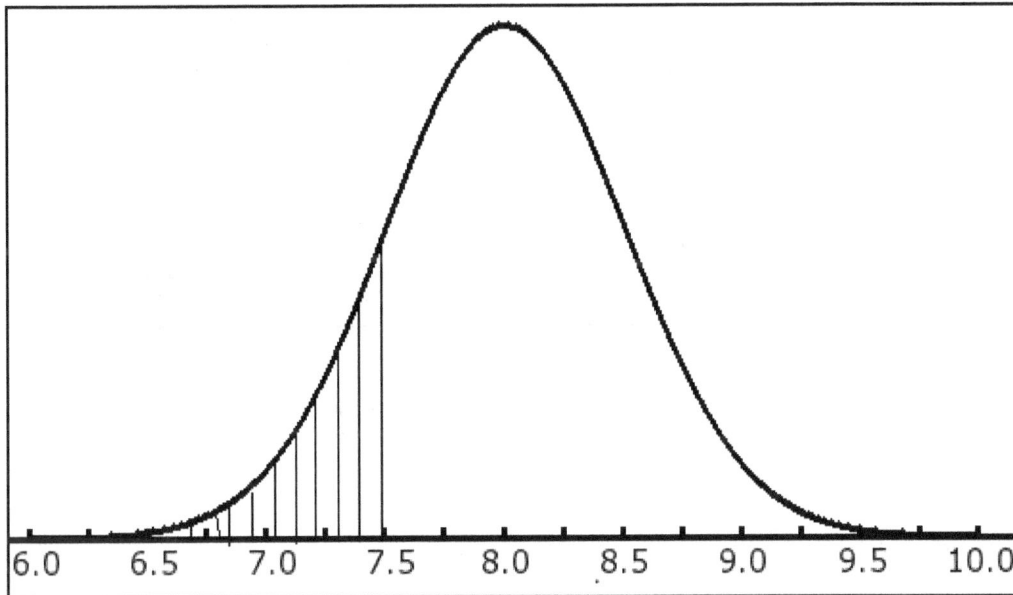

Data distribution

$$z = \frac{x - \mu}{\sigma} = \frac{7.5 - 8}{0.5} = -1$$

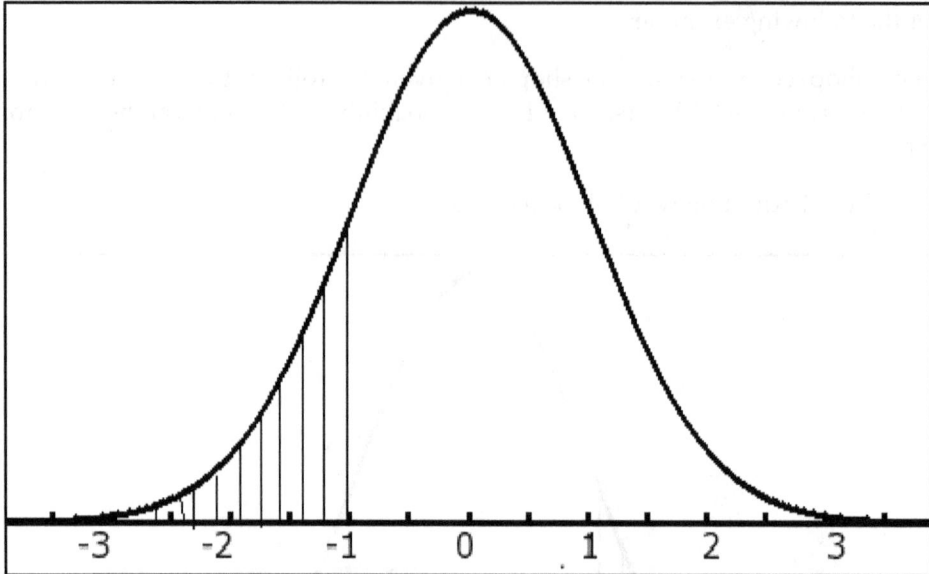

Standard normal distribution

So the probability that the shopkeeper stays at the shop for less than 7.5 hours is given by:

P(z = -1) = 0.1587 = 15.87

This was figured out using the Z-table.

Please note that normality in a dataset is mostly an approximation. You first need to check the normality of the data and then proceed further if your analysis is based on the assumption of normality in data. There are various different ways to check for normality: you can opt for techniques such as histogram (with a curve fitted with the mean and standard deviation of the data), normal probability plot, or QQ plot.

Chi-square distribution

Chi-square distribution is one of the most widely used distributions in statistical inference. It is a special case of gamma distribution, which is useful in modeling skewed distributions of the variables that are not negative. It states that, if a random variable X is normally distributed and Z is one of its standard normal variables, then Z_2 will have a X_2 distribution with one degree of freedom. Similarly, if we take many such random independent standard normal variables from the same distribution, square them and add them up, then that will also follow X_2 distribution as follows:

$Z_{12} + Z_{22} + ... + Z_{k2}$ will have X_2 distribution with k degrees of freedom.

Chi-square distribution is mainly used for the inference of population variance or population standard deviation given the sample variance or standard deviation. This is because X_2 distribution is defined in an alternative way, in terms of the ratio of sample variance to population variance.

To justify this point, let us take a random sample $(x_1, x_2,...,xn)$ from a normal distribution with variance σ^2

The sample mean would be given by:

$$\overline{X} = \frac{\sum_{i=1}^{n} x_i}{n}$$

However, the sample variance is given by:

$$S^2 = \frac{\sum_{i=1}^{n}(x_i - \overline{x})^2}{n-1}$$

Considering the preceding mentioned facts, we can define the chi-square statistic as follows:

$$\chi^2 = \frac{\sum_{i=1}^{n}(X_i - \overline{X})^2}{\sigma^2}$$

(Remember $z = \frac{x-\mu}{\sigma}$ and Z_2 will have X_2 distribution.)

So, $\chi^2 = \frac{(n-1)S^2}{\sigma^2}$

Therefore, the sampling distribution of the chi-square statistic will follow a chi-square distribution with *(n-1)* degrees of freedom.

The probability density function of a chi-square distribution with *n* degrees of freedom and gamma function Γ is given by:

$$f(x) = \frac{1}{2^{n/2}\ \Gamma(n/2)}\ x^{n/2-1}\ e^{-x/2}, \quad x > 0$$

For a $\chi 2$ distribution with *k* degrees of freedom, mean $(\mu) = k$ and variance $(\sigma 2) = 2k$.

Please note that chi-square distributions are positively skewed, but the degree of skewness decreases with the increase in the degree of freedom and approaches a normal distribution.

Sample problem

Find the 90 percent confidence interval for the variance and standard deviation for the price in dollars for adult single movie tickets. The data given represents a selected sample of nationwide movie theaters. Assume the variable is normally distributed.

Given sample (in $): 10, 08, 07, 11, 12, 06, 05, 09, 15, 12

Solution:

N = 10

Mean of sample:

$\bar{x} = (10+8+7+11+12+6+5+9+15+12)/10 = 9.5$

Variance of sample:

$S^2 = [(10 - \bar{x})^2 + (08 - \bar{x})^2 + \ldots + (12 - \bar{x})^2] / 9 = 9.61$

Standard deviation of sample:

S = sqrt(9.61)

Degree of freedom:

10-1 = 9

Now we need to find the 90 percent confidence interval, which means that 10 percent of the data will be left over in the tails.

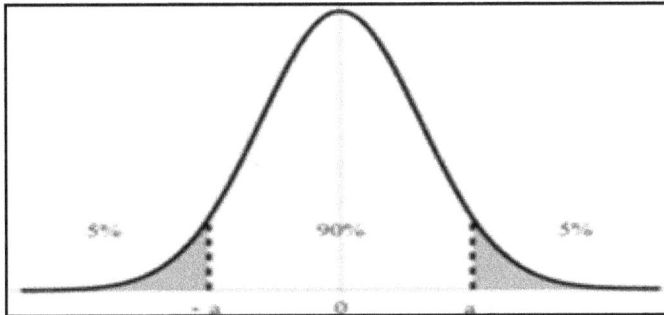

Now, let us use the formula:

$$\frac{(n-1)S^2}{X^2_{right}} < \sigma^2 < \frac{(n-1)S^2}{X^2_{left}}$$

$$=> \sqrt{\frac{(n-1)S^2}{X^2_{right}}} < \sigma < \sqrt{\frac{(n-1)S^2}{X^2_{left}}}$$

Then we can either find the chi-square value using a table or a computer program.

To find the middle 90 percent confidence interval, we can consider the left 95 percent and right 5 percent.

So after substituting the numbers, we get:

$$=> \sqrt{\frac{(9)(9.61)}{16.919}} < \sigma < \sqrt{\frac{(9)(9.61)}{3.325}}$$

$$=> \sqrt{\frac{(9)(9.61)}{16.92}} < \sigma < \sqrt{\frac{(9)(9.61)}{3.33}}$$

$$=> 2.26 < \sigma < 5.1$$

So, we can conclude that we are 90 percent confident that the standard deviation for the price of a single movie ticket of the population (all tickets in the nation) is between $2.26 and $5.10 based on a sample of 10 nationwide movie ticket prices.

Student's t-distribution

Student's t-distribution is used in estimating the mean of a normally distributed population in the case where the population standard deviation is not known or the sample size is too small. In such cases, both μ and σ are unknown and population parameters are estimated only through the sample.

This distribution is bell-shaped and symmetric like normal distribution, but has heavier tails. The t-distribution becomes a normal distribution when the sample size is large.

Let us take a random sample $(x1, x2,...,xn)$ from a normal distribution with mean μ and variance $\sigma2$.

The sample mean would be $\overline{X} = \frac{\sum_{i=1}^{n} x_i}{n}$ and sample variance $S^2 = \frac{\sum_{i=1}^{n}(X_i - \overline{X})^2}{n-1}$

Considering the above-mentioned facts, the t-statistic can be defined as:

$$t = \frac{\overline{X} - \mu}{S/\sqrt{n}}$$

The sampling distribution of the t-statistic will follow a t-distribution with $(n-1)$**degrees of freedom (df)**. The higher the degree of freedom, the closer will be the t-distribution to the standard normal distribution.

The mean of a t-distribution (μ) = and variance $(\sigma2) = df/df-2$

Now, just to make things clearer, let us look back for a moment and consider the scenario where the population σ is known. When the population is normally distributed, the sample mean x is mostly normally distributed regardless of the sample size and any linear transformation of x such as $\frac{\overline{X} - \mu}{\sigma/\sqrt{n}}$ will also follow a normal distribution.

What if the population is not normally distributed? Even then, the distribution of $\bar{x}$ (which is the sampling distribution) or $\frac{\bar{X}-\mu}{\sigma/\sqrt{n}}$ will follow a normal distribution as per CLT when the sample size is large enough!

The other scenario is that the population σ is unknown. With this, if the population is normally distributed, the sample mean $\bar{x}$ is mostly normally distributed, but the random variable $\frac{\bar{X}-\mu}{S/\sqrt{n}}$ will not follow a normal distribution; it follows a t-distribution with *(n-1)* degrees of freedom. The reason is because of the randomness of S in the denominator, it is different for different samples.

In the above case, if the population is not normally distributed, the distribution of $\frac{\bar{X}-\mu}{S/\sqrt{n}}$ will follow a normal distribution as per CLT with sufficiently large sample sizes (and not with the small sample size!). So, with the large sample size, the distribution of $\frac{\bar{X}-\mu}{S/\sqrt{n}}$ follows a normal distribution, and it is safe to assume that it follows t-distribution because t-distribution approaches normality with an increase in the sample size.

F-distribution

In statistical inference, F-distribution is used to study the variance of two normally distributed populations. It states that the sampling distribution of the sample variances from two independent normally distributed populations with the same population variance follow F-distribution.

If the sample variance of sample 1 is $S_1^2 = \frac{\sum_{i=1}^{n_1}(X_i-\bar{X}_1)^2}{n_1-1}$ and if the sample variance of sample 2 is $S_2^2 = \frac{\sum_{j=1}^{n_2}(X_j-\bar{X}_2)^2}{n_2-1}$ then, $\frac{S_1^2}{S_2^2}$ will have F-distribution ($\sigma 12 = \sigma 22$).

From the above fact, we can also say that $\frac{S_1^2/\sigma_1^2}{S_2^2/\sigma_2^2}$ will also follow F-distribution.

In the previous section of chi-square distribution, we can also say that

$\frac{\chi_1^2/(n_1-1)}{\chi_2^2/(n_2-1)}$ will also follow F-distribution with *n1-1* and *n2-1* degrees of freedom. For each combination of these degrees of freedoms, there would be different F-distributions.

Standard error

The standard deviation of the sampling distribution of a statistic (such as mean or variance) is called the **standard error** (**SE**), a measure of variability. In other words, the **standard error of the mean** (**SEM**) can be defined as the standard deviation of the sample mean's estimate of a population mean.

As you increase the sample sizes, the sampling distribution of the mean gets more and more normal and the standard deviation gets smaller. It is proved that:

$$\sigma_{\bar{X}}^{2} = \frac{\sigma_{population}^{2}}{n}$$

(*n* being the sample size)

$$\sigma_{\bar{X}} = \frac{\sigma_{Population}}{\sqrt{n}}$$

The smaller the standard error, the more representative the sample will be of the overall population. Also, the larger the sample size, the smaller the standard error.

SE is very important in other measures of statistical inference, such as margin of error and confidence interval.

Confidence level

It is a measure of how certain you would like to be (the probability) in estimating the population parameter through sample statistics so that the expected values would fall within a desired range or confidence interval. It is calculated by subtracting the significance level (α) from 1 (that is, *confidence level = 1 – α*). So, if $\alpha = 0.05$, the confidence level would be *1-0.05 = 0.95*

Usually, the higher the confidence level, the higher the sample size required. However, there are often trade-offs and you have to decide on how confident you would like to be so that you can estimate the sample size needed for your confidence level.

Margin of error and confidence interval

As discussed already, since a sample can never be a 100 percent representative of the population, estimating the population parameter through inference will always have some margin of error due to sampling errors. Usually, the bigger the sample size, the smaller the margin of error. However, you have to decide on how much error to allow, and estimating a proper sample size required would depend on that.

So, the range of values below and above the sample statistic based on the margin of error is called the **confidence interval**. In other words, a confidence interval is a range of numbers within which we believe the true population parameter to fall a certain percentage of the time (confidence level).

Please note here that a statement such as "I am 95 percent confident that the confidence interval contains the true value" could be misleading! The right way of stating this could be *"If I take an infinite number of samples of the same size, then 95 percent of the time the confidence interval would contains the true value"*.

For example, when you put the confidence level as 95 percent and the confidence interval as 4 percent for a sample statistic 58 (here, 58 is any sample statistic such as mean, variance, or standard deviation), you can say that you are 95 percent sure that the true percentage of the population is between 58 – 4 = 54 percent and 58 + 4 = 62 percent.

Variability in the population

The variability in the population is one of the most important factors we should consider in our inferential statistics. It plays an important role in estimating the sample size. No matter what sampling algorithm you choose that can best represent the population, the sample size still plays a crucial role – and this is obvious!

If the variation in the population is more, then the sample size required would also be more.

Estimating sample size

We already covered sampling techniques in the previous sections. In this section, we will discuss how to estimate the sample size. Assume you have to prove a concept or to assess the result of some action, then you take some relevant data and try to prove your point. However, how would you ensure you have enough data? Samples that are too big waste time and resources, and samples that are too small may lead to misleading results. Estimating the sample size depends majorly on factors such as the margin of error or confidence interval, confidence level, and variability in the population.

Consider the following example:

The college president asks the statistics teacher to estimate the average age of the students at their college. How large a sample is necessary? The statistics teacher would like to be 99 percent confident that the estimate should be accurate within 1 year. From a previous study, the standard deviation of the ages is known to be 3 years.

Solution:

Since $\alpha = 0.01$ (or $1 - 0.99$), $z_{\alpha/2} = 2.58$, and $E = 1$, substituting in the formula, one gets

$$n = \left(\frac{z_{\alpha/2} \cdot \sigma}{E}\right)^2 = \left[\frac{(2.58)(3)}{1}\right]^2 = 59.9$$

which is rounded up to 60. Therefore, to be 99% confident that the estimate is within 1 year of the true mean age, the teacher needs a sample size of at least 60 students.

Hypothesis testing

Hypothesis testing is about testing the assumptions made for the population parameters. This helps in determining whether a result is statistically significant or has occurred by chance. It is the most important instrument of statistical research. We will discuss some of the testing to see how variables are related to each other in the population.

Null and alternate hypotheses

The null hypothesis (denoted as H0) is often the initial claim about the population parameter, and it is mostly indicative of *no effect* or *no relation*. In our hypothesis testing, our aim is to invalidate and reject the null hypothesis to be able to accept the alternate hypothesis (denoted as H1). The alternate hypothesis is indicative of some effect in your experiment. While experimenting, please note here that you either reject the null hypothesis or fail to reject the null hypothesis. If you are successful in rejecting the null hypothesis then the alternate hypothesis is to be considered and if you fail to reject the null hypothesis then the null hypothesis is considered (though it may not be true!).

So, we usually hope to get a very small P-value (lower than the defined significance level alpha) to be able to reject the null hypothesis. If the P-value is greater than alpha, then you fail to reject the null hypothesis.

Chi-square test

Most of the statistical inference techniques are used to estimate the population parameters or to test a hypothesis using the sample statistics such as *mean*. However, the chi-square statistic takes a completely different approach by examining the whole distribution or the relationship between two distributions. In the field of inferential statistics, many test statistics resemble a chi-square distribution. The most common tests using this distribution are the chi-square test of goodness of fit (one-way tables) and chi-square test of independence (two-way tables). The *goodness of fit* test is done when you want to see if the sample data follows the same distribution in the population and the *independence* test is done when you want to see if two categorical variables are related to each other in the population.

The input data types determine whether to conduct a *goodness of fit* or *independence* test without specifying them as switches explicitly. So, if you provide a vector as input, then the *goodness of fit* test is conducted and if you provide a matrix as input, then the *independence* test is conducted. In either case, a vector of frequencies of events or a contingency matrix is provided as input which you need to compute first. Let us explore these through examples:

Python

```
//Chi-Square test
>>> from pyspark.mllib.linalg import Vectors, Matrices
>>> from pyspark.mllib.stat import Statistics
>>> import random
>>>
//Make a vector of frequencies of events
>>> vec = Vectors.dense( random.sample(xrange(1,101),10))
```

```
>>> vec
DenseVector([45.0, 40.0, 93.0, 66.0, 56.0, 82.0, 36.0, 30.0, 85.0, 15.0])
// Get Goodnesss of fit test results
>>> GFT_Result = Statistics.chiSqTest(vec)
// Here the 'goodness of fit test' is conducted because your input is a
vector
//Make a contingency matrix
>>> mat = Matrices.dense(5,6,random.sample(xrange(1,101),30))\
//Get independense test results\\
>>> IT_Result = Statistics.chiSqTest(mat)
// Here the 'independence test' is conducted because your input is a vector
//Examine the independence test results
>>> print(IT_Result)
Chi squared test summary:
method: pearson
degrees of freedom = 20
statistic = 285.9423808343265
pValue = 0.0
Very strong presumption against null hypothesis: the occurrence of the
outcomes is statistically independent..
```

Scala

```
scala> import org.apache.spark.mllib.linalg.{Vectors, Matrices}
import org.apache.spark.mllib.linalg.{Vectors, Matrices}

scala> import org.apache.spark.mllib.stat.Statistics

scala> val vec = Vectors.dense( Array.fill(10)(
scala.util.Random.nextDouble))vec: org.apache.spark.mllib.linalg.Vector =
[0.4925741159101148,....]

scala> val GFT_Result = Statistics.chiSqTest(vec)GFT_Result:
org.apache.spark.mllib.stat.test.ChiSqTestResult =Chi squared test summary:
method: pearson
degrees of freedom = 9
statistic = 1.9350768763253192
pValue = 0.9924531181394086
No presumption against null hypothesis: observed follows the same
distribution as expected..
// Here the 'goodness of fit test' is conducted because your input is a
vector
scala> val mat = Matrices.dense(5,6,
Array.fill(30)(scala.util.Random.nextDouble)) // a contingency matrix
mat: org.apache.spark.mllib.linalg.Matrix =.....
scala> val IT_Result = Statistics.chiSqTest(mat)
IT_Result: org.apache.spark.mllib.stat.test.ChiSqTestResult =Chi squared
test summary:
```

```
method: pearson
degrees of freedom = 20
statistic = 2.5401190679900663
pValue = 0.9999990459111089
No presumption against null hypothesis: the occurrence of the outcomes is
statistically independent..
// Here the 'independence test' is conducted because your input is a vector
```

F-test

We have already covered how to calculate the F-statistic in the previous sections. Now we will solve a sample problem.

Problem:

You want to test the belief that the income of Master's degree holders shows greater variability than the income of Bachelor's degree holders. A random sample of 21 graduates and a random sample of 30 Masters were taken. The standard deviation of the graduates sample was $180 and that of the Masters sample was $112.

Solution:

The null hypothesis is: $H : \sigma_1^2 = \sigma_2^2$

Given that $S_1 = \$180$, $n_1 = 21$, and $S_2 = \$112$, $n_2 = 30$

Considering the level of significance to be $\alpha = 0.05$

$F = S_1^2 / S_2^2 = 180^2 / 112^2 = 2.58$

From the F-table with the significance level 0.05, df1=20 and df2=29, we can see that the F-value is 1.94

Since the computed value of F is greater than the table value of F, we can reject the null hypothesis and conclude that $\sigma_1^2 > \sigma_2^2$.

Correlations

Correlations provide a way to measure the statistical dependence between two random variables that are numeric in nature. This shows the extent to which the two variables change with each other. There are basically two types of correlation measures: Pearson and Spearman. Pearson is more appropriate for interval scale data, such as temperature, height, and so on. Spearman is more appropriate for ordinal scale, such as a satisfaction survey where 1 is less satisfied and 5 is most satisfied. Also, Pearson is calculated based on true values and is useful in finding linear relationships whereas Spearman is based on rank order and is useful in finding monotonic relationships. The monotonic relationship means that the variables do change together, but not at a constant rate. Please note that both of these correlation measures can only measure linear or monotonic relationships and are not capable of depicting any other kind of relationships such as non-linear relationships.

In Spark, both of these are supported. If you input two `RDD[Double]`, the output is a *Double* and if you input an `RDD[Vector]`, the output is a *Correlation Matrix*. In both Scala and Python implementations, if you do not provide the type of correlation as input, then the default considered is always Pearson.

Python

```
>>> from pyspark.mllib.stat import Statistics
>>> import random
// Define two series
//Number of partitions and cardinality of both Ser_1 and Ser_2 should be
the same
>>> Ser_1 = sc.parallelize(random.sample(xrange(1,101),10))
// Define Series_1>>> Ser_2 =
sc.parallelize(random.sample(xrange(1,101),10))
// Define Series_2
>>> correlation = Statistics.corr(Ser_1, Ser_2, method = "pearson")
//if you are interested in Spearman method, use "spearman" switch instead
>>> round(correlation,2)-0.14
>>> correlation = Statistics.corr(Ser_1, Ser_2, method ="spearman")
>>> round(correlation,2)-0.19//Check on matrix//The following statement
creates 100 rows of 5 elements each
>>> data = sc.parallelize([random.sample(xrange(1,51),5) for x in
range(100)])
>>> correlMatrix = Statistics.corr(data, method = "pearson")
//method may be spearman as per you requirement
>>> correlMatrix
array([[ 1.        ,  0.09889342, -0.14634881,  0.00178334,
0.08389984],        [ 0.09889342,  1.         , -0.07068631, -0.02212963,
-0.1058252 ],        [-0.14634881, -0.07068631,  1.         , -0.22425991,
0.11063062],        [ 0.00178334, -0.02212963, -0.22425991,  1.         ,
-0.04864668],        [ 0.08389984, -0.1058252 ,  0.11063062, -0.04864668,
```

```
1.
]])
>>>
```

Scala

```
scala> val correlation = Statistics.corr(Ser_1, Ser_2,
"pearson")correlation: Double = 0.43217145308272087
//if you are interested in Spearman method, use "spearman" switch instead
scala> val correlation = Statistics.corr(Ser_1, Ser_2,
"spearman")correlation: Double = 0.4181818181818179
scala>
//Check on matrix
//The following statement creates 100 rows of 5 element Vectors
scala> val data =
sc.parallelize(Seq.fill(100)(Vectors.dense(Array.fill(5)(
scala.util.Random.nextDouble))))
data: org.apache.spark.rdd.RDD[org.apache.spark.mllib.linalg.Vector] =
ParallelCollectionRDD[37] at parallelize at <console>:27
scala> val correlMatrix = Statistics.corr(data, method="pearson")
//method may be spearman as per you requirement
correlMatrix: org.apache.spark.mllib.linalg.Matrix =1.0
-0.05478051936343809   ... (5 total)-0.05478051936343809
1.0                    .........
```

Summary

In this chapter, we briefly covered the steps involved in the data science life cycle, such as data acquisition, data preparation, and data exploration through descriptive statistics. We also learnt to estimate the population parameters through sample statistics using some popular tools and techniques.

We explained the basics of statistics from both theoretical and practical aspects by going deeper into the fundamentals in a few areas to be able to solve business problems. Finally, we learnt a few examples on how statistical analysis can be performed on Apache Spark, leveraging the out-of-the-box features, which was basically the objective behind this chapter.

We will discuss more details of the machine learning part of data science in the next chapter as we have already built statistical understanding in this chapter. Learnings from this chapter should help connect to the machine learning algorithms in a more informed way.

References

Supported statistics by Spark:

`http://spark.apache.org/docs/latest/mllib-statistics.html`

Plotting features of Databricks:

https://docs.cloud.databricks.com/docs/latest/databricks_guide/04%20Visualizations/4%20Matplotlib%20and%20GGPlot.html

Detailed information on OOTB library functions of MLLIB stats:

`http://spark.apache.org/docs/latest/api/scala/index.html#org.apache.spark.mllib.stat.Statistics$`

6
Machine Learning

We are the consumers of machine learning every day, whether we notice or not. E-mail providers such as Google automatically push some incoming mails into the `Spam` folder and online shopping sites such as Amazon or social networking sites such as Facebook jump in with unsolicited recommendations that are surprisingly useful. So, what enables these software products to reconnect long lost friends? These are just a few examples of machine learning in action.

Formally, machine learning is a part of **Artificial Intelligence** (**AI**) which deals with a class of algorithms that can learn from data and make predictions. The techniques and underlying concepts are drawn from the field of statistics. Machine learning exists at the intersection of computer science and statistics and is considered one of the most important components of data science. It has been around for quite some time now, but its complexity has only increased with increase in data and scalability requirements. Machine learning algorithms tend to be resource intensive and iterative in nature, which render them a poor fit for MapReduce paradigm. MapReduce works very well for single pass algorithms but does not cater so well for multi-pass counterparts. The Spark research program was started precisely to address this challenge. Apache Spark is equipped with efficient algorithms in its MLlib library that are designed to perform well even in iterative computational requirements.

The previous chapter outlined the data analytics' life cycle and its various components such as data cleaning, data transformation, sampling techniques, and graphical techniques to visualize the data, along with concepts covering descriptive statistics and inferential statistics. We also looked at some of the statistical testing that could be performed on the Spark platform. Further to the basics we built up in the previous chapter, we are going to cover in this chapter most of the machine learning algorithms and how to use them to build models on Spark.

As a prerequisite for this chapter, basic understanding of machine learning algorithms and computer science fundamentals are nice to have. However, we have covered some theoretical basics of the algorithms with right set of practical examples to make those more comprehendible and easy to implement. The topics covered in this chapter are:

- Introduction to machine learning
  - The evolution
  - Supervised learning
  - Unsupervised learning
- MLlib and the Pipeline API
  - MLlib
  - ML pipeline
- Introduction to machine learning
  - Parametric methods
  - Non-parametric methods
- Regression methods
  - Linear regression
  - Regularization on regression
- Classification methods
  - Logistic regression
  - Linear Support Vector Machines (SVMs)
- Decision trees
  - Impurity measures
  - Stopping rule
  - Split canditate
  - Advantages of decision tress
  - Example
- Ensembles
  - Random forests
  - Gradient boosted trees
- Multilayer perceptron classifier
- Clustering techniques
  - K-means clustering
- Summary

Introduction

Machine learning is all about learning by example data; examples that produce a particular output for a given input. There are various business use cases for machine learning. Let us look at a few examples to get an idea of what exactly it is:

- A recommendation engine that recommends users what they might be interested in buying
- Customer segmentation (grouping customers who share similar characteristics) for marketing campaigns
- Disease classification for cancer – malignant/benign
- Predictive modeling, for example, sales forecasting, weather forecasting
- Drawing business inferences, for example, understanding what effect will change the price of a product have on sales

The evolution

The concept of statistical learning was existent even before the first computer system was introduced. In the nineteenth century, the least squares technique (now called linear regression) had already been developed. For classification problems, Fisher came up with **Linear Discriminant Analysis (LDA)**. Around the 1940s, an alternative to LDA, known as **logistic regression**, was proposed and all these approaches not only improved with time, but also inspired the development of other new algorithms.

During those times, computation was a big problem as it was done using pen and paper. So fitting non-linear equations was not quite feasible as it required a lot of computations. After the 1980s, with improvements in technology and the introduction of computer systems, classification/regression trees were introduced. Slowly, with further advancements in technology and computing systems, statistical learning in a way converged with what is now known as machine learning.

Supervised learning

As discussed in the previous section, machine learning is all about learning by example data. Based on how the algorithms understand data and get trained on it, they are broadly divided into two categories: **supervised learning** and **unsupervised learning**.

Supervised statistical learning involves building a model based on one or more inputs for a particular output. This means that the output that we get can supervise our analysis based on the inputs we supply. In other words, for each observation of the predictor variables (for example, age, education, and expense variables), there is an associated response measurement of the outcome variable (for example, salary). Refer to the following table to get an idea of the example dataset where we are trying to predict the **Salary** based on the **Age**, **Education,** and **Expense** variables:

	Explanatory/Predictor Variables		Response/Outcome Variables
Age	**Education**	**Expense ($)**	**Salary($)**
25	Graduate	3,000	20,000
44	PhD	6,000	80,000
65	Masters	9,000	85,000
37	Masters	10,000	64,000
31	Graduate	5,000	39,000
50	PhD	8,500	?
41	Graduate	6,400	?

Supervised algorithms can be used for predicting, estimating, classifying, and other similar requirements which we will cover in the following sections.

Unsupervised learning

Unsupervised statistical learning involves building a model based on one or more inputs but with no intention to produce a specific output. This means that there is no response/output variable to predict explicitly; but the output is usually the groups of data points that share some similar characteristics. Unlike supervised learning, you are not aware of the groups/labels to classify the data points into, per say, and you leave it to the algorithm to decide by itself.

Here, there is no concept of a `training` dataset that is used to `relate` the outcome variable with the `predictor` variables by building a model and then validate the model using the `test` dataset. The output of unsupervised algorithm cannot supervise your analysis based on the inputs you supply. Such algorithms can learn relationships and structure from data. *Clustering* and *Association rule learning* are examples of unsupervised learning techniques.

The following image depicts how clustering is used to group the data items that share some similar characteristics:

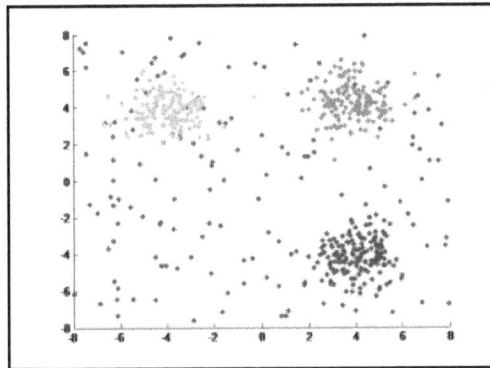

MLlib and the Pipeline API

Let us first learn some Spark fundamentals to be able to perform the machine learning operations on it. We will discuss the MLlib and the pipeline API in this section.

MLlib

MLlib is the machine learning library built on top of Apache Spark which homes most of the algorithms that can be implemented at scale. The seamless integration of MLlib with other components such as GraphX, SQL, and Streaming provides developers with an opportunity to assemble complex, scalable, and efficient workflows relatively easily. The MLlib library consists of common learning algorithms and utilities including classification, regression, clustering, collaborative filtering, and dimensionality reduction.

MLlib works in conjunction with the `spark.ml` package which provides a high level Pipeline API. The fundamental difference between these two packages is that MLlib (`spark.mllib`) works on top of RDDs whereas the ML (`spark.ml`) package works on top of DataFrames and supports ML Pipeline. Currently, both packages are supported by Spark but it is recommended to use the `spark.ml` package.

Fundamental data types in this library are vectors and matrices. Vectors are local, and may be dense or sparse. Dense vectors are stored as an array of values. Sparse vectors are stored as two arrays; the first array stores the non-zero value indices and the second array stores the actual values. All element values are stored as doubles and indices are stored as integers starting from zero. Understanding the fundamental structures goes a long way in effective use of the libraries and it should help code up any new algorithm from scratch. Let us see some example code for a better understanding of these two vector representations:

Scala

```
//Create vectors
scala> import org.apache.spark.ml.linalg.{Vector, Vectors}
import org.apache.spark.ml.linalg.{Vector, Vectors}

//Create dense vector
scala> val dense_v: Vector = Vectors.dense(10.0,0.0,20.0,30.0,0.0)
dense_v: org.apache.spark.ml.linalg.Vector = [10.0,0.0,20.0,30.0,0.0]
scala>

//Create sparse vector: pass size, position index array and value array
scala> val sparse_v1: Vector = Vectors.sparse(5,Array(0,2,3),
        Array(10.0,20.0,30.0))
sparse_v1: org.apache.spark.ml.linalg.Vector = (5,[0,2,3],[10.0,20.0,30.0])
scala>

//Another way to create sparse vector with position, value tuples
scala> val sparse_v2: Vector = Vectors.sparse(5,
         Seq((0,10.0),(2,20.0),(3,30.0)))
sparse_v2: org.apache.spark.ml.linalg.Vector = (5,[0,2,3],[10.0,20.0,30.0])
scala>

Compare vectors
---------------
cala> sparse_v1 == sparse_v2
res0: Boolean = true
scala> sparse_v1 == dense_v
res1: Boolean = true        //All three objects are equal butâ¦
scala> dense_v.toString()
res2: String = [10.0,0.0,20.0,30.0,0.0]
scala> sparse_v2.toString()
res3: String = (5,[0,2,3],[10.0,20.0,30.0]) //..internal representation
differs
scala> sparse_v2.toArray
res4: Array[Double] = Array(10.0, 0.0, 20.0, 30.0, 0.0)

Interchangeable
---------------
```

```scala
scala> dense_v.toSparse
res5: org.apache.spark.mllib.linalg.SparseVector = (5,[0,2,3]
[10.0,20.0,30.0])
scala> sparse_v1.toDense
res6: org.apache.spark.mllib.linalg.DenseVector = [10.0,0.0,20.0,30.0,0.0]
scala>
```

A common operation

```scala
scala> Vectors.sqdist(sparse_v1,
        Vectors.dense(1.0,2.0,3.0,4.0,5.0))
res7: Double = 1075.0
```

Python:

```python
//Create vectors
>>> from pyspark.ml.linalg import Vector, Vectors
//Create vectors
>>> dense_v = Vectors.dense(10.0,0.0,20.0,30.0,0.0)
//Pass size, position index array and value array
>>> sparse_v1 = Vectors.sparse(5,[0,2,3],
                    [10.0,20.0,30.0])
>>>

//Another way to create sparse vector with position, value tuples
>>> sparse_v2 = Vectors.sparse(5,
                    [[0,10.0],[2,20.0],[3,30.0]])
>>>
```

Compare vectors

```python
>>> sparse_v1 == sparse_v2
True
>>> sparse_v1 == dense_v
True      //All three objects are equal but…
>>> dense_v
DenseVector([10.0, 0.0, 20.0, 30.0, 0.0])
>>> sparse_v1
SparseVector(5, {0: 10.0, 2: 20.0, 3: 30.0}) //..internal representation
differs
>>> sparse_v2
SparseVector(5, {0: 10.0, 2: 20.0, 3: 30.0})
```

Interchangeable

```python
//Note: as of Spark 2.0.0, toDense and toSparse are not available in
pyspark
```

A common operation

```
>>> Vectors.squared_distance(sparse_v1,
        Vectors.dense(1.0,2.0,3.0,4.0,5.0))
1075.0
```

Matrices may be local or distributed, dense or sparse. A local matrix is stored on a single machine as a single dimensional array. A dense local matrix is stored in column major order (column members are contiguous) whereas a sparse matrix values are stored in **Compressed Sparse Column** (**CSC**) format in column major order. In this format, the matrix is stored in the form of three arrays. The first array contains row indices of non-zero values, the second array has the beginning value index for each column, and the third one is an array of all the non-zero values. Indices are of type integer starting from zero. The first array contains values from zero to the number of rows minus one. The third array has elements of type double. The second array requires some explanation. Every entry in this array corresponds to the index of the first non-zero element in each column. For example, assume that there is only one non-zero element in each column in a 3 by 3 matrix. Then the second array would contain 0,1,2 as its elements. The first array contains row positions and the third array contains three values. If none of the elements in a column are non-zero, you will note the same index repeating in the second array. Let us examine some example code:

Scala:

```
scala> import org.apache.spark.ml.linalg.{Matrix,Matrices}
import org.apache.spark.ml.linalg.{Matrix, Matrices}
```

Create dense matrix

```
//Values in column major order
Matrices.dense(3,2,Array(9.0,0,0,0,8.0,6))
res38: org.apache.spark.mllib.linalg.Matrix =
9.0  0.0
0.0  8.0
0.0  6.0
```

Create sparse matrix

```
//1.0 0.0 4.0
0.0 3.0 5.0
2.0 0.0 6.0//
val sm: Matrix = Matrices.sparse(3,3,
        Array(0,2,3,6), Array(0,2,1,0,1,2),
        Array(1.0,2.0,3.0,4.0,5.0,6.0))
sm: org.apache.spark.mllib.linalg.Matrix =
3 x 3 CSCMatrix
(0,0) 1.0
```

```
(2,0) 2.0
(1,1) 3.0
(0,2) 4.0
(1,2) 5.0
(2,2) 6.0
```

Sparse matrix, a column of all zeros
```
--------------------------------------
//third column all zeros
Matrices.sparse(3,4,Array(0,2,3,3,6),
    Array(0,2,1,0,1,2),values).toArray
res85: Array[Double] = Array(1.0, 0.0, 2.0, 0.0, 3.0, 0.0, 0.0, 0.0, 0.0,
4.0, 5.0, 6.0)
```

Python:

```
//Create dense matrix
>>> from pyspark.ml.linalg import Matrix, Matrices

//Values in column major order
>>> Matrices.dense(3,2,[9.0,0,0,0,8.0,6])
DenseMatrix(3, 2, [9.0, 0.0, 0.0, 0.0, 8.0, 6.0], False)
>>>

//Create sparse matrix
//1.0 0.0 4.0
0.0 3.0 5.0
2.0 0.0 6.0//
>>> sm = Matrices.sparse(3,3,
        [0,2,3,6], [0,2,1,0,1,2],
        [1.0,2.0,3.0,4.0,5.0,6.0])
>>>

//Sparse matrix, a column of all zeros
//third column all zeros
>>> Matrices.sparse(3,4,[0,2,3,3,6],
        [0,2,1,0,1,2],
    values=[1.0,2.0,3.0,4.0,5.0,6.0]).toArray()
array([[ 1.,   0.,   0.,   4.],
       [ 0.,   3.,   0.,   5.],
       [ 2.,   0.,   0.,   6.]])
>>>
```

Distributed matrices are the most sophisticated ones and choosing the right type of distributed matrix is very important. A distributed matrix is backed by one or more RDDs. The row and column indices are of the type long to support very large matrices. The basic type of distributed matrix is a RowMatrix, which is simply backed by an RDD of its rows.

Each row in turn is a local vector. This is suitable when the number of columns is very low. Remember, we need to pass RDDs to create distributed matrices, unlike the local ones. Let us look at an example:

Scala:

```
scala> import org.apache.spark.mllib.linalg.{Vector,Vectors}
import org.apache.spark.mllib.linalg.{Vector, Vectors}
scala> import org.apache.spark.mllib.linalg.distributed.RowMatrix
import org.apache.spark.mllib.linalg.distributed.RowMatrix

scala>val dense_vlist: Array[Vector] = Array(
    Vectors.dense(11.0,12,13,14),
    Vectors.dense(21.0,22,23,24),
    Vectors.dense(31.0,32,33,34))
dense_vlist: Array[org.apache.spark.mllib.linalg.Vector] =
Array([11.0,12.0,13.0,14.0], [21.0,22.0,23.0,24.0], [31.0,32.0,33.0,34.0])
scala>

//Distribute the vector list
scala> val rows  = sc.parallelize(dense_vlist)
rows: org.apache.spark.rdd.RDD[org.apache.spark.mllib.linalg.Vector] =
ParallelCollectionRDD[0] at parallelize at <console>:29
scala> val m: RowMatrix = new RowMatrix(rows)
m: org.apache.spark.mllib.linalg.distributed.RowMatrix =
org.apache.spark.mllib.linalg.distributed.RowMatrix@5c5043fe
scala> print("Matrix size is " + m.numRows()+"X"+m.numCols())
Matrix size is 3X4
scala>
```

Python:

```
>>> from pyspark.mllib.linalg import Vector,Vectors
>>> from pyspark.mllib.linalg.distributed import RowMatrix

>>> dense_vlist = [Vectors.dense(11.0,12,13,14),
        Vectors.dense(21.0,22,23,24), Vectors.dense(31.0,32,33,34)]
>>> rows  = sc.parallelize(dense_vlist)
>>> m = RowMatrix(rows)
>>> "Matrix size is {0} X {1}".format(m.numRows(), m.numCols())
'Matrix size is 3 X 4'
```

An `IndexedRowMatrix` stores a row index prefixed to the row entry. This is useful in executing joins. You need to pass `IndexedRow` objects to create an `IndexedRowMatrix`. An `IndexedRow` object is a wrapper with a long `Index` and a `Vector` of row elements.

A `CoordinatedMatrix` stores data as tuples of row, column indexes, and element value. A `BlockMatrix` represents a distributed matrix in blocks of local matrices. Methods to convert matrices from one type to another are provided but these are expensive operations and should be used with caution.

ML pipeline

A real life machine learning workflow is an iterative cycle of data extraction, data cleansing, pre-processing, exploration, feature extraction, model fitting, and evaluation. ML Pipeline on Spark is a simple API for users to set up complex ML workflows. It was designed to address some of the pain areas such as parameter tuning, or training many models based on different splits of data (cross-validation), or different sets of parameters. Writing scripts to automate this whole thing is no more a requirement and can be taken care of within the Pipeline API itself.

The Pipeline API consists of a series of pipeline stages (implemented as abstractions such as *transformers* and *estimators*) to get executed in a desired order.

In the ML Pipeline, you can invoke the data cleaning/transformation functions as discussed in the previous chapter and call the machine learning algorithms that are available in the MLlib. This can be done in an iterative fashion till you get the desired performance of your model.

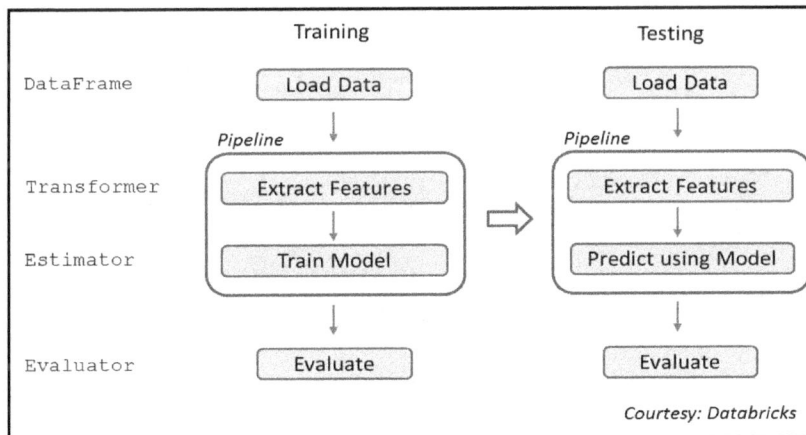

Transformer

A transformer is an abstraction which implements the `transform()` method to convert one DataFrame into another. If the method is a feature transformer, the resulting DataFrame might contain some additional transformed columns based on the operation you performed. However, if the method is a learning model, then the resulting DataFrame would contain an extra column with predicted outcomes.

Estimator

An Estimator is an abstraction that can be any learning algorithm which implements the `fit()` method to get trained on a DataFrame to produce a model. Technically, this model is a transformer for the given DataFrame.

Example: Logistic regression is a learning algorithm, hence an estimator. Calling `fit()` trains a logistic regression model, which is a resultant model, and hence a transformer which can produce a DataFrame containing a predicted column.

The following example demonstrates a simple, single stage pipeline.

Scala:

```
//Pipeline example with single stage to illustrate syntax
scala> import org.apache.spark.ml.Pipeline
import org.apache.spark.ml.Pipeline
scala> import org.apache.spark.ml.feature._
import org.apache.spark.ml.feature._

//Create source data frame
scala> val df = spark.createDataFrame(Seq(
        ("Oliver Twist","Charles Dickens"),
        ("Adventures of Tom Sawyer","Mark Twain"))).toDF(
        "Title","Author")

//Split the Title to tokens
scala> val tok = new Tokenizer().setInputCol("Title").
        setOutputCol("words")
tok: org.apache.spark.ml.feature.Tokenizer = tok_2b2757a3aa5f

//Define a pipeline with a single stage
scala> val p = new Pipeline().setStages(Array(tok))
p: org.apache.spark.ml.Pipeline = pipeline_f5e0de400666

//Run an Estimator (fit) using the pipeline
scala> val model = p.fit(df)
```

```
model: org.apache.spark.ml.PipelineModel = pipeline_d00989625bb2

//Examine stages
scala> p.getStages    //Returns a list of stage objects
res1: Array[org.apache.spark.ml.PipelineStage] = Array(tok_55af0061af6d)

// Examine the results
scala> val m = model.transform(df).select("Title","words")
m: org.apache.spark.sql.DataFrame = [Title: string, words: array<string>]
scala> m.select("words").collect().foreach(println)
[WrappedArray(oliver, twist)]
[WrappedArray(adventures, of, tom, sawyer)]
```

Python:

```
//Pipeline example with single stage to illustrate syntax
//Create source data frame
>>> from pyspark.ml.pipeline import Pipeline
>>> from pyspark.ml.feature import Tokenizer
>>>  df = sqlContext.createDataFrame([
    ("Oliver Twist","Charles Dickens"),
    ("Adventures of Tom Sawyer","Mark Twain")]).toDF("Title","Author")
>>>

//Split the Title to tokens
>>> tok = Tokenizer(inputCol="Title",outputCol="words")

//Define a pipeline with a single stage
>>> p = Pipeline(stages=[tok])

//Run an Estimator (fit) using the pipeline
>>> model = p.fit(df)

//Examine stages
>>> p.getStages()   //Returns a list of stage objects
[Tokenizer_4f35909c4c504637a263]

// Examine the results
>>> m = model.transform(df).select("Title","words")
>>> [x[0] for x in m.select("words").collect()]
[[u'oliver', u'twist'], [u'adventures', u'of', u'tom', u'sawyer']]
>>>
```

The above example showed pipeline creation and execution although with a single stage, a Tokenizer in this context. Spark provides several âøøfeature transformersâøø out of the box. These feature transformers are quite handy during data cleaning and data preparation phases.

The following example shows a real world example of converting raw text into feature vectors. If you are not familiar with TF-IDF, read this short tutorial from `http://www.tfidf.com`.

Scala:

```
scala> import org.apache.spark.ml.Pipeline
import org.apache.spark.ml.Pipeline
scala> import org.apache.spark.ml.feature._
import org.apache.spark.ml.feature._
scala>

//Create a dataframe
scala> val df2 = spark.createDataset(Array(
        (1,"Here is some text to illustrate pipeline"),
        (2, "and tfidf, which stands for term frequency inverse document
frequency"
        ))).toDF("LineNo","Text")

//Define feature transformations, which are the pipeline stages
// Tokenizer splits text into tokens
scala> val tok = new Tokenizer().setInputCol("Text").
            setOutputCol("Words")
tok: org.apache.spark.ml.feature.Tokenizer = tok_399dbfe012f8

// HashingTF maps a sequence of words to their term frequencies using
hashing
// Larger value of numFeatures reduces hashing collision possibility
scala> val tf = new
HashingTF().setInputCol("Words").setOutputCol("tf").setNumFeatures(100)
tf: org.apache.spark.ml.feature.HashingTF = hashingTF_e6ad936536ea
// IDF, Inverse Docuemnt Frequency is a statistical weight that reduces
weightage of commonly occuring words
scala> val idf = new IDF().setInputCol("tf").setOutputCol("tf_idf")
idf: org.apache.spark.ml.feature.IDF = idf_8af1fecad60a
// VectorAssembler merges multiple columns into a single vector column
scala> val va = new
VectorAssembler().setInputCols(Array("tf_idf")).setOutputCol("features")
va: org.apache.spark.ml.feature.VectorAssembler = vecAssembler_23205c3f92c8
//Define pipeline
scala> val tfidf_pipeline = new Pipeline().setStages(Array(tok,tf,idf,va))
val tfidf_pipeline = new Pipeline().setStages(Array(tok,tf,idf,va))
scala> tfidf_pipeline.getStages
res2: Array[org.apache.spark.ml.PipelineStage] = Array(tok_399dbfe012f8,
hashingTF_e6ad936536ea, idf_8af1fecad60a, vecAssembler_23205c3f92c8)
scala>

//Now execute the pipeline
```

```
scala> val result =
tfidf_pipeline.fit(df2).transform(df2).select("words","features").first()
result: org.apache.spark.sql.Row = [WrappedArray(here, is, some, text, to,
illustrate,
pipeline),(100,[0,3,35,37,69,81],[0.4054651081081644,0.4054651081081644,0.4
054651081081644,0.4054651081081644,0.4054651081081644,0.4054651081081644])]
```

Python:

```
//A realistic, multi-step pipeline that converts text to TF_ID
>>> from pyspark.ml.pipeline import Pipeline
>>> from pyspark.ml.feature import Tokenizer, HashingTF, IDF,
VectorAssembler, \
            StringIndexer, VectorIndexer

//Create a dataframe
>>> df2 = sqlContext.createDataFrame([
    [1,"Here is some text to illustrate pipeline"],
    [2,"and tfidf, which stands for term frequency inverse document
frequency"
    ]]).toDF("LineNo","Text")

//Define feature transformations, which are the pipeline stages
//Tokenizer splits text into tokens
>>> tok = Tokenizer(inputCol="Text",outputCol="words")

// HashingTF maps a sequence of words to their term frequencies using
hashing

// Larger the numFeatures, lower the hashing collision possibility
>>> tf = HashingTF(inputCol="words", outputCol="tf",numFeatures=1000)

// IDF, Inverse Docuemnt Frequency is a statistical weight that reduces
weightage of commonly occuring words
>>> idf = IDF(inputCol = "tf",outputCol="tf_idf")

// VectorAssembler merges multiple columns into a single vector column
>>> va = VectorAssembler(inputCols=["tf_idf"],outputCol="features")

//Define pipeline
>>> tfidf_pipeline = Pipeline(stages=[tok,tf,idf,va])
>>> tfidf_pipeline.getStages()
[Tokenizer_4f5fbfb6c2a9cf5725d6, HashingTF_4088a47d38e72b70464f,
IDF_41ddb3891541821c6613, VectorAssembler_49ae83b800679ac2fa0e]
>>>

//Now execute the pipeline
>>> result =
```

```
tfidf_pipeline.fit(df2).transform(df2).select("words","features").collect()
>>> [(x[0],x[1]) for x in result]
[([u'here', u'is', u'some', u'text', u'to', u'illustrate', u'pipeline'],
SparseVector(1000, {135: 0.4055, 169: 0.4055, 281: 0.4055, 388: 0.4055,
400: 0.4055, 603: 0.4055, 937: 0.4055})), ([u'and', u'tfidf,', u'which',
u'stands', u'for', u'term', u'frequency', u'inverse', u'document',
u'frequency'], SparseVector(1000, {36: 0.4055, 188: 0.4055, 333: 0.4055,
378: 0.4055, 538: 0.4055, 597: 0.4055, 727: 0.4055, 820: 0.4055, 960:
0.8109}))]
>>>
```

This example has created and executed a multi-stage pipeline that has converted text to a feature vector that can be processed by machine learning algorithms. Let us see a few more features before we move on.

Scala:

```
scala> import org.apache.spark.ml.feature._
import org.apache.spark.ml.feature._
scala>

//Basic examples illustrating features usage
//Look at model examples for more feature examples
//Binarizer converts continuous value variable to two discrete values based
on given threshold
scala> import scala.util.Random
import scala.util.Random
scala> val nums = Seq.fill(10)(Random.nextDouble*100)
...
scala> val numdf =
spark.createDataFrame(nums.map(Tuple1.apply)).toDF("raw_nums")
numdf: org.apache.spark.sql.DataFrame = [raw_nums: double]
scala> val binarizer = new Binarizer().setInputCol("raw_nums").
          setOutputCol("binary_vals").setThreshold(50.0)
binarizer: org.apache.spark.ml.feature.Binarizer = binarizer_538e392f56db
scala> binarizer.transform(numdf).select("raw_nums","binary_vals").show(2)
+------------------+-----------+
|          raw_nums|binary_vals|
+------------------+-----------+
|55.209245003482884|        1.0|
| 33.46202184060426|        0.0|
+------------------+-----------+
scala>

//Bucketizer to convert continuous value variables to desired set of
discrete values
scala> val split_vals:Array[Double] = Array(0,20,50,80,100) //define
intervals
```

```
split_vals: Array[Double] = Array(0.0, 20.0, 50.0, 80.0, 100.0)
scala> val b = new Bucketizer().
            setInputCol("raw_nums").
            setOutputCol("binned_nums").
            setSplits(split_vals)
b: org.apache.spark.ml.feature.Bucketizer = bucketizer_a4dd599e5977
scala> b.transform(numdf).select("raw_nums","binned_nums").show(2)
+------------------+-----------+
|          raw_nums|binned_nums|
+------------------+-----------+
|55.209245003482884|        2.0|
| 33.46202184060426|        1.0|
+------------------+-----------+
scala>

//Bucketizer is effectively equal to binarizer if only two intervals are
given
scala> new Bucketizer().setInputCol("raw_nums").
        setOutputCol("binned_nums").setSplits(Array(0,50.0,100.0)).
        transform(numdf).select("raw_nums","binned_nums").show(2)
+------------------+-----------+
|          raw_nums|binned_nums|
+------------------+-----------+
|55.209245003482884|        1.0|
| 33.46202184060426|        0.0|
+------------------+-----------+
scala>
```

Python:

```
//Some more features
>>> from pyspark.ml import feature, pipeline
>>>

//Basic examples illustrating features usage
//Look at model examples for more examples
//Binarizer converts continuous value variable to two discrete values based
on given threshold
>>> import random
>>> nums = [random.random()*100 for x in range(1,11)]
>>> numdf = sqlContext.createDataFrame(
            [[x] for x in nums]).toDF("raw_nums")
>>> binarizer = feature.Binarizer(threshold= 50,
        inputCol="raw_nums", outputCol="binary_vals")
>>> binarizer.transform(numdf).select("raw_nums","binary_vals").show(2)
+------------------+-----------+
|          raw_nums|binary_vals|
+------------------+-----------+
```

```
|  95.41304359504672|        1.0|
|41.906045589243405|        0.0|
+------------------+----------+
>>>


//Bucketizer to convert continuous value variables to desired set of
discrete values
>>> split_vals = [0,20,50,80,100] //define intervals
>>> b =
feature.Bucketizer(inputCol="raw_nums",outputCol="binned_nums",splits=split
vals)
>>> b.transform(numdf).select("raw_nums","binned_nums").show(2)
+------------------+----------+
|          raw_nums|binned_nums|
+------------------+----------+
|  95.41304359504672|        3.0|
|41.906045589243405|        1.0|
+------------------+----------+


//Bucketizer is effectively equal to binarizer if only two intervals are
given
>>> feature.Bucketizer(inputCol="raw_nums",outputCol="binned_nums",
                  splits=[0,50.0,100.0]).transform(numdf).select(
                  "raw_nums","binned_nums").show(2)
+------------------+----------+
|          raw_nums|binned_nums|
+------------------+----------+
|  95.41304359504672|        1.0|
|41.906045589243405|        0.0|
+------------------+----------+
>>>
```

Introduction to machine learning

In the previous sections of the book, we learnt how the response/outcome variable is related to the predictor variables, typically in a supervised learning context. There are various different names for both of those types of variables that people use these days. Let us see some of the synonymous terms for them and we will use them interchangeably in the book:

- **Input variables (X)**: Features, predictors, explanatory variables, independent variables
- **Output variables (Y)**: Response variable, dependent variable

If there is a relation between Y and X where $X = X_1, X_2, X_3, ..., X_n$ (n different predictors) then it can be written as follows:

$$Y = f(X) + \varepsilon$$

Here $f(X)$ is a function that represents how X describes Y and is unknown! This is what we figure out using the observed data points at hand. The term ε is a random error term with mean zero and is independent of X.

There are basically two types of errors associated with such an equation – reducible errors and irreducible errors. As the name suggests, a reducible error is associated with the function and can be minimized by improving the accuracy of $f(X)$ by using a better learning algorithm or by tuning the same algorithm. Since Y is also a function of ε, which is independent of X, there would still be some error associated that cannot be addressed. This is called an irreducible error (ε). There are always some factors which influence the outcome variable but are not considered in building the model (as they are unknown most of the time), and contribute to the irreducible error term. So, our approaches discussed throughout this book will only be focused on minimizing the reducible error.

Most of the machine learning models that we build can be used for either prediction or for inference, or a combination of both. For some of the algorithms, the function $f(X)$ can be represented as an equation which tells us how the dependent variable Y is related to the independent variables ($X1, X2,..., Xn$). In such cases, we can do both inference and prediction. However, some of the algorithms are black box, where we can only predict and no inference is possible, because how Y is related to X is unknown.

Note that the linear machine learning models can be more apt for an inference setting because they are more interpretable to business users. However, on a prediction setting, there can be better algorithms providing more accurate predictions but they are less interpretable. When inference is the target, we should prefer the restrictive models such as linear regression for better interpretability, and when only prediction is the goal, we may choose to use highly flexible models such as **Support Vector Machines** (**SVM**) that are less interpretable and more accurate (this may not hold true in all cases, however). You need to be careful in choosing an algorithm based on the business requirement, by accounting for the trade-off between interpretability and accuracy. Let us dive deeper into understanding the fundamentals behind these concepts.

Basically, we need a set of data points (training data) to build a model to estimate $f(X)$ so that $Y = f(X)$. Broadly, such learning methods can be either parametric or non-parametric.

Parametric methods

Parametric methods follow a two-step process. In the first step, you assume the shape of $f()$. For example, X is linearly related to Y, so the function of X, which is $f(X)$, can be represented with a linear equation as shown next:

$$f(X) = \beta_0 + \beta_1 X_1 + ... + \beta_n X_n$$

After the model is selected, the second step is to estimate the parameters $\hat{\beta}_0, \hat{\beta}_1, ..., \hat{\beta}_n$ by using the data points at hand to train the model, so that:

$$Y = \beta_0 + \beta_1 X_1 + ... + \beta_n X_n$$

The one disadvantage to this parametric approach is that our assumption of linearity for $f()$ might not hold true in real life situations.

Non-parametric methods

We do not make any assumptions about the linear relation between Y and X as well as data distributions of variables, and hence the form of $f()$ in non-parametric. Since it does not assume any form of $f()$, it can produce better results by fitting well with data points, which could be an advantage.

So, the non-parametric methods require more data points compared to parametric methods to estimate $f()$ accurately. Note however, it can lead to overfitting problems if not handled properly. We will discuss more on this as we move further.

Regression methods

Regression methods are a type of supervised learning. If the response variable is quantitative/continuous (takes on numeric values such as age, salary, height, and so on), then the problem can be called a regression problem regardless of the explanatory variables' type. There are various kinds of modeling techniques to address the regression problems. In this section, our focus will be on linear regression techniques and some different variations of it.

Regression methods can be used to predict any real valued outcomes. Following are a few examples:

- Predict the salary of an employee based on his educational level, location, type of job, and so on
- Predict stock prices
- Predict buying potential of a customer
- Predict the time a machine would take before failing

Linear regression

Further to what we discussed in the previous section *Parametric methods,* after the assumption of linearity is made for $f(X)$, we need the training data to fit a model that would describe the relation between explanatory variables (denoted as X) and the response variable (denoted as Y). When there is only one explanatory variable present, it is called simple linear regression and when there are multiple explanatory variables present, it is called multiple linear regression. The simple linear regression is all about fitting a straight line in a 2-D setting, and when there are say two predictor variables, it would fit a plane in a 3-D setting, and so on for higher dimensional settings when there are more than two variables.

The usual form of a linear regression equation can be represented as:

$$Y' = f(X) + \varepsilon$$

Here Y' represents the predicted outcome variable.

A linear regression equation with only one predictor variable can be given as:

$$Y' = \beta_0 + \beta_1 X_1 + \varepsilon$$

A linear regression equation with multiple predictor variables can be given as:

$$Y' = \beta_0 + \beta_1 X_1 + \ldots + \beta_n X_n + \varepsilon$$

Here ε is the irreducible error term independent of X and has a mean of zero. We do not have any control over it, but we can work towards optimizing $f(X)$. Since none of the models can achieve a 100 percent accuracy, there would always be some error associated with it because of the irreducible error component (ε).

The most common approach of fitting a linear regression is called **least squares**, also known as, the **Ordinary Least Squares (OLS)** approach. This method finds the regression line that best fits the observed data points by minimizing the sum of squares of the vertical deviations from each data point to the regression line. To get a better understanding on how the linear regression works, let us look at a simple linear regression of the following form for now:

$$Y' = \beta_0 + \beta_1 X_1$$

Where, $\hat{\beta}_0$ is the Y-intercept of the regression line and $\hat{\beta}_1$ defines the slope of the line. What it means is that $\hat{\beta}_1$ is the average change in Y for every one unit change in X. Let us take an example with X and Y:

X	Y
1	12
2	20
3	13
4	38
5	27

If we fit a linear regression line through the data points as shown in the preceding table, then it would appear as follows:

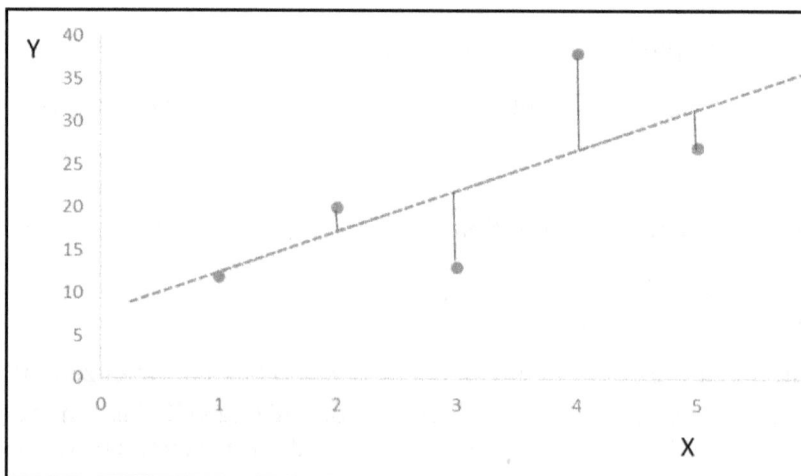

The red vertical lines in the preceding figure indicate the error of prediction which can be defined as the difference between the actual Y value and the predicted Y' value. If you square these differences and sum them up, it is called the **Sum of Squared Error (SSE)**, which is the most common measure that is used to find the best fitting line. The following table shows how to calculate the SSE:

X	Y	Y'	Y-Y'	(Y-Y') 2
1	12	12.4	0.4	0.16
2	20	17.2	2.8	7.84
3	13	22	-9	81
4	38	26.8	11.2	125.44
5	27	31.6	-4.6	21.16
			SUM	235.6

In the above table, the term **(Y-Y')** is called the residual. The **Residual Sum of Squares (RSS)** can be represented as:

$$RSS = residual_1^2 + residual_2^2 + residual_3^2 + \ldots\ldots + residual_n^2$$

Note that regression is highly susceptible to outliers and can introduce huge RSS error if not handled prior to applying regression.

After a regression line is fit into the observed data points, you should examine the residuals by plotting them on the Y-Axis against explanatory the variable on the X-Axis. If the plot is nearly a straight line, then your assumption about linear relationship is valid, or else it may indicate the presence of some kind of non-linear relationship. In case of the presence of nonlinear relationships, you may have to account for the non-linearity. One of the techniques is by adding higher order polynomials to the equation.

We saw that RSS was an important characteristic in fitting the regression line (while building the model). Now, to assess how good your regression fit is (once the model is built), you need two other statistics – **Residual Standard Error (RSE)** and R^2 statistic.

We discussed the irreducible error component $\hat{I}\mu$, because of which there would always be some level of error with your regression (even if your equation exactly fits your data points and you have estimated the coefficients properly). RSE is an estimate of standard deviation of $\hat{I}\mu$ which can be defined as follows:

$$RSE = \sqrt{\frac{1}{n-2}RSS}$$

This means that the actual values would deviate from the true regression line by a factor of RSE on an average.

Since RSE is actually measured in the units of Y (refer to how we calculated RSS in the previous section), it is difficult to say that it is the only best statistic for the model accuracy.

So, an alternative approach was introduced, called the R^2 statistic (also known as the coefficient of determination). The formula to calculate R^2 is as follows:

$$R^2 = \frac{TSS - RSS}{TSS} = 1 - \frac{RSS}{TSS}$$

The **Total Sum of Squares (TSS)** can be calculated as:

$$TSS = \sum (y_i - \bar{y})^2$$

Note here that TSS measures the total variance inherent in Y even before performing the regression to predict Y. Observe that there is no Y' in it. On the contrary, RSS represents the variability in Y that is unexplained after regression. This means that $(TSS - RSS)$ is able to explain the variability in response after regression is performed.

The R^2 statistic usually ranges from 0 to 1, but can be negative if the fit is worse than fitting just a horizontal line, but that is rarely the case. A value close to 1 indicates that the regression equation could explain a large proportion of the variability in the response variable and is a good fit. On the contrary, a value close to 0 indicates that the regression did not explain much of the variance in the response variable and is not a good fit. As an example, an R^2 of 0.25 means that 25 percent of the variance in Y is explained by X and is indicating to tune the model for improvement.

Let us now discuss how to address the non-linearity in the dataset through regression. As discussed earlier, when you find nonlinear relations, it needs to be handled properly. To model a non-linear equation using the same linear regression technique, you have to create the higher order features, which will be treated as just another variable by the regression technique. For example, if *salary* is a feature/variable that is predicting the *buying potential*, and we find that there is a non-linear relationship between them, then we might create a feature called (*salary3*) depending on how much of the non-linearity needs to be addressed. Note that while you create such higher order features, you also have to keep the base features. In this example, you have to use both (*salary*) and (*salary3*) in the regression equation.

So far, we have kind of assumed that all the predictor variables are continuous. What if there are categorical predictors? In such cases, we have to dummy-code those variables (say 1 for male and 0 for female) so that the regression technique generates two equations, one for gender = male (the equation will have the gender variable) and the other for gender = female (the equation will not have the gender variable as it will be dropped as coded 0). At times, with very few categorical variables, it may be a good idea to divide the dataset based on the levels of categorical variables and build separate models for them.

One major advantage of the least squares linear regression is that it explains how the outcome variable is related to the predictor variables. This makes it very interpretable and can be used to draw inferences as well as to do predictions.

Loss function

Many machine learning problems can be formulated as a convex optimization problem. The objective of this problem is to find the values of the coefficients for which the squared loss is minimum. This objective function has basically two components – regularizer and the loss function. The regularizer is there to control the complexity of the model (so it does not overfit) and the loss function is there to estimate the coefficients of the regression function for which squared loss (RSS) is minimum.

The loss function used for least squares is called **squared loss**, as shown next:

$$\tfrac{1}{2}\left(\mathbf{w}^{\mathrm{T}}\mathbf{x} - \mathbf{y}\right)^2$$

Here Y is the response variable (real valued), W is the weight vector (value of the coefficients), and X is the feature vector. So $W^T X$ gives the predicted values which we equate with the actual values Y to find the squared loss that needs to be minimized.

The algorithm used to estimate the coefficients is called **gradient descent**. There are different types of loss functions and optimization algorithms for different kinds of machine learning algorithms which we will cover as and when needed.

Optimization

Ultimately, the linear methods have to optimize the loss function. Under the hood, linear methods use convex optimization methods to optimize the objective functions. MLlib has **Stochastic Gradient Descent (SGD)** and **Limited Memory – Broyden-Fletcher-Goldfarb-Shanno (L-BFGS)** supported out of the box. Currently, most algorithm APIs support SGD and a few support L-BFGS.

SGD is a first-order optimization technique that works best for large scale data and distributed computing environment. Optimization problems whose objective function (loss function) is written as a sum are best suited to be solved using SGD.

L-BFGS is an optimization algorithm in the family of quasi-Newton methods to solve the optimization problems. L-BFGS often achieves a rapider convergence compared with other first-order optimization techniques such as SGD.

Some of the linear methods available in MLlib support both SGD and L-BFGS. You should choose one over the other depending on the objective function under consideration. In general, L-BFGS is recommended over SGD as it converges faster but you need to evaluate carefully based on the requirement.

Regularizations on regression

With large weights (coefficient values), it is easier to overfit the model. Regularization is a technique used mainly to eliminate the overfitting problem by controlling the complexity of the model. This is usually done when you see a difference between the model performance on training data and test data. If the training performance is more than that of the test data, it could be a case of overfitting (high variance case).

To address this, a regularization technique was introduced that would penalize the loss function. It is always recommended to use any of the regularizations techniques, especially when the training data has a small number of observations.

Before we discuss further on the regularization techniques, we have to understand what *bias* and *variance* mean in a supervised learning setting and why there is always a trade-off associated. While both are related to errors, a *biased* model means that it is biased towards some erroneous assumption and may miss the relation between the predictor variables and the response variable to some extent. This is a case of underfitting! On the other hand, a *high variance* model means that it tries to touch every data point and ends up modelling the random noise present in the dataset. It represents the case of overfitting.

Linear regression with the L2 penalty (L2 regularization) is called **ridge regression** and with the L1 penalty (L1 regularization) is called **lasso regression**. When both L1 and L2 penalties are used together, it is called **elastic net regression**. We will discuss them one by one in the following section.

L2 regularized problems are usually easy to solve compared to L1 regularized problems due to smoothness, but the L1 regularized problems can cause sparsity in weights leading to smaller and more interpretable models. Because of this, lasso is at times used for feature selection.

Ridge regression

When we add the L2 penalty (also known as the **shrinkage penalty**) to the loss function of least squares, it becomes the ridge regression, as shown next:

$$\text{RSS} + \lambda \sum_{j=1}^{p} \beta_j^2,$$

Here λ (greater than 0) is a tuning parameter which is determined separately. The second term in the preceding equation is called the shrinkage penalty and can be small only if the coefficients (β_0, β_1...and so on) are small and close to 0. When $\lambda = 0$, the ridge regression becomes least squares. As lambda approaches infinity, the regression coefficients approach zero (but are never zero).

The ridge regression generates different sets of coefficient values for each value of λ. So, the lambda value needs to be carefully selected using cross-validation. As we increase the lambda value, the flexibility of the regression line decreases, thereby decreasing variance and increasing bias.

Note that the shrinkage penalty is applied to all the explanatory variables except the intercept term $\hat{\beta}_0$.

The ridge regression works really well when the training data is less or even in the case where the number of predictors or features are more than the number of observations. Also, the computation needed for ridge is almost the same as that of least squares.

Since ridge does not reduce any coefficient value to zero, all the variables will be present in the model which can make it less interpretable if the number of variables is high.

Lasso regression

Lasso was introduced after ridge. When we add the L1 penalty to the loss function of least squares, it becomes lasso regression, as shown next:

$$\text{RSS} + \lambda \sum_{j=1}^{p} |\beta_j|.$$

The difference here is that instead of taking the squared coefficients, it takes the mod of the coefficient. Unlike ridge, it can force some of its coefficients to be exactly zero which can result in elimination of some of the variables. So, lasso can be used for variable selection as well!

Lasso generates different sets of coefficient values for each value of lambda. So lambda value needs to be carefully selected using cross-validation. Like ridge, as you increase lambda, variance decreases and bias increases.

Lasso produces better interpretable models compared to ridge because it usually has a subset of the total number of variables. When there are many categorical variables, it is advisable to choose lasso over ridge.

In reality, neither ridge nor lasso is always better over the other. Lasso usually performs well with a small number of predictor variables that have substantial coefficients and the rest have very small coefficients. Ridge usually performs better when there are many predictors and almost all have substantial yet similar coefficient sizes.

Ridge is good for grouped selection and can also address multicollinearity problems. Lasso, on the other hand, cannot do grouped selection and tends to pick only one of the predictors. Also, if a group of predictors are highly correlated amongst themselves, Lasso tends to pick only one of them and shrink the others to zero.

Elastic net regression

When we add both L1 and L2 penalties to the loss function of least squares, it becomes elastic net regression, as shown next:

$$\text{RSS} + \lambda_2 \sum_{j=1}^{p} \beta_j^2 + \lambda_1 \sum_{j=1}^{p} |\beta_j|.$$

Following are the advantages of elastic net regression:

- Enforces sparsity and helps remove least effective variables
- Encourages grouping effect
- Combines the strengths of both ridge and lasso

The Naive version of elastic net regression incurs a double shrinkage problem which leads to increased bias and poorer prediction accuracy. To address this, one approach could be rescaling the estimated coefficients by multiplying *(1+ λ2)* with them:

Scala

```
import org.apache.spark.mllib.linalg.Vectors
import org.apache.spark.mllib.regression.LabeledPoint
import org.apache.spark.mllib.regression.LinearRegressionModel
import org.apache.spark.mllib.regression.LinearRegressionWithSGD
scala> import
org.apache.spark.ml.regression.{LinearRegression,LinearRegressionModel}
import
org.apache.spark.ml.regression.{LinearRegression,LinearRegressionModel}
// Load the data
scala> val data =
spark.read.format("libsvm").load("data/mllib/sample_linear_regression_data.
txt")
data: org.apache.spark.sql.DataFrame = [label: double, features: vector]

// Build the model
scala> val lrModel = new LinearRegression().fit(data)
```

```
//Note: You can change ElasticNetParam, MaxIter and RegParam
// Defaults are 0.0, 100 and 0.0
lrModel: org.apache.spark.ml.regression.LinearRegressionModel =
linReg_aa788bcebc42

//Check Root Mean Squared Error
scala> println("Root Mean Squared Error = " +
lrModel.summary.rootMeanSquaredError)
Root Mean Squared Error = 10.16309157133015
```

Python:

```
>>> from pyspark.ml.regression import LinearRegression,
LinearRegressionModel
>>>

// Load the data
>>> data =
spark.read.format("libsvm").load("data/mllib/sample_linear_regression_data.
txt")
>>>

// Build the model
>>> lrModel = LinearRegression().fit(data)

//Note: You can change ElasticNetParam, MaxIter and RegParam
// Defaults are 0.0, 100 and 0.0
//Check Root Mean Squared Error
>>> print "Root Mean Squared Error = ",
lrModel.summary.rootMeanSquaredError
Root Mean Squared Error = 10.16309157133015
>>>
```

Classification methods

If the response variable is qualitative/categorical (takes on categorical values such as gender, loan default, marital status, and such), then the problem can be called a classification problem regardless of the explanatory variables' type. There are various types of classification methods, but we will focus on logistic regression and Support Vector Machines in this section.

Following are a few examples of some implications of classification methods:

- A customer buys a product or does not buy it
- A person is diabetic or not diabetic

- An individual applying for a loan would default or not
- An e-mail receiver would read the e-mail or not

Logistic regression

Logistic regression measures the relation between the explanatory variables and the categorical response variable. We do not use linear regression for the categorical response variable because the response variable is not on a continuous scale and hence the error terms are not normally distributed.

So logistic regression is a classification algorithm. Instead of modelling the response variable Y directly, logistic regression models the probability distribution of $P(Y|X)$ that Y belongs to a particular category. The conditional distribution of $(Y|X)$ is a Bernoulli distribution rather than a Gaussian distribution. The logistic regression equation can be represented as follows:

$$p(X) = \beta_0 + \beta_1 X.$$

For a two class classification, the output of the model should be restricted to only one of the two classes (say either 0 or 1). Since logistic regression predicts probabilities and not classes directly, we use a logistic function (also known as the, *sigmoid function*) to restrict the output to a single class:

$$p(X) = \frac{e^{\beta_0 + \beta_1 X}}{1 + e^{\beta_0 + \beta_1 X}}$$

Solving for the preceding equation gives us the following:

$$= \frac{1}{1 + e^{-(\beta_0 + x \cdot \beta)}}$$

It can be further simplified as:

$$\frac{p(X)}{1 - p(X)} = e^{\beta_0 + \beta_1 X}$$

The quantity on the left *P(X)/1-P(X)* is called the *odds*. The value of odds ranges from 0 to infinity. The values close to 0 indicate very less probability and the ones bigger in numbers indicate high probability. At times odds are used directly instead of probabilities, depending on the situation.

If we take the log of the odds, it becomes log-odd or logit and can be shown as follows:

$$\log \left(\frac{p(X)}{1 - p(X)} \right) = \beta_0 + \beta_1 X_1 + \cdots + \beta_p X_p$$

You can see from the previous equation that logit is linearly related to X.

In the situation where there are two classes, 1 and 0, then we predict *Y = 1* if *p >= 0.5* and *Y = 0* when *p < 0.5*. So logistic regression is actually a linear classifier with decision boundary at *p = 0.5*. There could be business cases where *p* is just not set to 0.5 by default and you may have to figure out the right value using some mathematical techniques.

A method known as maximum likelihood is used to fit the model by computing the regression coefficients, and the algorithm can be a gradient descent like in a linear regression setting.

In logistic regression, the loss function should address the misclassification rate. So, the loss function used for logistic regression is called *logistic loss*, as shown next:

$$L(\mathbf{w}; \mathbf{x}, y) := \log(1 + \exp(-y\mathbf{w}^T\mathbf{x}))$$

Note that logistic regression is also prone to overfitting when you use higher order polynomial to better fit a model. To solve this, you can use regularization terms like you did in linear regression. As of this writing, Spark does not support regularized logistic regression so we will skip this part for now.

Linear Support Vector Machines (SVM)

Support Vector Machines (**SVM**) is a type of supervised machine learning algorithm and can be used for both classification and regression. However, it is more popular in addressing the classification problems, and since Spark offers it as an SVM classifier, we will limit our discussion to the classification setting only. When used as a classifier, unlike logistic regression, it is a non-probabilistic classifier.

The SVM has evolved from a simple classifier called the **maximal margin classifier**. Since the maximal margin classifier required that the classes be separable by a linear boundary, it could not be applied to many datasets. So it was extended to an improved version called the **support vector classifier** that could address the cases where the classes overlapped and there were no clear separation between the classes. The support vector classifier was further extended to what we call an SVM to accommodate the non-linear class boundaries. Let us discuss the evolution of the SVM step by step so we get a clear understanding of how it works.

If there are p dimensions (features) in a dataset, then we fit a hyperplane in that p-dimensional space whose equation can be defined as follows:

$$\beta_0 + \beta_1 X_1 + \beta_2 X_2 + \ldots + \beta_p X_p = 0$$

This hyperplane is called the separating hyperplane that forms the decision boundary. The result will be classified based on the result; if greater than 0, then on one side and if less than 0, then on the other side, as shown in the following figure:

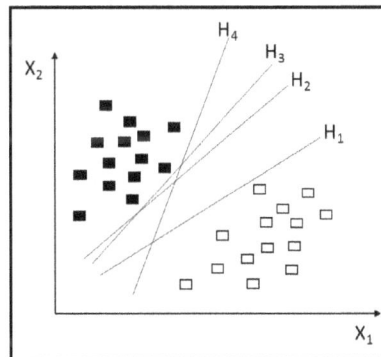

Observe in the preceding figure that there can be multiple hyperplanes (they can be infinite). There should be a reasonable way to choose the best hyperplane. This is where we select the maximal margin hyperplane. If you compute the perpendicular distance of all data points to the separating hyperplane, then the smallest distance would be called as the margin. So, for the maximal margin classifier, the hyperplane should have the highest margin.

The training observations that are close yet equidistant from the separating hyperplane are known as support vectors. For any slight change in the support vectors, the hyperplane would also get reoriented. These support vectors actually define the margin. Now, what if the two classes under consideration are not separable? We would probably want a classifier that does not perfectly separate the two classes and has a softer boundary that allows some level of misclassification as well. This requirement led to the introduction of the support vector classifier (also known as the soft margin classifier).

Mathematically, it is the slack variable in the equation that allows for misclassification. Also, there is a tuning parameter in the support vector classifier which should be selected using cross‌validation. This tuning parameter is the one that trades off between bias and variance and should be handled with care. When it is large, the margin is wider and includes many support vectors, and has low variance and high bias. If it is small, then the margin will have fewer support vectors and the classifier will have low bias but high variance.

The loss function for the SVM can be represented as follows:

$$L(\mathbf{w}; \mathbf{x}, y) := \max\{0, 1 - y\mathbf{w}^T\mathbf{x}\}.$$

As of this writing, Spark supports only linear SVMs. By default, linear SVMs are trained with an L2 regularization. Spark also supports alternative L1 regularization.

So far so good! But how would the support vector classifier work when there is a non-linear boundary between the classes, as shown in the following image:

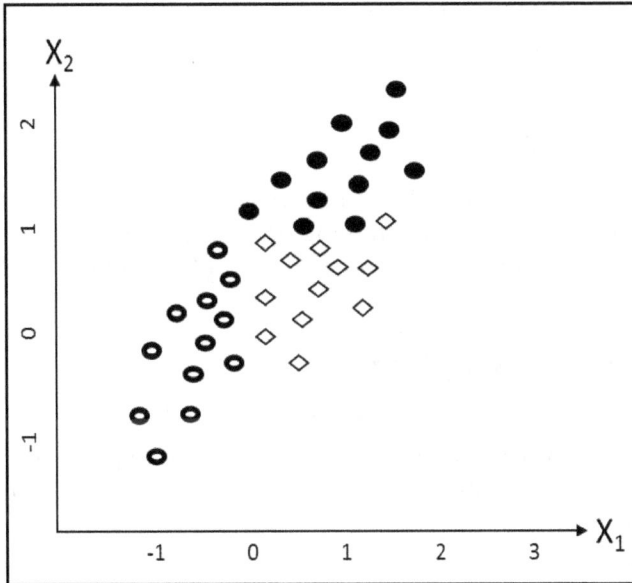

Any linear classifier, such as a support vector classifier, would perform very poorly in the preceding situation. If it draws a straight line through the data points, then the classes would not be separated properly. This is a case of non-linear class boundaries. A solution to this problem is the SVM. In other words, when a support vector classifier is fused with a non-linear kernel, it becomes an SVM.

Similar to the way we introduced higher order polynomial terms in the regression equation to account for the non-linearity, something can also be done in the SVM context. The SVM uses something called kernels to take care of different kinds of non-linearity in the dataset; different kernels for different kinds of non-linearity. Kernel methods map the data into higher dimensional space as the data might get well separated if it does so. Also, it makes distinguishing different classes easier. Let us discuss a few of the important kernels so as to be able to select the right one.

Linear kernel

This is one of the most basic type of kernels that allows us to pick out only lines or hyperplanes. It is equivalent to a support vector classifier. It cannot address the non-linearity if present in the dataset.

Polynomial kernel

This allows us to address some level of non-linearity to the extent of the order of polynomials. This works well when the training data is normalized. This kernel usually has more hyperparameters and therefore increases the complexity of the model.

Radial Basis Function kernel

When you are not really sure of which kernel to use, **Radial Basis Function** (**RBF**) can be a good default choice. It allows you to pick out even circles or hyperspheres. Though this usually performs better than linear or polynomial kernel, it does not perform well when the number of features is huge.

Sigmoid kernel

The sigmoid kernel has its roots in neural networks. So, an SVM with a sigmoid kernel is equivalent to a neural network with a two layered perceptron.

Training an SVM

While training an SVM, the modeler has to take a number of decisions:

- How to pre-process the data (transformation and scaling). The categorical variables should be converted to numeric ones by dummifying them. Also, scaling the numeric values is needed (either 0 to 1 or -1 to +1).
- Which kernel to use (check using cross‑validation if you are unable to visualize the data and/ or conclude on it).
- What parameters to set for the SVM: penalty parameter and the kernel parameter (find using cross‑validation or grid search)

If needed, you can use an entropy based feature selection to include only the important features in your model.

Scala:

```
scala> import org.apache.spark.mllib.classification.{SVMModel, SVMWithSGD}
import org.apache.spark.mllib.classification.{SVMModel, SVMWithSGD}
scala> import org.apache.spark.mllib.evaluation.BinaryClassificationMetrics
import org.apache.spark.mllib.evaluation.BinaryClassificationMetrics
scala> import org.apache.spark.mllib.util.MLUtils
import org.apache.spark.mllib.util.MLUtils
scala>

// Load training data in LIBSVM format.
scala> val data = MLUtils.loadLibSVMFile(sc,
"data/mllib/sample_libsvm_data.txt")
data:
org.apache.spark.rdd.RDD[org.apache.spark.mllib.regression.LabeledPoint] =
MapPartitionsRDD[6] at map at MLUtils.scala:84
scala>

// Split data into training (60%) and test (40%).
scala> val splits = data.randomSplit(Array(0.6, 0.4), seed = 11L)
splits:
Array[org.apache.spark.rdd.RDD[org.apache.spark.mllib.regression.LabeledPoi
nt]] = Array(MapPartitionsRDD[7] at randomSplit at <console>:29,
MapPartitionsRDD[8] at randomSplit at <console>:29)
scala> val training = splits(0).cache()
training:
org.apache.spark.rdd.RDD[org.apache.spark.mllib.regression.LabeledPoint] =
MapPartitionsRDD[7] at randomSplit at <console>:29
scala> val test = splits(1)
test:
org.apache.spark.rdd.RDD[org.apache.spark.mllib.regression.LabeledPoint] =
MapPartitionsRDD[8] at randomSplit at <console>:29
scala>

// Run training algorithm to build the model
scala> val model = SVMWithSGD.train(training, numIterations=100)
model: org.apache.spark.mllib.classification.SVMModel =
org.apache.spark.mllib.classification.SVMModel: intercept = 0.0,
numFeatures = 692, numClasses = 2, threshold = 0.0
scala>

// Clear the default threshold.
scala> model.clearThreshold()
res1: model.type = org.apache.spark.mllib.classification.SVMModel:
intercept =
0.0, numFeatures = 692, numClasses = 2, threshold = None
scala>
```

```
// Compute raw scores on the test set.
scala> val scoreAndLabels = test.map { point =>
        val score = model.predict(point.features)
        (score, point.label)
        }
scoreAndLabels: org.apache.spark.rdd.RDD[(Double, Double)] =
MapPartitionsRDD[213] at map at <console>:37
scala>

// Get evaluation metrics.
scala> val metrics = new BinaryClassificationMetrics(scoreAndLabels)
metrics: org.apache.spark.mllib.evaluation.BinaryClassificationMetrics =
org.apache.spark.mllib.evaluation.BinaryClassificationMetrics@3106aebb
scala> println("Area under ROC = " + metrics.areaUnderROC())
Area under ROC = 1.0
scala>
```

`mllib` has already entered maintenance mode and SVM is still not available under ml so only Scala code is provided for illustration.

Decision trees

A decision tree is a non-parametric supervised learning algorithm which can be used for both classification and regression. Decision trees are like inverted trees with the root node at the top and leaf nodes forming downwards. There are different algorithms to split the dataset into branch-like segments. Each leaf node is assigned to a class that represents the most appropriate target values.

Decision trees do not require any scaling or transformations of the dataset and work as the data is. They can handle both categorical and continuous features, and also address non-linearity in the dataset. At its core, a decision tree is a greedy algorithm (it considers the best split at the moment and does not take into consideration the future scenarios) that performs a recursive binary partitioning of the feature space. Splitting is done based on information gain at each node because information gain measures how well a given attribute separates the training examples as per the target class or value. The first split happens for the feature that generates maximum information gain and becomes the root node.

The information gain at a node is the difference between the parent node impurity and the weighted sum of two child node impurities. To estimate information gain, Spark currently has two impurity measures for classification problems and one impurity measure for regression, as explained next.

Impurity measures

Impurity is a measure of homogeneity and the best criteria for recursive partitioning. By calculating the impurity, the best split candidate is decided. Most of the impurity measures are probability based:

Probability of a class = number of observations of that class / total number of observations

Let us spend some time on different types of important impurity measures that are supported by Spark.

Gini Index

The Gini Index is mainly intended for the continuous attributes or features in a dataset. If not, it would assume that all the attributes and features are continuous. The split makes the child nodes more *purer* than the parent node. Gini tends to find the largest class – the class of response variable that has got the maximum observations. It can be defined as follows:

$$Gini\ Index = 1 - \sum_j p_j^2$$

If all observations of a response belong to a single class, then probability P of that class j, that is (Pj), will be 1 as there is only one class, and $(Pj)2$ would also be 1. This makes the Gini Index to be zero.

Entropy

Entropy is mainly intended for the categorical attributes or features in a dataset. It can be defined as follows:

$$Entropy = \sum_j -p_j log_2 p_j$$

If all observations of a response belong to a single class, then the probability of that class (*Pj*) will be 1, and *log(P)* would be zero. This makes the entropy to be zero.

The following graph depicts the probability of a fair coin toss:

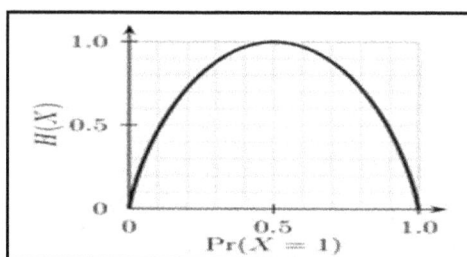

Just to explain the preceding graph, if you toss a fair coin, the probability of a head or a tail would be 0.5, so there will be maximum observations at a probability of 0.5.

If the data sample is completely homogeneous then the entropy will be zero, and if the sample can be equally divided into two, then the entropy will be one.

It is a little slower to compute than Gini because it has to compute the log as well.

Variance

Unlike the Gini Index and entropy, variance is used for calculating information gain for regression problems. Variance can be defined as:

$\frac{1}{N} \sum_{i=1}^{N} (y_i - \mu)^2$ y_i is label for an instance, N is the number of instances and μ is the mean given by $\frac{1}{N} \sum_{i=1}^{N} y_i$.

Stopping rule

The recursive tree construction is stopped at a node when one of the following conditions is met:

- The node depth is equal to the `maxDepth` training parameter
- No split candidate leads to an information gain greater than `minInfoGain`
- No split candidate produces child nodes, each of which have at least a `minInstancesPerNode` training instances

Split candidates

A dataset typically has a mixture of categorical and continuous features. How the features get split further into split candidates is something we should understand because we at times need some level of control over them to build a better model.

Categorical features

For a categorical feature with M possible values (categories), one could come up with $2(M-1)-1$ split candidates. Whether for binary classification or regression, the number of split candidates can be reduced to $M-1$ by ordering the categorical feature values by the average label.

For example, consider a binary classification (0/1) problem with one categorical feature that has three categories A, B, and C, and their corresponding proportions of label-1 response variables are 0.2, 0.6, and 0.4 respectively. In this case, the categorical features can be ordered as A, C, B. So, the two split candidates (*M-1 = 3-1 = 2*) can be *A | (C, B)* and *A, (C | B)* where '|' denotes the split.

Continuous features

For a continuous feature variable, there can be a chance that no two values are the same (at least we can assume so). If there are n observations, then n split candidates might not be a good idea, especially in a big data setting.

In Spark, it is done by performing a quantile calculation on a sample of data, and binning the data accordingly. You can still have control over the maximum bins that you would like to allow, using the `maxBins` parameter. The maximum default value for `maxBins` is 32.

Advantages of decision trees

- They are simple to understand and interpret, so easy to explain to business users
- They works for both classification and regression
- Both qualitative and quantitative data can be accommodated in constructing the decision trees

Information gains in decision trees are biased in favor of the attributes with more levels.

Disadvantages of decision trees

- They do not work that greatly for effectively continuous outcome variables
- Performance is poor when there are many classes and the dataset is small
- Axis parallel split reduces the accuracy
- They suffer from high variance as they try to fit almost all data points

Example

Implementation â©® wise there are no major differences between classification and regression trees. Let us have a look at the practical implementation of it on Spark.

Scala:

```scala
//Assuming ml.Pipeline and ml.features are already imported
scala> import org.apache.spark.ml.classification.{
        DecisionTreeClassifier, DecisionTreeClassificationModel}
import org.apache.spark.ml.classification.{DecisionTreeClassifier,
DecisionTreeClassificationModel}
scala>
/prepare train data
scala> val f:String = "<Your path>/simple_file1.csv"
f: String = <your path>/simple_file1.csv
scala> val trainDF = spark.read.options(Map("header"->"true",
        "inferSchema"->"true")).csv(f)
trainDF: org.apache.spark.sql.DataFrame = [Text: string, Label: int]

scala>

 //define DecisionTree pipeline
//StringIndexer maps labels(String or numeric) to label indices
//Maximum occurrence label becomes 0 and so on
```

```
scala> val lblIdx = new StringIndexer().
               setInputCol("Label").
               setOutputCol("indexedLabel")
lblIdx: org.apache.spark.ml.feature.StringIndexer = strIdx_3a7bc9c1ed0d
scala>

// Create labels list to decode predictions
scala> val labels = lblIdx.fit(trainDF).labels
labels: Array[String] = Array(2, 1, 3)
scala>

//Define Text column indexing stage
scala> val fIdx = new StringIndexer().
               setInputCol("Text").
               setOutputCol("indexedText")
fIdx: org.apache.spark.ml.feature.StringIndexer = strIdx_49253a83c717

// VectorAssembler
scala> val va = new VectorAssembler().
               setInputCols(Array("indexedText")).
               setOutputCol("features")
va: org.apache.spark.ml.feature.VectorAssembler = vecAssembler_764720c39a85

//Define Decision Tree classifier. Set label and features vector
scala> val dt = new DecisionTreeClassifier().
               setLabelCol("indexedLabel").
               setFeaturesCol("features")
dt: org.apache.spark.ml.classification.DecisionTreeClassifier =
dtc_84d87d778792

//Define label converter to convert prediction index back to string
scala> val lc = new IndexToString().
               setInputCol("prediction").
               setOutputCol("predictedLabel").
               setLabels(labels)
lc: org.apache.spark.ml.feature.IndexToString = idxToStr_e2f4fa023665
scala>

//String the stages together to form a pipeline
scala> val dt_pipeline = new Pipeline().setStages(
         Array(lblIdx,fIdx,va,dt,lc))
dt_pipeline: org.apache.spark.ml.Pipeline = pipeline_d4b0e884dcbf
scala>
//Apply pipeline to the train data
scala> val resultDF = dt_pipeline.fit(trainDF).transform(trainDF)

//Check results. Watch Label and predictedLabel column values match
resultDF: org.apache.spark.sql.DataFrame = [Text: string, Label: int ... 6
```

```
more
fields]
scala>
resultDF.select("Text","Label","features","prediction","predictedLabel").sh
ow()
+----+-----+--------+----------+--------------+
|Text|Label|features|prediction|predictedLabel|
+----+-----+--------+----------+--------------+
|   A|    1|   [1.0]|       1.0|             1|
|   B|    2|   [0.0]|       0.0|             2|
|   C|    3|   [2.0]|       2.0|             3|
|   A|    1|   [1.0]|       1.0|             1|
|   B|    2|   [0.0]|       0.0|             2|
+----+-----+--------+----------+--------------+
scala>

//Prepare evaluation data
scala> val eval:String = â??<Your path>/simple_file2.csv"
eval: String = <Your path>/simple_file2.csv
scala> val evalDF = spark.read.options(Map("header"->"true",
             "inferSchema"->"true")).csv(eval)
evalDF: org.apache.spark.sql.DataFrame = [Text: string, Label: int]
scala>

//Apply the same pipeline to the evaluation data
scala> val eval_resultDF = dt_pipeline.fit(evalDF).transform(evalDF)
eval_resultDF: org.apache.spark.sql.DataFrame = [Text: string, Label: int
... 7
more fields]

//Check evaluation results
scala>
eval_resultDF.select("Text","Label","features","prediction","predictedLabel
").sh
w()
+----+-----+--------+----------+--------------+
|Text|Label|features|prediction|predictedLabel|
+----+-----+--------+----------+--------------+
|   A|    1|   [0.0]|       1.0|             1|
|   A|    1|   [0.0]|       1.0|             1|
|   A|    2|   [0.0]|       1.0|             1|
|   B|    2|   [1.0]|       0.0|             2|
|   C|    3|   [2.0]|       2.0|             3|
+----+-----+--------+----------+--------------+
//Note that predicted label for the third row is 1 as against Label(2) as
expected
```

Python:

```
//Model training example
>>> from pyspark.ml.pipeline import Pipeline
>>> from pyspark.ml.feature import StringIndexer, VectorIndexer,
VectorAssembler,
IndexToString
>>> from pyspark.ml.classification import DecisionTreeClassifier,
DecisionTreeClassificationModel
>>>

//prepare train data
>>> file_location = "../work/simple_file1.csv"
>>> trainDF = spark.read.csv(file_location,header=True,inferSchema=True)

 //Read file
>>>

//define DecisionTree pipeline
//StringIndexer maps labels(String or numeric) to label indices
//Maximum occurrence label becomes 0 and so on
>>> lblIdx = StringIndexer(inputCol = "Label",outputCol = "indexedLabel")

// Create labels list to decode predictions
>>> labels = lblIdx.fit(trainDF).labels
>>> labels
[u'2', u'1', u'3']
>>>

//Define Text column indexing stage
>>> fidx = StringIndexer(inputCol="Text",outputCol="indexedText")

// Vector assembler
>>> va = VectorAssembler(inputCols=["indexedText"],outputCol="features")

//Define Decision Tree classifier. Set label and features vector
>>> dt =
DecisionTreeClassifier(labelCol="indexedLabel",featuresCol="features")

//Define label converter to convert prediction index back to string
>>> lc = IndexToString(inputCol="prediction",outputCol="predictedLabel",
                       labels=labels)

//String the stages together to form a pipeline
>>> dt_pipeline = Pipeline(stages=[lblIdx,fidx,va,dt,lc])
>>>
>>>
```

```
//Apply decision tree pipeline
>>> dtModel = dt_pipeline.fit(trainDF)
>>> dtDF = dtModel.transform(trainDF)
>>> dtDF.columns
['Text', 'Label', 'indexedLabel', 'indexedText', 'features',
'rawPrediction',
'probability', 'prediction', 'predictedLabel']
>>> dtDF.select("Text","Label","indexedLabel","prediction",
"predictedLabel").show()
+----+-----+------------+----------+--------------+
|Text|Label|indexedLabel|prediction|predictedLabel|
+----+-----+------------+----------+--------------+
|   A|    1|         1.0|       1.0|             1|
|   B|    2|         0.0|       0.0|             2|
|   C|    3|         2.0|       2.0|             3|
|   A|    1|         1.0|       1.0|             1|
|   B|    2|         0.0|       0.0|             2|
+----+-----+------------+----------+--------------+

>>>

>>> //prepare evaluation dataframe
>>> eval_file_path = "../work/simple_file2.csv"
>>> evalDF = spark.read.csv(eval_file_path,header=True, inferSchema=True)

//Read eval file
>>> eval_resultDF = dt_pipeline.fit(evalDF).transform(evalDF)
>>> eval_resultDF.columns
['Text', 'Label', 'indexedLabel', 'indexedText', 'features',
'rawPrediction', 'probability', 'prediction', 'predictedLabel']
>>> eval_resultDF.select("Text","Label","indexedLabel","prediction",
"predictedLabel").show()
+----+-----+------------+----------+--------------+
|Text|Label|indexedLabel|prediction|predictedLabel|
+----+-----+------------+----------+--------------+
|   A|    1|         1.0|       1.0|             1|
|   A|    1|         1.0|       1.0|             1|
|   A|    2|         0.0|       1.0|             1|
|   B|    2|         0.0|       0.0|             2|
|   C|    3|         2.0|       2.0|             3|
+----+-----+------------+----------+--------------+
>>>

Accompanying data files:
simple_file1.csv
Text,Label
A,1
B,2
```

```
C,3
A,1
B,2simple_file2.csv
Text,Label
A,1
A,1
A,2
B,2
C,3
```

Ensembles

As the name suggests, ensemble methods use multiple learning algorithms to obtain a more accurate model in terms of prediction accuracy. Usually these techniques require more computing power and make the model more complex, which makes it difficult to interpret. Let us discuss the various types of ensemble techniques available on Spark.

Random forests

A random forest is an ensemble technique for the decision trees. Before we get to random forests, let us see how it has evolved. We know that decision trees usually have high variance issues and tend to overfit the model. To address this, a concept called *bagging* (also known as bootstrap aggregating) was introduced. For the decision trees, the idea was to take multiple training sets (bootstrapped training sets) from the dataset and create separate decision trees out of those, and then average them out for regression trees. For the classification trees, we can take the majority vote or the most commonly occurring class from all the trees. These trees grew deep and were not pruned at all. This definitely reduced the variance though the individual trees might have high variance.

One problem with the plain bagging approach was that for most of the bootstrapped training sets, the strong predictors took their positions at the top split which almost made the bagged trees look similar. This meant that the prediction also looked similar and if you averaged them out, then it did not reduce the variance to the extent expected. To address this, a technique was needed which would take a similar approach as that of bagged trees but eliminate the correlation amongst the trees, hence the *random forest*.

In this approach, you build bootstrapped training samples to create decision trees, but the only difference is that every time a split happens, a random sample of P predictors are chosen from a total of say K predictors. This is how a random forest injects randomness to this approach. As a thumb rule, we can take P as the square root of Q.

Like in the case of bagging, in this approach you also average the predictions if your goal is regression and take the majority vote if the goal is classification. Spark provides some tuning parameters to tune this model, which are as follows:

- `numTrees`: You can specify the number of trees to consider in the random forest. If the numbers are high then the variance in prediction would be less, but the time required would be more.
- `maxDepth`: You can specify the maximum depth of each tree. An increased depth makes the trees more powerful in terms of prediction accuracy. Though they tend to overfit the individual trees, the overall output is still good because we average the results anyway, which reduces the variance.

- `subsamplingRate`: This parameter is mainly used to speed up training. It is used to set the bootstrapped training sample size. A value less than 1.0 speeds up the performance.
- `featureSubsetStrategy`: This parameter can also help speed up the execution. It is used to set the number of features to use as split candidates for every node. It should be set carefully as too low or too high a value can impact the accuracy of the model.

Advantages of random forests

- They run faster as the execution happens in parallel
- They are less prone to overfitting
- They are easy to tune
- Prediction accuracy is more compared to trees or bagged trees
- They work well even when the predictor variables are a mixture of categorical and continuous features, and do not require scaling

Gradient-Boosted Trees

Like random forests, **Gradient-Boosted Trees** (**GBTs**) are also an ensemble of trees. They can be applied to both classification and regression problems. Unlike bagged trees or random forests, where trees are built in parallel on independent datasets and are independent of each other, GBTs are built sequentially. Each tree is grown using the result of the previously grown tree. Note that GBTs do not work on bootstrapped samples.

On each iteration, GBTs use the current ensemble at hand to predict the labels for the training instances and compares them with true labels and estimates the error. The training instances with poor prediction accuracy get relabeled so that the decision trees get corrected in the next iteration based on the error rate for the previous mistakes.

The mechanism behind finding the error rate and relabeling the instances is based on the loss function. GBTs are designed to reduce this loss function for every iteration. The following types of loss functions are supported by Spark:

- **Log loss**: This is used for classification problems.

- **Squared error (L2 loss)**: This is used for regression problems and is set by default. It is the summation of the squared differences between the actual and predicted output for all the observations. Outliers should be treated well for this loss function to perform well.
- **Absolute error (L1 loss)**: This is also used for regression problems. It is the summation of the absolute differences between the actual and predicted output for all the observations. It is more robust to outliers compared to squared error.

Spark provides some tuning parameters to tune this model, which are as follows:

- `loss`: You can pass a loss function as discussed in the previous section, depending on the dataset you are dealing with and whether you intend to do classification or regression.
- `numIterations`: Each iteration produces only one tree! If you set this very high, then the time needed for execution will also be high as the operation would be sequential and can also lead to overfitting. It should be carefully set for better performance and accuracy.
- `learningRate`: This is not really a tuning parameter. If the algorithm's behavior is unstable then reducing this can help stabilize the model.
- `algo`: *Classification* or *regression* is set based on what you want.

GBTs can overfit the models with a greater number of trees, so Spark provides the `runWithValidation` method to prevent overfitting.

> As of this writing, GBTs on Spark do not yet support multiclass classification.

Let us look at an example to illustrate GBTs in action. The example dataset contains average marks and attendance of twenty students. The data also contains result as Pass or Fail, which follow a set of criteria. However, a couple of students (ids 1009 and 1020) were âøøgrantedâøø Pass status event though they did not really qualify. Now our task is to check if the models pick up these two students are not.

The Pass criteria are as follows:

- Marks should be at least 40 and Attendance should be at least âøøEnoughâøø
- If Marks are between 40 and 60, then attendance should be âøøFullâøø to pass

The following example also emphasizes on reuse of pipeline stages across multiple models. So, we build a DecisionTree classifier first and then a GBT. We build two different pipelines that share stages.

Input:

```
// Marks < 40 = Fail
// Attendence == Poor => Fail
// Marks >40 and attendence Full => Pass
// Marks > 60 and attendence Enough or Full => Pass
// Two exceptions were studentId 1009 and 1020 who were granted Pass
//This example also emphasizes the reuse of pipeline stages
// Initially the code trains a DecisionTreeClassifier
// Then, same stages are reused to train a GBT classifier
```

Scala:

```
scala> import org.apache.spark.ml.feature._
scala> import org.apache.spark.ml.Pipeline
scala> import org.apache.spark.ml.classification.{DecisionTreeClassifier,
                            DecisionTreeClassificationModel}
scala> case class StResult(StudentId:String, Avg_Marks:Double,
        Attendance:String, Result:String)
scala> val file_path = "../work/StudentsPassFail.csv"
scala> val source_ds = spark.read.options(Map("header"->"true",
            "inferSchema"->"true")).csv(file_path).as[StResult]
source_ds: org.apache.spark.sql.Dataset[StResult] = [StudentId: int,
Avg_Marks:
double ... 2 more fields]
scala>
//Examine source data
scala> source_ds.show(4)
+---------+---------+----------+------+
|StudentId|Avg_Marks|Attendance|Result|
+---------+---------+----------+------+
|     1001|     48.0|      Full|  Pass|
```

```
|    1002|    21.0|    Enough|  Fail|
|    1003|    24.0|    Enough|  Fail|
|    1004|     4.0|      Poor|  Fail|
+--------+--------+----------+------+

scala>
//Define preparation pipeline
scala> val marks_bkt = new Bucketizer().setInputCol("Avg_Marks").
        setOutputCol("Mark_bins").setSplits(Array(0,40.0,60.0,100.0))
marks_bkt: org.apache.spark.ml.feature.Bucketizer = bucketizer_5299d2fbd1b2
scala> val att_idx = new StringIndexer().setInputCol("Attendance").
        setOutputCol("Att_idx")
att_idx: org.apache.spark.ml.feature.StringIndexer = strIdx_2db54ba5200a
scala> val label_idx = new StringIndexer().setInputCol("Result").
        setOutputCol("Label")
label_idx: org.apache.spark.ml.feature.StringIndexer = strIdx_20f4316d6232
scala>

//Create labels list to decode predictions
scala> val resultLabels = label_idx.fit(source_ds).labels
resultLabels: Array[String] = Array(Fail, Pass)
scala> val va = new
VectorAssembler().setInputCols(Array("Mark_bins","Att_idx")).
                setOutputCol("features")
va: org.apache.spark.ml.feature.VectorAssembler = vecAssembler_5dc2dbbef48c
scala> val dt = new DecisionTreeClassifier().setLabelCol("Label").
        setFeaturesCol("features")
dt: org.apache.spark.ml.classification.DecisionTreeClassifier =
dtc_e8343ae1a9eb
scala> val lc = new IndexToString().setInputCol("prediction").
            setOutputCol("predictedLabel").setLabels(resultLabels)
lc: org.apache.spark.ml.feature.IndexToString = idxToStr_90b6693d4313
scala>

//Define pipeline
scala>val dt_pipeline = new
Pipeline().setStages(Array(marks_bkt,att_idx,label_idx,va,dt,lc))
dt_pipeline: org.apache.spark.ml.Pipeline = pipeline_95876bb6c969
scala> val dtModel = dt_pipeline.fit(source_ds)
dtModel: org.apache.spark.ml.PipelineModel = pipeline_95876bb6c969
scala> val resultDF = dtModel.transform(source_ds)
resultDF: org.apache.spark.sql.DataFrame = [StudentId: int, Avg_Marks:
double ...
10 more fields]
scala> resultDF.filter("Label !=
prediction").select("StudentId","Label","prediction","Result","predictedLab
el").show()
+--------+-----+----------+------+--------------+
```

```
|StudentId|Label|prediction|Result|predictedLabel|
+---------+-----+----------+------+--------------+\
|    1009| 1.0|       0.0| Pass|          Fail|
|    1020| 1.0|       0.0| Pass|          Fail|
+---------+-----+----------+------+--------------+
```

```
//Note that the difference is in the student ids that were granted pass
```

```
//Same example using Gradient boosted tree classifier, reusing the pipeline
stages
scala> import org.apache.spark.ml.classification.GBTClassifier
import org.apache.spark.ml.classification.GBTClassifier
scala> val gbt = new GBTClassifier().setLabelCol("Label").
                setFeaturesCol("features").setMaxIter(10)
gbt: org.apache.spark.ml.classification.GBTClassifier = gbtc_cb55ae2174a1
scala> val gbt_pipeline = new
Pipeline().setStages(Array(marks_bkt,att_idx,label_idx,va,gbt,lc))
gbt_pipeline: org.apache.spark.ml.Pipeline = pipeline_dfd42cd89403
scala> val gbtResultDF = gbt_pipeline.fit(source_ds).transform(source_ds)
gbtResultDF: org.apache.spark.sql.DataFrame = [StudentId: int, Avg_Marks:
double ... 8 more fields]
scala> gbtResultDF.filter("Label !=
prediction").select("StudentId","Label","Result","prediction","predictedLab
el").show()
+---------+-----+------+----------+--------------+
|StudentId|Label|Result|prediction|predictedLabel|
+---------+-----+------+----------+--------------+
|    1009| 1.0| Pass|       0.0|          Fail|
|    1020| 1.0| Pass|       0.0|          Fail|
+---------+-----+------+----------+--------------+
```

Python:

```python
>>> from pyspark.ml.pipeline import Pipeline
>>> from pyspark.ml.feature import Bucketizer, StringIndexer,
VectorAssembler, IndexToString
>>> from pyspark.ml.classification import DecisionTreeClassifier,
DecisionTreeClassificationModel
>>>

//Get source file
>>> file_path = "../work/StudentsPassFail.csv"
>>> source_df = spark.read.csv(file_path,header=True,inferSchema=True)
>>>

//Examine source data
>>> source_df.show(4)
+---------+---------+----------+------+
```

```
|StudentId|Avg_Marks|Attendance|Result|
+---------+---------+----------+------+
|     1001|     48.0|      Full|  Pass|
|     1002|     21.0|    Enough|  Fail|
|     1003|     24.0|    Enough|  Fail|
|     1004|      4.0|      Poor|  Fail|
+---------+---------+----------+------+

//Define preparation pipeline
>>> marks_bkt = Bucketizer(inputCol="Avg_Marks",
        outputCol="Mark_bins", splits=[0,40.0,60.0,100.0])
>>> att_idx = StringIndexer(inputCol = "Attendance",
        outputCol="Att_idx")
>>> label_idx = StringIndexer(inputCol="Result",
                    outputCol="Label")
>>>

//Create labels list to decode predictions
>>> resultLabels = label_idx.fit(source_df).labels
>>> resultLabels
[u'Fail', u'Pass']
>>>
>>> va = VectorAssembler(inputCols=["Mark_bins","Att_idx"],
                    outputCol="features")
>>> dt = DecisionTreeClassifier(labelCol="Label", featuresCol="features")
>>> lc = IndexToString(inputCol="prediction",outputCol="predictedLabel",
            labels=resultLabels)
>>> dt_pipeline = Pipeline(stages=[marks_bkt, att_idx, label_idx,va,dt,lc])
>>> dtModel = dt_pipeline.fit(source_df)
>>> resultDF = dtModel.transform(source_df)
>>>

//Look for obervatiuons where prediction did not match
>>> resultDF.filter("Label != prediction").select(
        "StudentId","Label","prediction","Result","predictedLabel").show()
+---------+-----+----------+------+--------------+
|StudentId|Label|prediction|Result|predictedLabel|
+---------+-----+----------+------+--------------+
|     1009|  1.0|       0.0|  Pass|          Fail|
|     1020|  1.0|       0.0|  Pass|          Fail|
+---------+-----+----------+------+--------------+

//Note that the difference is in the student ids that were granted pass
>>>
//Same example using Gradient boosted tree classifier, reusing the pipeline
stages
>>> from pyspark.ml.classification import GBTClassifier
>>> gbt = GBTClassifier(labelCol="Label",
```

```
featuresCol="features",maxIter=10)
>>> gbt_pipeline = Pipeline(stages=[marks_bkt,att_idx,label_idx,va,gbt,lc])
>>> gbtResultDF = gbt_pipeline.fit(source_df).transform(source_df)
>>> gbtResultDF.columns
['StudentId', 'Avg_Marks', 'Attendance', 'Result', 'Mark_bins', 'Att_idx',
'Label', 'features', 'prediction', 'predictedLabel']
>>> gbtResultDF.filter("Label !=
prediction").select("StudentId","Label","Result","prediction","predictedLab
el").show()
+---------+-----+------+----------+--------------+
|StudentId|Label|Result|prediction|predictedLabel|
+---------+-----+------+----------+--------------+
|     1009|  1.0|  Pass|       0.0|          Fail|
|     1020|  1.0|  Pass|       0.0|          Fail|
+---------+-----+------+----------+--------------+
```

Multilayer perceptron classifier

A **multilayer perceptron classifier** (**MLPC**) is a feedforward artificial neural network with multiple layers of nodes connected to each other in a directed fashion. It uses a supervised learning technique called *backpropagation* for training the network.

Nodes in the intermediary layer use the sigmoid function to restrict the output between 0 and 1, and the nodes in the output layer use the `softmax` function, which is a generalized version of the sigmoid function.

Scala:

```
scala> import
org.apache.spark.ml.classification.MultilayerPerceptronClassifier
import org.apache.spark.ml.classification.MultilayerPerceptronClassifier
scala> import
org.apache.spark.ml.evaluation.MulticlassClassificationEvaluator
import org.apache.spark.ml.evaluation.MulticlassClassificationEvaluator
scala> import org.apache.spark.mllib.util.MLUtils
import org.apache.spark.mllib.util.MLUtils

// Load training data
scala> val data = MLUtils.loadLibSVMFile(sc,
"data/mllib/sample_multiclass_classification_data.txt").toDF()
data: org.apache.spark.sql.DataFrame = [label: double, features: vector]

//Convert mllib vectors to ml Vectors for spark 2.0+. Retain data for
previous versions
scala> val data2 = MLUtils.convertVectorColumnsToML(data)
```

```
data2: org.apache.spark.sql.Dataset[org.apache.spark.sql.Row] = [label:
double, features: vector]

// Split the data into train and test
scala> val splits = data2.randomSplit(Array(0.6, 0.4), seed = 1234L)
splits: Array[org.apache.spark.sql.Dataset[org.apache.spark.sql.Row]] =
Array([label: double, features: vector], [label: double, features: vector])
scala> val train = splits(0)
train: org.apache.spark.sql.Dataset[org.apache.spark.sql.Row] = [label:
double, features: vector]
scala> val test = splits(1)
test: org.apache.spark.sql.Dataset[org.apache.spark.sql.Row] = [label:
double, features: vector]

// specify layers for the neural network:
// input layer of size 4 (features), two intermediate of size 5 and 4 and
output of size 3 (classes)
scala> val layers = Array[Int](4, 5, 4, 3)
layers: Array[Int] = Array(4, 5, 4, 3)

// create the trainer and set its parameters
scala> val trainer = new MultilayerPerceptronClassifier().
           setLayers(layers).setBlockSize(128).
           setSeed(1234L).setMaxIter(100)
trainer: org.apache.spark.ml.classification.MultilayerPerceptronClassifier
= mlpc_edfa49fbae3c

// train the model
scala> val model = trainer.fit(train)
model:
org.apache.spark.ml.classification.MultilayerPerceptronClassificationModel
= mlpc_edfa49fbae3c

// compute accuracy on the test set
scala> val result = model.transform(test)
result: org.apache.spark.sql.DataFrame = [label: double, features: vector
... 1 more field]
scala> val predictionAndLabels = result.select("prediction", "label")
predictionAndLabels: org.apache.spark.sql.DataFrame = [prediction: double,
label: double]
scala> val evaluator = new
MulticlassClassificationEvaluator().setMetricName("accuracy")
evaluator: org.apache.spark.ml.evaluation.MulticlassClassificationEvaluator
= mcEval_a4f43d85f261
scala> println("Accuracy:" + evaluator.evaluate(predictionAndLabels))
Accuracy:0.9444444444444444
```

Python:

```
>>> from pyspark.ml.classification import MultilayerPerceptronClassifier
>>> from pyspark.ml.evaluation import MulticlassClassificationEvaluator
>>> from pyspark.mllib.util import MLUtils
>>>

  //Load training data
>>> data = spark.read.format("libsvm").load(
"data/mllib/sample_multiclass_classification_data.txt")

//Convert mllib vectors to ml Vectors for spark 2.0+. Retain data for
previous versions
>>> data2 = MLUtils.convertVectorColumnsToML(data)
>>>

 // Split the data into train and test
>>> splits = data2.randomSplit([0.6, 0.4], seed = 1234L)
>>> train, test = splits[0], splits[1]
>>>

 // specify layers for the neural network:
 // input layer of size 4 (features), two intermediate of size 5 and 4 and
output of size 3 (classes)
>>> layers = [4,5,4,3]

// create the trainer and set its parameters
>>> trainer = MultilayerPerceptronClassifier(layers=layers, blockSize=128,
               seed=1234L, maxIter=100)
// train the model
>>> model = trainer.fit(train)
>>>

// compute accuracy on the test set
>>> result = model.transform(test)
>>> predictionAndLabels = result.select("prediction", "label")
>>> evaluator =
MulticlassClassificationEvaluator().setMetricName("accuracy")
>>> print "Accuracy:",evaluator.evaluate(predictionAndLabels)
Accuracy: 0.901960784314
>>>
```

Clustering techniques

Clustering is an unsupervised learning technique where there is no response variable to supervise the model. The idea is to cluster the data points that have some level of similarity. Apart from exploratory data analysis, it is also used as a part of a supervised pipeline where classifiers or regressors can be built on the distinct clusters. There are a bunch of clustering techniques available. Let us look into a few important ones that are supported by Spark.

K-means clustering

K-means is one of the most common clustering techniques. The k-means problem is to find cluster centers that minimize the intra-class variance, that is, the sum of squared distances from each data point being clustered to its cluster center (the center that is closest to it). You have to specify in advance the number of clusters you want in the dataset.

Since it uses the Euclidian distance measure to find the differences between the data points, the features need to be scaled to a comparable unit prior to using k-means. The Euclidian distance can be better explained in a graphical way as follows:

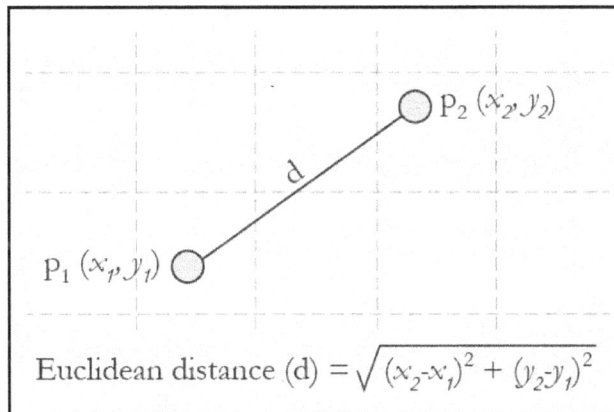

$$\text{Euclidean distance } (d) = \sqrt{(x_2 \text{-} x_1)^2 + (y_2 \text{-} y_1)^2}$$

Given a set of data points (*x1, x2, ..., xn*) with as many dimensions as the number of variables, k-means clustering aims to partition the n observations into k (less than *n*) sets where *S* = {*S1, S2, ..., Sk*}, so as to minimize the **within-cluster sum of squares (WCSS)**. In other words, its objective is to find:

$$\arg\min_{S} \sum_{i=1}^{k} \sum_{x \in S_i} \|x - \mu_i\|^2$$

Spark requires the following parameters to be passed to this algorithm:

- `k`: This is the number of desired clusters.
- `maxIterations`: This is the maximum number of iterations to run.
- `initializationMode`: This specifies either random initialization or initialization via k-means||.
- `runs`: This is the number of times to run the k-means algorithm (k-means is not guaranteed to find a globally optimal solution, and when run multiple times on a given dataset, the algorithm returns the best clustering result).
- `initializationSteps`: This determines the number of steps in the k-means|| algorithm.
- `epsilon`: This determines the distance threshold within which we consider k-means to have converged.
- `initialModel`: This is an optional set of cluster centers used for initialization. If this parameter is supplied, only one run is performed.

Disadvantages of k-means

- It works only on the numeric features
- It requires scaling before implementing the algorithm
- It is susceptible to local optima (the solution to this is k-means++)

Example

Let us run k-means clustering on the same students data.

```scala
scala> import org.apache.spark.ml.clustering.{KMeans, KMeansModel}
import org.apache.spark.ml.clustering.{KMeans, KMeansModel}
scala> import org.apache.spark.ml.linalg.Vectors
import org.apache.spark.ml.linalg.Vectors
scala>

//Define pipeline for kmeans. Reuse the previous stages in ENSEMBLES
scala> val km = new KMeans()
km: org.apache.spark.ml.clustering.KMeans = kmeans_b34da02bd7c8
scala> val kmeans_pipeline = new
Pipeline().setStages(Array(marks_bkt,att_idx,label_idx,va,km,lc))
kmeans_pipeline: org.apache.spark.ml.Pipeline = pipeline_0cd64aa93a88

//Train and transform
scala> val kmeansDF = kmeans_pipeline.fit(source_ds).transform(source_ds)
kmeansDF: org.apache.spark.sql.DataFrame = [StudentId: int, Avg_Marks:
double ... 8 more fields]

//Examine results
scala> kmeansDF.filter("Label != prediction").count()
res17: Long = 13
```

Python:

```python
>>> from pyspark.ml.clustering import KMeans, KMeansModel
>>> from pyspark.ml.linalg import Vectors
>>>

//Define pipeline for kmeans. Reuse the previous stages in ENSEMBLES
>>> km = KMeans()
>>> kmeans_pipeline = Pipeline(stages = [marks_bkt, att_idx,
label_idx,va,km,lc])

//Train and transform
>>> kmeansDF = kmeans_pipeline.fit(source_df).transform(source_df)
>>> kmeansDF.columns
['StudentId', 'Avg_Marks', 'Attendance', 'Result', 'Mark_bins', 'Att_idx',
'Label', 'features', 'prediction', 'predictedLabel']
>>> kmeansDF.filter("Label != prediction").count()
4
```

Summary

In this chapter, we explained various machine learning algorithms, how they are implemented in the MLlib library and how they can be used with the pipeline API for a streamlined execution. The concepts were covered with Python and Scala code examples for a ready reference.

In the next chapter, we will discuss how Spark supports R programming language focusing on some of the algorithms and their executions similar to what we covered in this chapter.

References

Supported algorithms in MLlib:

- http://spark.apache.org/docs/latest/mllib-guide.html
- http://spark.apache.org/docs/latest/mllib-decision-tree.html

Spark ML Programming Guide:

- http://spark.apache.org/docs/latest/ml-guide.html

Advanced datascience on spark.pdf from June 2015 summit slides:

- https://databricks.com/blog/2015/07/29/new-features-in-machine-learning-pipelines-in-spark-1-4.html
- https://databricks.com/blog/2015/06/02/statistical-and-mathematical-functions-with-dataframes-in-spark.html
- https://databricks.com/blog/2015/01/07/ml-pipelines-a-new-high-level-api-for-mllib.html

7
Extending Spark with SparkR

Statisticians and data scientists have been using R to solve challenging problems in almost every field, ranging from bioinformatics to election campaigns. They prefer R due to its powerful visualization capabilities, strong community, and rich package ecosystem for statistics and machine learning. Many academic institutions around the world teach data science and statistics using the R language.

R was originally created by and for statisticians in around the mid-1990s with a goal to deliver a better and more user-friendly way to perform data analysis. R was initially used in academics and research. As businesses became increasingly aware of the role of data science in their business growth, the number of data analysts using R in the corporate sector started growing as well. The R language user base is considered to be more than two million strong, after being in existence for two decades.

One of the driving factors behind all this success is the fact that R is designed to make the life of the analyst easier but not that of the computer. R is inherently single-threaded and it can only process datasets that completely fit in a single machine's memory. But nowadays, R users are working with increasingly larger datasets. Seamless integration of modern-day distributed processing power underneath the well-established R language allows data scientists to leverage the best of both worlds. They can keep up with their ever-increasing business demands and continue to benefit from the flexibility of their favorite R language.

This chapter introduces SparkR, an R API to Spark for R programmers so that they can harness the power of Spark, without learning a new language. Since prior knowledge of R, R Studio, and data analysis skills are already assumed, this chapter does not attempt to introduce R. A very brief overview of the Spark compute engine is provided as a quick recap. The reader should go through the first three chapters of this book to gain a deeper understanding of the Spark programming model and DataFrames. This knowledge is extremely important because the developer has to understand which part of his code is executing in the local R environment and which part is being handled by the Spark compute engine. The topics covered in this chapter are as follows:

- SparkR basics
- Advantages of R with Spark and its limitations
- Programming with SparkR
- SparkR DataFrames
- Machine learning

SparkR basics

R is a language and environment for statistical computing and graphics. SparkR is an R package that provides a lightweight frontend to enable Apache Spark access from R. The goal of SparkR is to combine the flexibility and ease of use provided by the R environment and the scalability and fault tolerance provided by the Spark compute engine. Let us recap the Spark architecture before discussing how SparkR realizes its goal.

Apache Spark is a fast, general-purpose, fault-tolerant framework for interactive and iterative computations on large, distributed datasets. It supports a wide variety of data sources as well as storage layers. It provides unified data access to combine different data formats, streaming data and defining complex operations using high-level, composable operators. You can develop your applications interactively using Scala, Python, or R shell (or Java without a shell). You can deploy it on your home desktop or you can run it on large clusters of thousands of nodes crunching petabytes of data.

SparkR originated in the AMPLab (`https://amplab.cs.berkeley.edu/`) to explore different techniques to integrate the usability of R with the scalability of Spark. It was released as an alpha component in Apache Spark 1.4, which was released in June 2015. The Spark 1.5 release had improved R usability and introduced the MLlib machine learning package with **Generalized Linear Models (GLMs)**. The Spark 1.6 release that happened in January 2016 added some more features, such as model summary and feature interactions. The Spark 2.0 release that happened in July 2016 brought several important features, such as UDF, improved model coverage, DataFrames Window functions API, and so on.

Accessing SparkR from the R environment

You can start SparkR from R shell or R Studio. The entry point to SparkR is the SparkSession object, which represents the connection to the Spark cluster. The node on which R is running becomes the driver. Any objects created by the R program reside on this driver. Any objects created via SparkSession are created on the worker nodes in the cluster. The following diagram depicts the runtime view of R interaction with Spark running on a cluster. Note that R interpreter exists on every worker node in the cluster. The following figure does not show the cluster manager and it does not show the storage layer either. You could use any cluster manager (for example, Yarn or Mesos) and any storage option, such as HDFS, Cassandra, or Amazon S3:

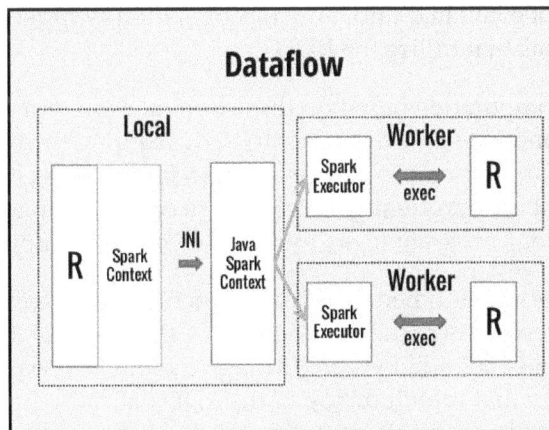

Source: http://www.slideshare.net/Hadoop_Summit/w-145p210-avenkataraman.

A SparkSession object is created by passing information such as application name, memory, number of cores, and the cluster manager to connect to. Any interaction with the Spark engine is initiated via this SparkSession object. A SparkSession object is already created for you if you use SparkR shell. You have to explicitly create it otherwise. This object replaces SparkContext and SQLContext objects that existed in Spark 1.x releases. These objects still exist for backward compatibility. Even the preceding figure depicts SparkContext, which you should treat as SparkSession post Spark 2.0.

Now that we have understood how to access Spark from the R environment, let us examine the core data abstractions provided by the Spark engine.

RDDs and DataFrames

At the core of the Spark engine is its main data abstraction, called a **Resilient Distributed Dataset** (**RDD**). An RDD is composed of one or more data sources and is defined by the user as a series of transformations (aka lineage) on one or more stable (concrete) data sources. Every RDD or RDD partition knows how to recreate itself on failure using the lineage graph, thereby providing fault tolerance. RDD is an immutable data structure, implying that it is sharable between threads without synchronization overheads and hence amenable for parallelization. Operations on RDDs are either transformations or actions. Transformations are individual steps in the lineage. In other words, they are operations that create RDDs because every transformation is getting data from a stable data source or transforming an immutable RDD and creating another RDD. Transformations are simply declarations; they are not evaluated until an *action* operation is applied on that RDD. Actions are the operations that utilize the RDDs.

Spark optimizes RDD computation based on the action on hand. For example, if the action is to read the first line, only one partition is computed, skipping the rest. It automatically performs in-memory computation with graceful degradation (spills it to disk when memory is insufficient) and distributes processing across all the cores. You may cache an RDD if it is frequently accessed in your program logic, thereby avoiding recomputing overhead.

The R language provides a two-dimensional data structure called a *DataFrame* which makes data manipulation convenient. Apache Spark comes with its own DataFrames that are inspired by the DataFrame in R and Python (through Pandas). A Spark DataFrame is a specialized data structure that is built on top of the RDD data structure abstraction. It provides distributed DataFrame implementation that looks very similar to R DataFrame from the developer perspective and at the same time can support very large datasets. The Spark dataset API adds structure to DataFrames and this structure provides information for more optimization under the hood.

Getting started

Now that we have understood the underlying data structures and the runtime view, it is time to run a few commands. In this section, we assume that you already have R and Spark successfully installed and added to the path. We also assume that the SPARK_HOME environment variable is set. Let us see how to access SparkR from R shell or R Studio:

```
> R  // Start R shell
> Sys.getenv("SPARK_HOME") //Confirm SPARK_HOME is set
  <Your SPARK_HOME path>
> library(SparkR, lib.loc =
    c(file.path(Sys.getenv("SPARK_HOME"), "R", "lib")))

Attaching package: 'SparkR'
The following objects are masked from 'package:stats':

    cov, filter, lag, na.omit, predict, sd, var, window

The following objects are masked from 'package:base':

    as.data.frame, colnames, colnames<-, drop, endsWith, intersect,
    rank, rbind, sample, startsWith, subset, summary, transform, union
>

> //Try help(package=SparkR) if you want to more information
//initialize SparkSession object
>   sparkR.session()
Java ref type org.apache.spark.sql.SparkSession id 1
>
Alternatively, you may launch sparkR shell which comes with predefined
SparkSession.

> bin/sparkR  // Start SparkR shell
>       // For simplicity sake, no Log messages are shown here
> //Try help(package=SparkR) if you want to more information
>
```

This is all you need to do to access the power of Spark DataFrames from within the R environment.

Advantages and limitations

The R language has long been the lingua franca of data scientists. Its simple-to-understand DataFrame abstraction, expressive APIs, and vibrant package ecosystem are exactly what the analysts needed. The main challenge was with the scalability. SparkR bridges that gap by providing distributed in-memory DataFrames without leaving the R eco-system. Such a symbiotic relationship allows users to gain the following benefits:

- There is no need for the analyst to learn a new language
- The SparkR APIs are similar to R APIs
- You can access SparkR from R studio, along with the autocomplete feature
- Performing interactive, exploratory analysis of a very large dataset is no longer hindered by memory limitations or long turnaround times
- Accessing data from different types of data sources becomes a lot easier. Most of the tasks which were imperative before have become declarative. Check `Chapter 4`, *Unified Data Access*, to learn more
- You can freely mix dplyr such as Spark functions, SQL, and R libraries that are still not available in Spark

In spite of all the exciting advantages of combining the best of both worlds, there are still some limitations with this combination. These limitations may not impact every use case, but we need to be aware of them anyway:

- The inherent dynamic nature of R limits the information available for the catalyst optimizer. We may not get the full advantage of optimizations such as predicate pushback when compared to statically typed languages such as Scala.
- SparkR does not have support for all the machine learning algorithms that are already available in other APIs such as the Scala API.

In summary, using Spark for data preprocessing and using R for analysis and visualization seems to be the best approach in the near future.

Programming with SparkR

So far, we have understood the runtime model of SparkR and the basic data abstractions that provide the fault tolerance and scalability. We have understood how to access the Spark API from R shell or R studio. It's time to try out some basic and familiar operations:

```
>
> //Open the shell
>
> //Try help(package=SparkR) if you want to more information
>
> df <- createDataFrame(iris) //Create a Spark DataFrame
> df     //Check the type. Notice the column renaming using underscore
SparkDataFrame[Sepal_Length:double, Sepal_Width:double,
Petal_Length:double, Petal_Width:double, Species:string]
>
> showDF(df,4) //Print the contents of the Spark DataFrame
+------------+-----------+------------+-----------+-------+
|Sepal_Length|Sepal_Width|Petal_Length|Petal_Width|Species|
+------------+-----------+------------+-----------+-------+
|         5.1|        3.5|         1.4|        0.2| setosa|
|         4.9|        3.0|         1.4|        0.2| setosa|
|         4.7|        3.2|         1.3|        0.2| setosa|
|         4.6|        3.1|         1.5|        0.2| setosa|
+------------+-----------+------------+-----------+-------+
>
> head(df,2)   //Returns an R data.frame. Default 6 rows
  Sepal_Length Sepal_Width Petal_Length Petal_Width Species
1          5.1         3.5          1.4         0.2  setosa
2          4.9         3.0          1.4         0.2  setosa
> //You can use take(df,2) to get the same results
//Check the dimensions
> nrow(df) [1] 150 > ncol(df) [1] 5
```

The operations look very similar to R DataFrame functions because spark DataFrames are modeled based on R DataFrames and Python (Pandas) DataFrames. But the similarity may create confusion if you are not careful. You may accidentally end up choking your local machine by running a compute-intensive function on an R `data.frame`, thinking that the load will be distributed. For example, the intersect function has the same signature in both packages. You need to pay attention to whether the object is of class `SparkDataFrame` (Spark DataFrame) or `data.frame` (R DataFrame). You also need to minimize back and forth conversions between local R `data.frame` objects and Spark DataFrame objects. Let us get a feel for this distinction by trying out some examples:

```
>
> //Open the SparkR shell
> df <- createDataFrame(iris) //Create a Spark DataFrame
> class(df) [1] "SparkDataFrame" attr(,"package") [1] "SparkR"
> df2 <- head(df,2) //Create an R data frame
> class(df2)
 [1] "data.frame"
> //Now try running some R command on both data frames
> unique(df2$Species)    //Works fine as expected [1] "setosa" >
unique(df$Species)     //Should fail Error in unique.default(df$Species) :
unique() applies only to vectors > class(df$Species)    //Each column is a
Spark's Column class [1] "Column" attr(,"package") [1] "SparkR" >
class(df2$Species) [1] "character"
```

Function name masking

Now that we have tried some basic operations, let us digress a little bit. We have to understand what happens when a loaded library has overlapping function names with the base package or some other package that was already loaded. This is sometimes referred to as function name overlapping, function masking, or name conflict. You might have noticed the messages mentioning the objects masked when the SparkR package is loaded. This is common for any package loaded into the R environment, and is not specific to SparkR alone. If the R environment already contains any function that has the same name as a function in the package being loaded, then any subsequent calls to that function exhibit the behavior of the function in the latest package loaded. If you want to access the previous function instead of the `SparkR` function, you need to explicitly prefix that function with its package name, as shown:

```
//First try in R environment, without loading sparkR
//Try sampling from a column in an R data.frame
>sample(iris$Sepal.Length,6,FALSE) //Returns any n elements [1] 5.1 4.9 4.7
4.6 5.0 5.4 >sample(head(iris),3,FALSE) //Returns any 3 columns
//Try sampling from an R data.frame
```

```
//The Boolean argument is for with_replacement
> sample(head
> head(sample(iris,3,TRUE)) //Returns any 3 columns
  Species Species.1 Petal.Width
1  setosa    setosa        0.2
2  setosa    setosa        0.2
3  setosa    setosa        0.2
4  setosa    setosa        0.2
5  setosa    setosa        0.2
6  setosa    setosa        0.4

//Load sparkR, initialize sparkSession and then execute this
> df <- createDataFrame(iris) //Create a Spark DataFrame
> sample_df <- sample(df,TRUE,0.3) //Different signature
> dim(sample_df)   //Different behavior [1] 44   5
> //Returned 30% of the original data frame and all columns
> //Try with base prefix
> head(base::sample(iris),3,FALSE)   //Call base package's sample
  Species Petal.Width Petal.Length
1  setosa        0.2          1.4
2  setosa        0.2          1.4
3  setosa        0.2          1.3
4  setosa        0.2          1.5
5  setosa        0.2          1.4
6  setosa        0.4          1.7
```

Subsetting data

Subsetting operations on R DataFrames are quite flexible and SparkR tries to retain these operations with the same or similar equivalents. We have already seen some operations in the preceding examples but this section presents them in an ordered fashion:

```
//Subsetting data examples
> b1 <- createDataFrame(beaver1)
//Get one column
> b1$temp
Column temp     //Column class and not a vector
> //Select some columns. You may use positions too
> select(b1, c("day","temp"))
SparkDataFrame[day:double, temp:double]
>//Row subset based on conditions
> head(subset(b1,b1$temp>37,select= c(2,3)))
  time  temp
1 1730 37.07
2 1740 37.05
3 1940 37.01
```

```
4 1950 37.10
5 2000 37.09
6 2010 37.02
> //Multiple conditions with AND and OR
> head(subset(b1, between(b1$temp,c(36.0,37.0)) |
        b1$time %in% 900 & b1$activ == 1,c(2:4)),2)
  time  temp activ
1  840 36.33     0
2  850 36.34     0
```

At the time of writing this book (Apache Spark 2.0 release), row index based slicing is not available. You will not be able to get a specific row or range of rows using the `df[n,]` or `df[m:n,]` syntax.

```
//For example, try on a normal R data.frame
> beaver1[2:4,]
  day time  temp activ
2 346  850 36.34     0
3 346  900 36.35     0
4 346  910 36.42     0
//Now, try on Spark Data frame
> b1[2:4,] //Throws error
Expressions other than filtering predicates are not supported in the first
parameter of extract operator [ or subset() method.
>
```

Column functions

You will have already noticed the column functions `between` in the subsetting data section. These functions operate on the `Column` class. As the name suggests, these functions operate on a single column at a time and are usually used in subsetting DataFrames. There are several other handy column functions for common operations such as sorting, casting, and formatting. In addition to working on the values within a column, you can append columns to a DataFrame or drop one or more columns from a DataFrame. Negative column subscripts may be used to omit columns, similar to R. The following examples show the use of `Column` class functions in subset operations followed by adding and dropping columns:

```
> //subset using Column operation using airquality dataset as df
> head(subset(df,isNull(df$Ozone)),2)
  Ozone Solar_R Wind Temp Month Day
1    NA      NA 14.3   56     5   5
2    NA     194  8.6   69     5  10
>
> //Add column and drop column examples
```

```
> b1 <- createDataFrame(beaver1)

//Add new column
> b1$inRetreat <- otherwise(when(b1$activ == 0,"No"),"Yes")
 head(b1,2)
  day time  temp activ inRetreat
1 346  840 36.33     0        No
2 346  850 36.34     0        No
>
//Drop a column.
> b1$day <- NULL
> b1  // Example assumes b1$inRetreat does not exist
SparkDataFrame[time:double, temp:double, activ:double]
> //Drop columns using negative subscripts
> b2 <- b1[,-c(1,4)]  > head(b2)
   time  temp
1   840 36.33
2   850 36.34
3   900 36.35
4   910 36.42
5   920 36.55
6   930 36.69
>
```

Grouped data

DataFrame data can be subgrouped using the `group_by` function similar to SQL. There are multiple ways of performing such operations. We introduce a slightly complex example in this section. Moreover, we use `%>%`, aka the forward pipe operator, provided by the `magrittr` library, which provides a mechanism for chaining commands:

```
> //GroupedData example using iris data as df
> //Open SparkR shell and create df using iris dataset
> groupBy(df,"Species")
GroupedData     //Returns GroupedData object
> library(magrittr)  //Load the required library
//Get group wise average sepal length
//Report results sorted by species name
>df2 <- df %>% groupBy("Species") %>%
        avg("Sepal_Length") %>%
        withColumnRenamed("avg(Sepal_Length)","avg_sepal_len") %>%
        orderBy ("Species")
//Format the computed double column
df2$avg_sepal_len <- format_number(df2$avg_sepal_len,2)
showDF(df2)
+----------+-------------+
```

```
|   Species|avg_sepal_len|
+----------+-------------+
|    setosa|         5.01|
|versicolor|         5.94|
| virginica|         6.59|
+----------+-------------+
```

You can keep chaining the operations using the forward pipe operator. Look at the column renamed part of the code carefully. The column name argument is the output of previous operations, which would have completed before commencement of this operation and thus you can safely assume that the avg(sepal_len) column already exists. The format_number works as expected, and this is yet another handy Column operation.

The next section has another similar example with GroupedData and its equivalent implementation using dplyr.

SparkR DataFrames

In this section, we try out some useful, commonly used operations. First, we try out the traditional R/dplyr operations and then show equivalent operations using the SparkR API:

```
> //Open the R shell and NOT SparkR shell
> library(dplyr,warn.conflicts=FALSE)  //Load dplyr first
//Perform a common, useful operation
> iris %>%
+    group_by(Species) %>% +    summarise(avg_length = mean(Sepal.Length),
+             avg_width = mean(Sepal.Width)) %>% +
arrange(desc(avg_length))
Source: local data frame [3 x 3]
      Species avg_length avg_width
       (fctr)      (dbl)     (dbl)
1   virginica      6.588     2.974
2 versicolor      5.936     2.770
3     setosa      5.006     3.428

//Remove from R environment
> detach("package:dplyr",unload=TRUE)
```

This operation is very similar to the SQL group and is followed by order. Its equivalent implementation in SparkR is also very similar to the dplyr example. Look at the following example. Pay attention to the method names and compare their positioning with respect to the preceding dplyr example:

```
> //Open SparkR shell and create df using iris dataset
```

```
> collect(arrange(summarize(groupBy(df,df$Species),    +     avg_sepal_length
= avg(df$Sepal_Length), +     avg_sepal_width = avg(df$Sepal_Width)), +
"avg_sepal_length", decreasing = TRUE))
      Species avg_sepal_length avg_sepal_width
1       setosa            5.006           3.428
2 versicolor            5.936           2.770
3  virginica            6.588           2.974
```

SparkR is intended to be as close to the existing R API as possible. So, the method names
look very similar to `dplyr` methods. For example, look at the example which has `groupBy`
whereas `dplyr` has `group_by`. SparkR supports redundant function names. For example, it
has `group_by` as well as `groupBy` to cater to developers coming from different
programming environments. The method names in `dplyr` and SparkR are again very close
to the SQL keyword GROUP BY. But the sequence of these method calls is not the same. The
example also showed an additional step of converting a Spark DataFrame to an R
`data.frame` using `collect`. The methods are arranged inside out, in the sense that first
the data is grouped, then summarized, and then arranged. This is understandable because
in SparkR, the DataFrame created in the innermost method becomes the argument for its
immediate predecessor and so on.

SQL operations

If you are not very happy with the syntax in the preceding example, you may want to try
writing an SQL string as shown, which does exactly the same as the preceding but uses the
good old SQL syntax:

```
> //Register the Spark DataFrame as a table/View
> createOrReplaceTempView(df,"iris_vw")
//Look at the table structure and some rows
> collect(sql(sqlContext, "SELECT * FROM iris_tbl LIMIT 5"))
    Sepal_Length Sepal_Width Petal_Length Petal_Width Species
1            5.1          3.5          1.4          0.2  setosa
2            4.9          3.0          1.4          0.2  setosa
3            4.7          3.2          1.3          0.2  setosa
4            4.6          3.1          1.5          0.2  setosa
5            5.0          3.6          1.4          0.2  setosa
> //Try out the above example using SQL syntax
> collect(sql(sqlContext, "SELECT Species,       avg(Sepal_Length)
avg_sepal_length,     avg(Sepal_Width) avg_sepal_width        FROM iris_tbl
GROUP BY Species       ORDER BY avg_sepal_length desc"))

   Species avg_sepal_length avg_sepal_width

1  virginica            6.588           2.974
```

```
2 versicolor          5.936          2.770
3    setosa           5.006          3.428
```

The preceding example looks like the most natural way of implementing the operation on hand, if you are used to fetching data from RDBMS tables. But how are we doing this? The first statement tells Spark to register a temporary table (or, as the name suggests, a view, a logical abstraction of a table). This is not exactly the same as a database table. It is temporary in the sense that it is destroyed when the SparkSession object is destroyed. You are not explicitly writing data into any RDBMS datastore (you have to use SaveAsTable for that). But when once you register a Spark DataFrame as a temporary table, you are free to use SQL syntax to operate on that DataFrame. The next statement is a basic SELECT statement that displays column names followed by five rows, as dictated by the LIMIT keyword. The next SQL statement created a Spark DataFrame containing a Species column followed by two average columns sorted on the average sepal length. This DataFrame is in turn collected as an R data.frame by using collect. The final result is exactly the same as the preceding example. You are free to use either syntax. For more information and examples, check out the SQL section in Chapter 4, *Unified Data Access*.

Set operations

The usual set operations, such as union, intersection, and minus, are available out of the box in SparkR. In fact, when SparkR is loaded, the warning message shows intersect as one of the masked functions. The following examples are based on beaver datasets:

```
> //Create b1 and b2 DataFrames using beaver1 and beaver2 datasets
> b1 <- createDataFrame(beaver1)
> b2 <- createDataFrame(beaver2)
//Get individual and total counts
> > c(nrow(b1), nrow(b2), nrow(b1) + nrow(b2))
[1] 114 100 214
//Try adding both data frames using union operation
> nrow(unionAll(b1,b2))
[1] 214        //Sum of two datsets
> //intersect example
//Remove the first column (day) and find intersection
showDF(intersect(b1[,-c(1)],b2[,-c(1)]))

+------+-----+-----+
|  time| temp|activ|
+------+-----+-----+
|1100.0|36.89|  0.0|
+------+-----+-----+
> //except (minus or A-B) is covered in machine learning examples
```

Merging DataFrames

The next example illustrates the joining of two DataFrames using the merge command. The first part of the example shows the R implementation and the next part shows the SparkR implementation:

```
> //Example illustrating data frames merging using R (Not SparkR)
> //Create two data frames with a matching column
//Products df with two rows and two columns
> products_df <- data.frame(rbind(c(101,"Product 1"),
                  c(102,"Product 2")))
> names(products_df) <- c("Prod_Id","Product")
> products_df
 Prod_Id    Product
1      101 Product 1
2      102 Product 2

//Sales df with sales for each product and month 24x3
> sales_df <- data.frame(cbind(rep(101:102,each=12), month.abb,
                  sample(1:10,24,replace=T)*10))
> names(sales_df) <- c("Prod_Id","Month","Sales")

//Look at first 2 and last 2 rows in the sales_df
> sales_df[c(1,2,23,24),]
    Prod_Id Month Sales
1       101   Jan    60
2       101   Feb    40
23      102   Nov    20
24      102   Dec   100

> //merge the data frames and examine the data
> total_df <- merge(products_df,sales_df)
//Look at the column names
> colnames(total_df)
> [1] "Prod_Id" "Product" "Month"    "Sales"

//Look at first 2 and last 2 rows in the total_df
> total_df[c(1,2,23,24),]
    Prod_Id    Product Month Sales
1       101 Product 1   Jan    10
2       101 Product 1   Feb    20
23      102 Product 2   Nov    60
24      102 Product 2   Dec    10
```

The preceding piece of code completely relies on R's base package. We have used the same names for join columns in both DataFrames for simplicity. The next piece of code demonstrates the same example using SparkR. It looks similar to the preceding code so look carefully for the differences:

```
> //Example illustrating data frames merging using SparkR
> //Create an R data frame first and then pass it on to Spark
> //Watch out the base prefix for masked rbind function
> products_df <- createDataFrame(data.frame(
    base::rbind(c(101,"Product 1"),
    c(102,"Product 2"))))
> names(products_df) <- c("Prod_Id","Product")
>showDF(products_df)
+-------+---------+
|Prod_Id|  Product|
+-------+---------+
|    101|Product 1|
|    102|Product 2|
+-------+---------+
> //Create Sales data frame
> //Notice the as.data.frame similar to other R functions
> //No cbind in SparkR so no need for base:: prefix
> sales_df <- as.DataFrame(data.frame(cbind(
            "Prod_Id" = rep(101:102,each=12),
"Month" = month.abb,
"Sales" = base::sample(1:10,24,replace=T)*10)))
> //Check sales dataframe dimensions and some random rows
> dim(sales_df)
[1] 24   3
> collect(sample(sales_df,FALSE,0.20))
  Prod_Id Month Sales
1     101   Sep    50
2     101   Nov    80
3     102   Jan    90
4     102   Jul   100
5     102   Nov    20
6     102   Dec    50
> //Merge the data frames. The following merge is from SparkR library
> total_df <- merge(products_df,sales_df)
// You may try join function for the same purpose
//Look at the columns in total_df
> total_df
SparkDataFrame[Prod_Id_x:string, Product:string, Prod_Id_y:string,
Month:string, Sales:string]
//Drop duplicate column
> total_df$Prod_Id_y <- NULL
> head(total_df)
  Prod_Id_x   Product Month Sales
```

```
1        101 Product 1   Jan    40
2        101 Product 1   Feb    10
3        101 Product 1   Mar    90
4        101 Product 1   Apr    10
5        101 Product 1   May    50
6        101 Product 1   Jun    70
> //Note: As of Spark 2.0 version, SparkR does not support
    row sub-setting
```

You may want to play with different types of joins, such as left outer join and right outer join, or different column names to get a better understanding of this function.

Machine learning

SparkR provides wrappers on existing MLLib functions. R formulas are implemented as MLLib feature transformers. A transformer is an ML pipeline (`spark.ml`) stage that takes a DataFrame as input and produces another DataFrame as output, which generally contains some appended columns. Feature transformers are a type of transformers that convert input columns to feature vectors and these feature vectors are appended to the source DataFrame. For example, in linear regression, string input columns are one-hot encoded and numeric values are converted to doubles. A label column will be appended (if not there in the data frame already) as a replica of the response variable.

In this section, we cover example code for the Naive Bayes and Gaussian GLM models. We do not explain the models as such or the summaries they produce. Instead, we go straight away to how it can be done using SparkR.

The Naive Bayes model

The Naïve Bayes model is an intuitively simple model that works with categorical data. We'll be training a sample dataset using the Naïve Bayes model. We will not explain how the model works but move straight away to training the model using SparkR. If you want more information, please refer to `Chapter 6`, *Machine Learning*.

This example takes a dataset with the average marks and attendance of twenty students. In fact, this dataset has already been introduced in `Chapter 6`, *Machine Learning*, for training ensembles. However, let us revisit its contents.

The students are awarded Pass or Fail based on a set of well-defined rules. Two students with IDs 1009 and 1020 are granted Pass, even though they would have failed otherwise. Even though we do not provide the actual rules to the model, we expect the model to predict these two students' result as Fail. Here are the Pass / Fail criteria:

- Marks < 40 => Fail
- Poor attendance => Fail
- Marks above 40 and attendance Full => Pass
- Marks > 60 and attendance at least Enough => PassThe following is an example to train Naive Bayes model:

```
//Example to train NaÃ¯ve Bayes model

//Read file
> myFile <- read.csv("../work/StudentsPassFail.csv") //R data.frame
> df <- createDataFrame(myFile) //sparkDataFrame
//Look at the data
> showDF(df,4)
+---------+---------+----------+------+
|StudentId|Avg_Marks|Attendance|Result|
+---------+---------+----------+------+
|     1001|     48.0|      Full|  Pass|
|     1002|     21.0|    Enough|  Fail|
|     1003|     24.0|    Enough|  Fail|
|     1004|      4.0|      Poor|  Fail|
+---------+---------+----------+------+

//Make three buckets out of Avg_marks
// A >60; 40 < B < 60; C > 60
> df$marks_bkt <- otherwise(when(df$Avg_marks < 40, "C"),
                           when(df$Avg_marks > 60, "A"))
> df$marks_bkt <- otherwise(when(df$Avg_marks < 40, "C"),
                           when(df$Avg_marks > 60, "A"))
> df <- fillna(df,"B",cols="marks_bkt")
//Split train and test
> trainDF <- sample(df,TRUE,0.7)
> testDF <- except(df, trainDF)

//Build model by supplying RFormula, training data
> model <- spark.naiveBayes(Result ~ Attendance + marks_bkt, data =
trainDF)
> summary(model)
$apriori
          Fail      Pass
[1,] 0.6956522 0.3043478
```

```
$tables
     Attendance_Poor Attendance_Full marks_bkt_C marks_bkt_B
Fail 0.5882353     0.1764706       0.5882353   0.2941176
Pass 0.125         0.875           0.125       0.625

//Run predictions on test data
> predictions <- predict(model, newData= testDF)
//Examine results
> showDF(predictions[predictions$Result != predictions$prediction,
    c("StudentId","Attendance","Avg_Marks","marks_bkt",
"Result","prediction")])
+---------+----------+---------+---------+------+----------+
|StudentId|Attendance|Avg_Marks|marks_bkt|Result|prediction|
+---------+----------+---------+---------+------+----------+
|     1010|      Full|     19.0|        C|  Fail|      Pass|
|     1019|    Enough|     45.0|        B|  Fail|      Pass|
|     1014|      Full|     12.0|        C|  Fail|      Pass|
+---------+----------+---------+---------+------+----------+
//Note that the predictions are not exactly what we anticipate but models
are usually not 100% accurate
```

The Gaussian GLM model

In this example, we try to predict temperature based on the values of ozone, solar radiation, and wind:

```
> //Example illustrating Gaussian GLM model using SparkR
> a <- createDataFrame(airquality)
//Remove rows with missing values
> b <- na.omit(a)
> //Inspect the dropped rows with missing values
> head(except(a,b),2)     //MINUS set operation
  Ozone Solar_R Wind Temp Month Day
1    NA     186  9.2   84     6   4
2    NA     291 14.9   91     7  14

> //Prepare train data and test data
traindata <- sample(b,FALSE,0.8) //Not base::sample
testdata <- except(b,traindata)

> //Build model
> model <- glm(Temp ~ Ozone + Solar_R + Wind,
        data = traindata, family = "gaussian")
> // Get predictions
> predictions <- predict(model, newData = testdata)
> head(predictions[,c(predictions$Temp, predictions$prediction)],
```

```
                      5)
    Temp prediction
1     90   81.84338
2     79   80.99255
3     88   85.25601
4     87   76.99957
5     76   71.75683
```

Summary

To date, SparkR does not support all algorithms available in Spark, but active development is happening to bridge the gap. The Spark 2.0 release has improved algorithm coverage, including NaÃ¯ve Bayes, k-means clustering, and survival regression. Check out the latest documentation for the supported algorithms. More work is underway in bringing out a CRAN release of SparkR, with better integration with R packages and Spark packages, and better RFormula support.

References

- *SparkR: The Past, Present and Future by Shivaram Venkataraman:* http://shivaram.org/talks/sparkr-summit-2015.pdf
- *Enabling Exploratory Data Science with Spark and R by Shivaram Venkataraman and Hossein Falaki:*http://www.slideshare.net/databricks/enabling-explorator y-data-science-with-spark-and-r
- *SparkR: Scaling R Programs with Spark by Shivaram Venkataraman* and others: http://shivaram.org/publications/sparkr-sigmod.pdf
- *Recent Developments in SparkR for Advanced Analytics by Xiangrui Meng:* http://files.meetup.com/4439192/Recent%20Development%20in%20SparkR%20for%20Advanced%20Analytics.pdf
- To understand RFormula, try out the following links:
    - https://stat.ethz.ch/R-manual/R-devel/library/stats/html/formula.html
    - http://spark.apache.org/docs/latest/ml-features.html#rfo rmula

8
Analyzing Unstructured Data

In this Big Data era, the proliferation of unstructured data is overwhelming. Numerous methods such as data mining, **Natural Language Processing** (**NLP**), information retrieval, and so on, exist for analyzing unstructured data. Due to the rapid growth of unstructured data in all kinds of businesses, scalable solutions have become the need of the hour. Apache Spark is equipped with out of the box algorithms for text analytics, and it also supports custom development of algorithms that are not available by default.

In the previous chapter we have shown how SparkR, an R API to Spark for R programmers can harness the power of Spark, without learning a new language . In this chapter, we are going to step into a whole new dimension and explore algorithms and techniques to extract information out of unstructured data by leveraging Spark.

As a prerequisite for this chapter, a basic understanding of programming in Python or Scala and an overall understanding of text analytics and machine learning are nice to have. However, we have covered some theoretical basics with the right set of practical examples to make those more comprehendible and easy to implement. The topics covered in this chapter are:

- Sources of unstructured data
- Processing unstructured data
    - Count vectorizer
    - TF-IDF
    - Stop-word removal
    - Normalization/scaling
    - Word2Vec
    - n-gram modeling

- Text classification
    - Naive Bayes classifier
- Text clustering
    - K-means
- Dimensionality reduction
    - Singular value decomposition
    - Principal component analysis
- Summary

Sources of unstructured data

Data analytics has come very far since the spreadsheets and the BI tools in the eighties and nineties. Tremendous improvements in computing power, sophisticated algorithms, and an open source culture fueled unprecedented growth in data analytics, as well as in other fields. These advances in technologies paved the way for new opportunities and new challenges. Businesses started looking at generating insights from hitherto impossible to handle data sources such as internal memos, emails, customer satisfaction surveys, and the like. Data analytics now encompass this unstructured, usually text based data along with traditional rows and columns of data. Between the highly structured data stored in RDBMS table and completely unstructured plain text, we have semi-structured data sources in NoSQL data stores, XML or JSON documents, and graph or network data sources. As per current estimates, unstructured data forms about 80 percent of enterprise data and is growing rapidly. Satellite images, atmospheric data, social networks, blogs and other web pages, patient records and physicians' notes, companies' internal communications, and so on – all these combined are just a subset of unstructured data sources.

We have already been seeing successful data products that leverage unstructured data along with structured data. Some of the companies leverage the power of social networks to provide actionable insights to their customers. New fields such as **Sentiment Analysis** and **Multimedia Analytics** are emerging to draw insights from unstructured data. However, analyzing unstructured data is still a daunting feat. For example, contemporary text analytics tools and techniques cannot identify sarcasm. However, the potential benefits undoubtedly outweigh the limitations.

Processing unstructured data

Unstructured data does not lend itself to most of the programming tasks. It has to be processed in various different ways as applicable, to be able to serve as an input to any machine learning algorithm or for visual analysis. Broadly, the unstructured data analysis can be viewed as a series of steps as shown in the following diagram:

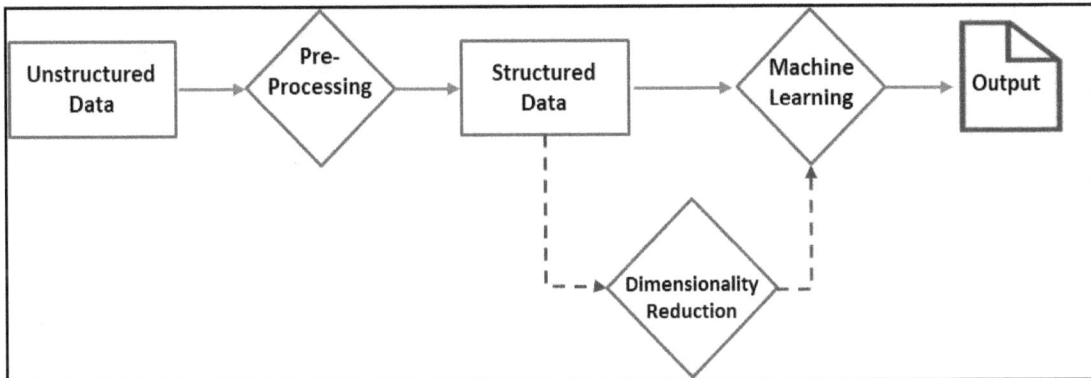

Data pre-processing is the most vital step in any unstructured data analysis. Fortunately, there have been several proven techniques accumulated over time that come in handy. Spark offers most of these techniques out of the box through the `ml.features` package. Most of the techniques aim to convert text data to concise numerical vectors that can be easily consumed by machine learning algorithms. Developers should understand the specific requirements of their organizations to arrive at the best pre-processing workflow. Remember that better, relevant data is the key to generate better insights.

Let us explore a couple of examples that process raw text and convert them into data frames. First example takes some text as input and extracts all date-like strings whereas the second example extracts tags from twitter text. First example is just a warm-up, using a simple, regex (regular expression) tokenizer feature transformer without using any spark-specific libraries. It also draws your attention to the possibility of misinterpretation. For example, a product code of the form 1-11-1111 may be interpreted as a date. The second example illustrates a non-trivial, multi-step extraction process that resulted in just the required tags. **User defined functions** (**udf**) and ML pipelines come in handy in developing such multi-step extraction processes. Remaining part of this section describes some more handy tools supplied out of box in apache Spark.

Example-1: Extract date like strings from text

Scala:

```
scala> import org.apache.spark.ml.feature.RegexTokenizer
import org.apache.spark.ml.feature.RegexTokenizer
scala> val date_pattern: String = "\\d{1,4}[/ -]\\d{1,4}[/ -]\\d{1,4}"
date_pattern: String = \d{1,4}[/ -]\d{1,4}[/ -]\d{1,4}
scala> val textDF  = spark.createDataFrame(Seq(
     (1, "Hello 1996-12-12 this 1-21-1111 is a 18-9-96 text "),
     (2, "string with dates in different 01/02/89 formats"))).
     toDF("LineNo","Text")
textDF: org.apache.spark.sql.DataFrame = [LineNo: int, Text: string]
scala> val date_regex = new RegexTokenizer().
        setInputCol("Text").setOutputCol("dateStr").
        setPattern(date_pattern).setGaps(false)
date_regex: org.apache.spark.ml.feature.RegexTokenizer =
regexTok_acdbca6d1c4c
scala> date_regex.transform(textDF).select("dateStr").show(false)
+---------------------------------+
|dateStr                          |
+---------------------------------+
|[1996-12-12, 1-21-1111, 18-9-96]|
|[01/02/89]                       |
+---------------------------------+
```

Python:

```
// Example-1: Extract date like strings from text
>>> from pyspark.ml.feature import RegexTokenizer
>>> date_pattern = "\\d{1,4}[/ -]\\d{1,4}[/ -]\\d{1,4}"
>>> textDF  = spark.createDataFrame([
        [1, "Hello 1996-12-12 this 1-21-1111 is a 18-9-96 text "],
        [2, "string with dates in different 01/02/89 formats"]]).toDF(
        "LineNo","Text")
>>> date_regex = RegexTokenizer(inputCol="Text",outputCol="dateStr",
         gaps=False, pattern=date_pattern)
>>> date_regex.transform(textDF).select("dateStr").show(5,False)
+---------------------------------+
|dateStr                          |
+---------------------------------+
|[1996-12-12, 1-21-1111, 18-9-96]|
|[01/02/89]                       |
+---------------------------------+
```

The preceding example defined a regular expression pattern to recognize date strings. The regex pattern and the sample text DataFrame are passed to the `RegexTokenizer` to extract matching, date like strings. The `gaps=False` option picks matching strings and a value of `False` would use the given pattern as a separator. Note that `1-21-1111`, which is obviously not a date, is also selected.

Next example extracts tags from twitter text and identifies most popular tags. You can use the same approach to collect hash (#) tags too.

This example uses a built in function `explode`, which converts a single row with an array of values into multiple rows, one value per array element.

Example-2: Extract tags from twitter â✴✴textâ✴✴

Scala:

```
//Step1: Load text containing @ from source file
scala> val path = "<Your path>/tweets.json"
path: String = <Your path>/tweets.json
scala> val raw_df = spark.read.text(path).filter($"value".contains("@"))
raw_df: org.apache.spark.sql.Dataset[org.apache.spark.sql.Row] = [value:
string]
//Step2: Split the text to words and filter out non-tag words
scala> val df1 = raw_df.select(explode(split('value, " ")).as("word")).
        filter($"word".startsWith("@"))
df1: org.apache.spark.sql.Dataset[org.apache.spark.sql.Row] = [word:
string]
//Step3: compute tag-wise counts and report top 5
scala> df1.groupBy($"word").agg(count($"word")).
        orderBy($"count(word)".desc).show(5)
+------------+-----------
+
|         word|count(word)|
+------------+-----------+
|@ApacheSpark|         15|
|     @SSKapci|          9|
|@databricks:|          4|
|      @hadoop|          4|
| @ApacheApex|          4|
+------------+-----------+
```

Python:

```
>> from pyspark.sql.functions import explode, split
//Step1: Load text containing @ from source file
>>> path ="<Your path>/tweets.json"
>>> raw_df1 = spark.read.text(path)
```

```
>>> raw_df = raw_df1.where("value like '%@%'")
>>>
//Step2: Split the text to words and filter out non-tag words
>>> df = raw_df.select(explode(split("value"," ")))
>>> df1 = df.where("col like '@%'").toDF("word")
>>>
//Step3: compute tag-wise counts and report top 5
>>> df1.groupBy("word").count().sort(
       "count",ascending=False).show(5)
+------------+-----+
|        word|count|
+------------+-----+
|@ApacheSpark|   15|
|    @SSKapci|    9|
|@databricks:|    4|
| @ApacheApex|    4|
|     @hadoop|    4|
+------------+-----+
```

Count vectorizer

Count vectorizer extracts vocabulary (tokens) from documents and generates a CountVectorizerModel model when a dictionary is not available priori. As the name indicates, a text document is converted into a vector of tokens and counts. The model produces a sparse representation of the documents over the vocabulary.

You can fine tune the behavior to limit the vocabulary size, minimum token count, and much more as applicable in your business case.

//Example 3: Count Vectorizer example

Scala

```
scala> import org.apache.spark.ml.feature.{CountVectorizer,
CountVectorizerModel}
import org.apache.spark.ml.feature.{CountVectorizer, CountVectorizerModel}
scala> import org.apache.spark.sql.DataFrame
import org.apache.spark.sql.DataFrame
scala> import org.apache.spark.ml.linalg.Vector
import org.apache.spark.ml.linalg.Vector
scala> val df: DataFrame = spark.createDataFrame(Seq(
   (0, Array("ant", "bat", "cat", "dog", "eel")),
   (1, Array("dog","bat", "ant", "bat", "cat"))
)).toDF("id", "words")
df: org.apache.spark.sql.DataFrame = [id: int, words: array<string>]
```

```
scala>
// Fit a CountVectorizerModel from the corpus
// Minimum occurrences (DF) is 2 and pick 10 top words(vocabsize) only
scala> val cvModel: CountVectorizerModel = new CountVectorizer().
        setInputCol("words").setOutputCol("features").
        setMinDF(2).setVocabSize(10).fit(df)
cvModel: org.apache.spark.ml.feature.CountVectorizerModel =
cntVec_7e79157ba561
// Check vocabulary. Words are arranged as per frequency
// eel is dropped because it is below minDF = 2
scala> cvModel.vocabulary
res6: Array[String] = Array(bat, dog, cat, ant)
//Apply the model on document
scala> val cvDF: DataFrame = cvModel.transform(df)
cvDF: org.apache.spark.sql.DataFrame = [id: int, words: array<string> ... 1
more field]
//Check the word count
scala> cvDF.select("features").collect().foreach(row =>
println(row(0).asInstanceOf[Vector].toDense))

[1.0,1.0,1.0,1.0]
[2.0,1.0,1.0,1.0]
```

Python:

```
>>> from pyspark.ml.feature import CountVectorizer,CountVectorizerModel
>>> from pyspark.ml.linalg import Vector
>>>
// Define source DataFrame
>>> df = spark.createDataFrame([
    [0, ["ant", "bat", "cat", "dog", "eel"]],
    [1, ["dog","bat", "ant", "bat", "cat"]]
  ]).toDF("id", "words")
>>>
// Fit a CountVectorizerModel from the corpus
// Minimum occurrences (DF) is 2 and pick 10 top words(vocabsize) only
>>> cvModel = CountVectorizer(inputCol="words", outputCol="features",
        minDF = 2, vocabSize = 10).fit(df)
>>>
// Check vocabulary. Words are arranged as per frequency
// eel is dropped because it is below minDF = 2
>>> cvModel.vocabulary
[u'bat', u'ant', u'cat', u'dog']
//Apply the model on document
>>> cvDF = cvModel.transform(df)
//Check the word count
>>> cvDF.show(2,False)
+---+-----------------------+----------------------------+
```

```
|id |words                   |features                       |
+---+------------------------+-------------------------------+
|0  |[ant, bat, cat, dog, eel]|(4,[0,1,2,3],[1.0,1.0,1.0,1.0])|
|1  |[dog, bat, ant, bat, cat]|(4,[0,1,2,3],[2.0,1.0,1.0,1.0])|
+---+------------------------+-------------------------------+
```

Input:

```
|id | text                                                   |
+---+------------------------------+-------------------------+
|0  | "ant", "bat", "cat", "dog", "eel"
|1  | "dog","bat", "ant", "bat", "cat"
```

Output:

```
id| text                          | Vector
--|-------------------------------|--------------------
0 | "ant", "bat", "cat", "dog", "eel" |[1.0,1.0,1.0,1.0]
1 | "dog","bat", "ant", "bat", "cat"  |[2.0,1.0,1.0,1.0]
```

The preceding example demonstrates how CountVectorizer works as an estimator to extract the vocabulary and generate a CountVectorizerModel. Note that the features vector order corresponds to vocabulary and not the input sequence. Let's also look at how the same can be achieved by building a dictionary a-priori. However, keep in mind that they have their own use cases.

Example 4: define CountVectorizerModel with a-priori vocabulary

Scala:

```scala
// Example 4: define CountVectorizerModel with a-priori vocabulary
scala> val cvm: CountVectorizerModel = new CountVectorizerModel(
        Array("ant", "bat", "cat")).
        setInputCol("words").setOutputCol("features")
cvm: org.apache.spark.ml.feature.CountVectorizerModel =
cntVecModel_ecbb8e1778d5

//Apply on the same data. Feature order corresponds to a-priory vocabulary
order
scala> cvm.transform(df).select("features").collect().foreach(row =>
        println(row(0).asInstanceOf[Vector].toDense))
[1.0,1.0,1.0]
[1.0,2.0,1.0]
```

Python:

Not available as of Spark 2.0.0

TF-IDF

The **Term Frequency-Inverse Document Frequency** (**TF-IDF**) is perhaps one of the most popular measures in text analytics. This metric indicates the importance of a given term in a given document within a set of documents. This consists two measurements, **Term Frequency** (**TF**) and **Inverse Document Frequency** (**IDF**). Let us discuss them one by one and then see their combined effect.

TF is a measure of the relative importance of a term in a document, which is usually the frequency of that term divided by the number of terms in that document. Consider a text document containing 100 words wherein the word *apple* appears eight times. The TF for *apple* would be $TF = (8 / 100) = 0.08$. So, the more frequently a term occurs in a document, the larger is its TF coefficient.

IDF is a measure of the importance of a particular term in the entire collection of documents, that is, how infrequently the word occurs across all the documents. The importance of a term is inversely proportional to its frequency. Spark provides two separate methods to perform these tasks. Assume we have 6 million documents and the word *apple* appears in 6000 of these. Then, IDF is calculated as $IDF = Log(6,000,000 / 6,000) = 3$. If you observe this carefully, the lower the denominator, the higher is the IDF value. This means that the fewer the number of documents containing a particular word, the higher would be its importance.

Thus, the TF-IDF score would be $TF * IDF = 0.08 * 3 = 0.24$. Note that it would penalize the words that are more frequent across documents and less important, such as *the*, *this*, *a*, and so on, and give more weight to the ones that are important.

In Spark, TF is implemented as HashingTF. It takes a sequence of terms (often the output of a tokenizer) and produces a fixed length features vector. It performs feature hashing to convert the terms into fixed length indices. IDF then takes that features vector (the output of HashingTF) as input and scales it based on the term frequency in the set of documents. The previous chapter has an example of this transformation.

Stop-word removal

Common words such as *is, was,* and *the* are called stop-words. They do not usually add value to analysis and should be dropped during the data preparation step. Spark provides StopWordsRemover transformer, which does just that. It takes a sequence of tokens as a series of string inputs, such as the output of a tokenizer, and removes all the stop words. Spark has a stop-words list by default that you may override by providing your own stop-words list as a parameter. You may optionally turn on caseSensitive match which is off by default.

Example 5: Stopword Remover

Scala:

```
scala> import org.apache.spark.ml.feature.StopWordsRemover
import org.apache.spark.ml.feature.StopWordsRemover
scala> import org.apache.spark.sql.DataFrame
import org.apache.spark.sql.DataFrame
scala> import org.apache.spark.ml.linalg.Vector
import org.apache.spark.ml.linalg.Vector
scala> val rawdataDF = spark.createDataFrame(Seq(
        (0, Array("I", "ate", "the", "cake")),
        (1, Array("John ", "had", "a", " tennis", "racquet")))).
        toDF("id","raw_text")
rawdataDF: org.apache.spark.sql.DataFrame = [id: int, raw_text:
array<string>]
scala> val remover = new StopWordsRemover().setInputCol("raw_text").
            setOutputCol("processed_text")
remover: org.apache.spark.ml.feature.StopWordsRemover =
stopWords_55edbac88edb
scala> remover.transform(rawdataDF).show(truncate=false)
+---+-------------------------------+-------------------------+
|id |raw_text                       |processed_text           |
+---+-------------------------------+-------------------------+
|0  |[I, ate, the, cake]            |[ate, cake]              |
|1  |[John , had, a,  tennis, racquet]|[John ,  tennis, racquet]|
+---+-------------------------------+-------------------------+
```

Python:

```
>>> from pyspark.ml.feature import StopWordsRemover
>>> RawData = sqlContext.createDataFrame([
    (0, ["I", "ate", "the", "cake"]),
    (1, ["John ", "had", "a", " tennis", "racquet"])
    ], ["id", "raw_text"])
>>>
>>> remover = StopWordsRemover(inputCol="raw_text",
        outputCol="processed_text")
>>> remover.transform(RawData).show(truncate=False)
+---+-----------------------------------------+------------------------------+
|id |raw_text                                 |processed_text                |
+---+-----------------------------------------+------------------------------+
|0  |[I, ate, the, cake]                      |[ate, cake]                   |
|1  |[John , had, a,  tennis, racquet]        |[John ,  tennis, racquet]     |
+---+-----------------------------------------+------------------------------+
```

Assume that we have the following DataFrame with columns id and raw_text:

```
id  |  raw_text
----|-----------
 0  | [I, ate, the, cake]
 1  | [John, had, a, tennis, racquet]
```

After applying StopWordsRemover with raw_text as the input column and
processed_text as the output column for the preceding example, we should get the
following output:

```
id  |  raw_text                         |  processed_text
----|-----------------------------------|--------------------
 0  | [I, ate, the, cake]               |  [ate, cake]
 1  | [John, had, a, tennis, racquet]   | [John, tennis, racquet]
```

Normalization/scaling

Normalization is a common and preliminary step in data preparation. Most of the machine learning algorithms work better when all features are on the same scale. For example, if there are two features where the value of one is about 100 times greater than the other, bringing them to the same scale reflects meaningful relative activity between the two variables. Any non-numeric values, such as high, medium, and low, should ideally be converted to appropriate numerical quantification as a best practice. However, you need to be careful in doing so as it may require domain expertise. For example, if you assign 3, 2, and 1 for high, medium, and low respectively, then it should be checked that these three units are equidistant from each other.

The common methods of feature normalization are *scaling*, *mean subtraction*, and *feature standardization*, just to name a few. In scaling, each numerical feature vector is rescaled such that its value range is between *-1* to *+1* or to *1* or something similar. In mean subtraction, you compute mean of a numerical feature vector and subtract that mean from each of the values. We are interested in the relative deflection from the mean, while the absolute value could be immaterial. Feature standardization refers to setting the data to zero mean and unit (1) variance.

Spark provides a `Normalizer` feature transformer to normalize each vector to have unit norm; `StandardScaler` to have unit norm and zero mean; and `MinMaxScaler` to rescale each feature to a specific range of values. By default, min and max are 0 and 1 but you may set the value parameters yourself as per the data requirement.

Word2Vec

The Word2Vec is a type of PCA (you will find out more about this shortly) that takes a sequence of words and produces a map (of string, vector). The string is the word and the vector is a unique fixed size vector. The resulting word vector representation is useful in many machine learning and NLP applications, such as named entity recognition and tagging. Let us look at an example.

Example 6: Word2Vec

Scala

```
scala> import org.apache.spark.ml.feature.Word2Vec
import org.apache.spark.ml.feature.Word2Vec

//Step1: Load text file and split to words
scala> val path = "<Your path>/RobertFrost.txt"
```

```
path: String = <Your path>/RobertFrost.txt
scala> val raw_text = spark.read.text(path).select(
        split('value, " ") as "words")
raw_text: org.apache.spark.sql.DataFrame = [words: array<string>]
```

//Step2: Prepare features vector of size 4
```
scala> val resultDF = new Word2Vec().setInputCol("words").
        setOutputCol("features").setVectorSize(4).
        setMinCount(2).fit(raw_text).transform(raw_text)
resultDF: org.apache.spark.sql.DataFrame = [words: array<string>, features:
vector]
```

//Examine results
```
scala> resultDF.show(5)
+--------------------+--------------------+
|               words|            features|
+--------------------+--------------------+
|[Whose, woods, th...|[-0.0209098898340...|
|[His, house, is, ...|[-0.0013444167044...|
|[He, will, not, s...|[-0.0058525378408...|
|[To, watch, his, ...|[-0.0189630933296...|
|[My, little, hors...|[-0.0084691265597...|
+--------------------+--------------------+
```

Python:

```
>>> from pyspark.ml.feature import Word2Vec
>>> from pyspark.sql.functions import explode, split
>>>
```

//Step1: Load text file and split to words
```
>>> path = "<Your path>/RobertFrost.txt"
>>> raw_text = spark.read.text(path).select(
        split("value"," ")).toDF("words")
```

//Step2: Prepare features vector of size 4
```
>>> resultDF = Word2Vec(inputCol="words",outputCol="features",
                vectorSize=4, minCount=2).fit(
                raw_text).transform(raw_text)
```

//Examine results
```
scala> resultDF.show(5)
+--------------------+--------------------+
|               words|            features|
+--------------------+--------------------+
|[Whose, woods, th...|[-0.0209098898340...|
|[His, house, is, ...|[-0.0013444167044...|
|[He, will, not, s...|[-0.0058525378408...|
```

```
|[To, watch, his, ...|[-0.0189630933296...|
|[My, little, hors...|[-0.0084691265597...|
+-------------------+--------------------+
```

n-gram modelling

An n-gram is a contiguous sequence of *n* items from a given sequence of text or speech. An n-gram of size *1* is referred to as a *unigram*, size *2* is a *bigram*, and size *3* is a *trigram*. Alternatively, they can be referred to by the value of *n*, for example, four-gram, five-gram, and so on. Let us take a look at an example to understand the possible outcomes of this model:

```
input |1-gram sequence  | 2-gram sequence | 3-gram sequence
------|-----------------|-----------------|----------------
apple | a,p,p,l,e       |  ap,pp,pl,le    | app,ppl,ple
```

This is an example of words to n-gram letters. The same is the case for sentence (or tokenized words) to n-gram words. For example, the 2-gram equivalent of the sentence *Kids love to eat chocolates* is:

'Kids love', 'love to', 'to eat', 'eat chocolates'.

There are various applications of n-gram modelling in text mining and NLP. One of the examples is predicting the probability of each word occurring given a prior context (conditional probability).

In Spark, NGram is a feature transformer that converts the input array (for example, the output of a Tokenizer) of strings into an array of n-grams. Null values in the input array are ignored by default. It returns an array of n-grams where each n-gram is represented by a space-separated string of words.

Example 7: NGram

Scala

```scala
scala> import org.apache.spark.ml.feature.NGram
import org.apache.spark.ml.feature.NGram
scala> val wordDF = spark.createDataFrame(Seq(
        (0, Array("Hi", "I", "am", "a", "Scientist")),
        (1, Array("I", "am", "just", "learning", "Spark")),
        (2, Array("Coding", "in", "Scala", "is", "easy"))
        )).toDF("label", "words")

//Create an ngram model with 3 words length (default is 2)
scala> val ngramModel = new NGram().setInputCol(
```

```
                    "words").setOutputCol("ngrams").setN(3)
ngramModel: org.apache.spark.ml.feature.NGram = ngram_dc50209cf693
```

//Apply on input data frame
```
scala> ngramModel.transform(wordDF).select("ngrams").show(false)
+------------------------------------------------+
|ngrams                                          |
+------------------------------------------------+
|[Hi I am, I am a, am a Scientist]               |
|[I am just, am just learning, just learning Spark]|
|[Coding in Scala, in Scala is, Scala is easy]   |
+------------------------------------------------+
```

//Apply the model on another dataframe, Word2Vec raw_text
```
scala>ngramModel.transform(raw_text).select("ngrams").take(1).foreach(print
ln)
[WrappedArray(Whose woods these, woods these are, these are I, are I think,
I think I, think I know.)]
```

Python:

```
>>> from pyspark.ml.feature import NGram
>>> wordDF = spark.createDataFrame([
        [0, ["Hi", "I", "am", "a", "Scientist"]],
        [1, ["I", "am", "just", "learning", "Spark"]],
        [2, ["Coding", "in", "Scala", "is", "easy"]]
        ]).toDF("label", "words")
```

//Create an ngram model with 3 words length (default is 2)
```
>>> ngramModel = NGram(inputCol="words", outputCol= "ngrams",n=3)
>>>
```

//Apply on input data frame
```
>>> ngramModel.transform(wordDF).select("ngrams").show(4,False)
+------------------------------------------------+
|ngrams                                          |
+------------------------------------------------+
|[Hi I am, I am a, am a Scientist]               |
|[I am just, am just learning, just learning Spark]|
|[Coding in Scala, in Scala is, Scala is easy]   |
+------------------------------------------------+
```

//Apply the model on another dataframe from Word2Vec example
```
>>> ngramModel.transform(resultDF).select("ngrams").take(1)
[Row(ngrams=[u'Whose woods these', u'woods these are', u'these are I',
u'are I think', u'I think I', u'think I know.'])]
```

Text classification

Text classification is about assigning a topic, subject category, genre, or something similar to the text blob. For example, spam filters assign spam or not spam to an email.

Apache Spark supports various classifiers through MLlib and ML packages. The SVM classifier and Naive Bayes classifier are popular classifiers, and the former was already covered in the previous chapter. Let's take a look at the latter now.

Naive Bayes classifier

The **Naive Bayes** (**NB**) classifier is a multiclass probabilistic classifier and is one of the best classification algorithms. It assumes strong independence between every pair of features. It computes the conditional probability distribution of each feature and a given label, and then applies Bayes' theorem to compute the conditional probability of a label given an observation. In terms of document classification, an observation is a document to be classified into some class. Despite its strong assumptions on data, it is quite popular. It works with small amount of training data – whether real or discrete. It works very efficiently because it takes a single pass through the training data; one constraint is that the feature vectors must be non-negative. By default, ML package supports multinomial NB. However, you may set the parameter `modelType` to `Bernoulli` if bernoulli NB is required.

The **laplace smoothing** technique may be applied by specifying the smoothing parameters and is extremely useful in situations where you want to assign a small non-zero probability to a rare word or new word so that the posterior probabilities do not suddenly drop to zero.

Spark also provides some other hyper parameters such as `thresholds` also to gain fine grain control. Here is an example that categorizes twitter text. This example contains some hand-coded rules that assign a category to the train data. A particular category is assigned if any of the corresponding words are found in the text. For example, the category is âoosurveyâoo if text contains âoosurveyâoo or âoopollâoo. The model is trained based on this train data and evaluated on a different text sample collected at a different time:

Example 8: Naive Bayes

Scala:

```
// Step 1: Define a udf to assign a category
// One or more similar words are treated as one category (eg survey, poll)
// If input list contains any of the words in a category list, it is
assigned to that category
// "General" is assigned if none of the categories matched
```

```scala
scala> import scala.collection.mutable.WrappedArray
import scala.collection.mutable.WrappedArray
scala> val findCategory = udf ((words: WrappedArray[String]) =>
    { var idx = 0; var category : String = ""
    val categories : List[Array[String]] =  List(
     Array("Python"), Array("Hadoop","hadoop"),
     Array("survey","poll"),
      Array("event","training", "Meetup", "summit",
          "talk", "talks", "Setting","sessions", "workshop"),
     Array("resource","Guide","newsletter", "Blog"))
    while(idx < categories.length && category.isEmpty ) {
        if (!words.intersect(categories(idx)).isEmpty) {
          category = categories(idx)(0) }  //First word in the category list
     idx += 1 }
    if (category.isEmpty) {
    category = "General"  }
    category
  })
findCategory: org.apache.spark.sql.expressions.UserDefinedFunction =
UserDefinedFunction(<function1>,StringType,Some(List(ArrayType(StringType,t
rue))))
```

//UDF to convert category to a numerical label
```scala
scala> val idxCategory = udf ((category: String) =>
        {val catgMap = Map({"General"->1},{"event"->2},{"Hadoop"->3},
                          {"Python"->4},{"resource"->5})
        catgMap(category)})
idxCategory: org.apache.spark.sql.expressions.UserDefinedFunction =
UserDefinedFunction(<function1>,IntegerType,Some(List(StringType)))
scala> val labels = Array("General","event","Hadoop","Python","resource")
```

//Step 2: Prepare train data
//Step 2a: Extract "text" data and split to words
```scala
scala> val path = "<Your path>/tweets_train.txt"
path: String = <Your path>../work/tweets_train.txt
scala> val pattern = ""text":"
pattern: String = "text":
scala> val raw_text =
spark.read.text(path).filter($"value".contains(pattern)).
                select(split('value, " ") as "words")
raw_text: org.apache.spark.sql.DataFrame = [words: array<string>]
scala>
```

//Step 2b: Assign a category to each line
```scala
scala> val train_cat_df = raw_text.withColumn("category",

findCategory(raw_text("words"))).withColumn("label",idxCategory($"category"
```

```
))
train_cat_df: org.apache.spark.sql.DataFrame = [words: array<string>,
category:
string ... 1 more field]
```

//Step 2c: Examine categories
```
scala> train_cat_df.groupBy($"category").agg(count("category")).show()
+--------+---------------
+
|category|count(category)|
+--------+---------------+
| General|            146|
|resource|              1|
|  Python|              2|
|   event|             10|
|  Hadoop|              6|
+--------+---------------+
```

//Step 3: Build pipeline
```
scala> import org.apache.spark.ml.Pipeline
import org.apache.spark.ml.Pipeline
scala> import org.apache.spark.ml.feature.{StopWordsRemover,
CountVectorizer,
                IndexToString}
import org.apache.spark.ml.feature.{StopWordsRemover, CountVectorizer,
StringIndexer, IndexToString}
scala> import org.apache.spark.ml.classification.NaiveBayes
import org.apache.spark.ml.classification.NaiveBayes
scala>
```

//Step 3a: Define pipeline stages
//Stop words should be removed first
```
scala> val stopw = new StopWordsRemover().setInputCol("words").
                setOutputCol("processed_words")
stopw: org.apache.spark.ml.feature.StopWordsRemover =
stopWords_2fb707daa92e
```
//Terms to term frequency converter
```
scala> val cv = new CountVectorizer().setInputCol("processed_words").
                setOutputCol("features")
cv: org.apache.spark.ml.feature.CountVectorizer = cntVec_def4911aa0bf
```
//Define model
```
scala> val model = new NaiveBayes().
                setFeaturesCol("features").
                setLabelCol("label")
model: org.apache.spark.ml.classification.NaiveBayes = nb_f2b6c423f12c
```
//Numerical prediction label to category converter
```
scala> val lc = new IndexToString().setInputCol("prediction").
                setOutputCol("predictedCategory").
```

```
        setLabels(labels)
lc: org.apache.spark.ml.feature.IndexToString = idxToStr_3d71be25382c
```

//Step 3b: Build pipeline with desired stages
```
scala> val p = new Pipeline().setStages(Array(stopw,cv,model,lc))
p: org.apache.spark.ml.Pipeline = pipeline_956942e70b3f
```

//Step 4: Process train data and get predictions
//Step 4a: Execute pipeline with train data
```
scala> val resultsDF = p.fit(train_cat_df).transform(train_cat_df)
resultsDF: org.apache.spark.sql.DataFrame = [words: array<string>,
category:
string ... 7 more fields]
```

//Step 4b: Examine results
```
scala> resultsDF.select("category","predictedCategory").show(3)
+--------+-----------------+
|category|predictedCategory|
+--------+-----------------+
|   event|            event|
|   event|            event|
| General|          General|
+--------+-----------------+
```

//Step 4c: Look for prediction mismatches
```
scala> resultsDF.filter("category != predictedCategory").select(
        "category","predictedCategory").show(3)
+--------+-----------------+
|category|predictedCategory|
+--------+-----------------+
| General|            event|
| General|           Hadoop|
|resource|           Hadoop|
+--------+-----------------+
```

//Step 5: Evaluate model using test data
//Step5a: Prepare test data
```
scala> val path = "<Your path> /tweets.json"
path: String = <Your path>/tweets.json
scala> val raw_test_df =
spark.read.text(path).filter($"value".contains(pattern)).
                select(split('value, " ") as "words"

raw_test_df: org.apache.spark.sql.DataFrame = [words: array<string>]
scala> val test_cat_df = raw_test_df.withColumn("category",
```

```
findCategory(raw_test_df("words")))withColumn("label",idxCategory($"categor
y"))
test_cat_df: org.apache.spark.sql.DataFrame = [words: array<string>,
category:
string ... 1 more field]
scala> test_cat_df.groupBy($"category").agg(count("category")).show()
+--------+---------------
+
|category|count(category)|
+--------+---------------+
| General|              6|
|   event|             11|
+--------+---------------+
```

//Step 5b: Run predictions on test data
```
scala> val testResultsDF = p.fit(test_cat_df).transform(test_cat_df)
testResultsDF: org.apache.spark.sql.DataFrame = [words: array<string>,
category: string ... 7 more fields]
//Step 5c:: Examine results
scala> testResultsDF.select("category","predictedCategory").show(3)
+--------+-----------------+
|category|predictedCategory|
+--------+-----------------+
| General|            event|
|   event|          General|
|   event|          General|
+--------+-----------------+
```

//Step 5d: Look for prediction mismatches
```
scala> testResultsDF.filter("category != predictedCategory").select(
        "category","predictedCategory").show()
+--------+-----------------+
|category|predictedCategory|
+--------+-----------------+
|   event|          General|
|   event|          General|
+--------+-----------------+
```

Python:

```
// Step 1: Initialization
//Step1a: Define a udfs to assign a category
// One or more similar words are treated as one category (eg survey, poll)
// If input list contains any of the words in a category list, it is
assigned to that category
// "General" is assigned if none of the categories matched
>>> def findCategory(words):
```

```
        idx = 0; category  = ""
        categories = [["Python"], ["Hadoop","hadoop"],
          ["survey","poll"],["event","training", "Meetup", "summit",
          "talk", "talks", "Setting","sessions", "workshop"],
          ["resource","Guide","newsletter", "Blog"]]
        while(not category and idx < len(categories)):
          if len(set(words).intersection(categories[idx])) > 0:
            category = categories[idx][0] #First word in the category list
          else:
            idx+=1
        if not category:   #No match found
          category = "General"
        return category
>>>
```

//Step 1b: Define udf to convert string category to a numerical label
```
>>> def idxCategory(category):
        catgDict = {"General" :1, "event" :2, "Hadoop" :2,
            "Python": 4, "resource" : 5}
        return catgDict[category]
>>>
```
//Step 1c: Register UDFs
```
>>> from pyspark.sql.functions import udf
>>> from pyspark.sql.types import StringType, IntegerType
>>> findCategoryUDF = udf(findCategory, StringType())
>>> idxCategoryUDF = udf(idxCategory, IntegerType())
```

//Step 1d: List categories
```
>>> categories =["General","event","Hadoop","Python","resource"]
```
//Step 2: Prepare train data
//Step 2a: Extract "text" data and split to words
```
>>> from pyspark.sql.functions import split
>>> path = "../work/tweets_train.txt"
>>> raw_df1 = spark.read.text(path)
>>> raw_df = raw_df1.where("value like '%"text":%'").select(
            split("value", " ")).toDF("words")
```

//Step 2b: Assign a category to each line
```
>>> train_cat_df = raw_df.withColumn("category",\
        findCategoryUDF("words")).withColumn(
        "label",idxCategoryUDF("category"))
```

//Step 2c: Examine categories
```
scala> train_cat_df.groupBy("category").count().show()
+--------+---------------
+
|category|count(category)|
+--------+---------------+
| General|            146|
```

```
|resource|              1|
|  Python|              2|
|   event|             10|
|  Hadoop|              6|
+--------+---------------+
```

//Step 3: Build pipeline
```
>>> from pyspark.ml import Pipeline
>>> from pyspark.ml.feature import StopWordsRemover, CountVectorizer,
IndexToString
>>> from pyspark.ml.classification import NaiveBayes
>>>
```

//Step 3a: Define pipeline stages
//Stop words should be removed first
```
>>> stopw = StopWordsRemover(inputCol = "words",
                outputCol = "processed_words")
```
//Terms to term frequency converter
```
>>> cv = CountVectorizer(inputCol = "processed_words",
            outputCol = "features")
```
//Define model
```
>>> model = NaiveBayes(featuresCol="features",
                    labelCol = "label")
```
//Numerical prediction label to category converter
```
>>> lc = IndexToString(inputCol = "prediction",
            outputCol = "predictedCategory",
            labels = categories)
>>>
```

//Step 3b: Build pipeline with desired stages
```
>>> p = Pipeline(stages = [stopw,cv,model,lc])
>>>
```

//Step 4: Process train data and get predictions
//Step 4a: Execute pipeline with train data
```
>>> resultsDF = p.fit(train_cat_df).transform(train_cat_df)
```

//Step 4b: Examine results
```
>>> resultsDF.select("category","predictedCategory").show(3)
+--------+-----------------+
|category|predictedCategory|
+--------+-----------------+
|   event|            event|
|   event|            event|
| General|          General|
+--------+-----------------+
```

//Step 4c: Look for prediction mismatches
```
>>> resultsDF.filter("category != predictedCategory").select(
        "category","predictedCategory").show(3)
+--------+-----------------+
|category|predictedCategory|
+--------+-----------------+
|  Python|           Hadoop|
|  Python|           Hadoop|
|  Hadoop|            event|
+--------+-----------------+
```

//Step 5: Evaluate model using test data
//Step5a: Prepare test data
```
>>> path = "<Your path>/tweets.json">>> raw_df1 = spark.read.text(path)
>>> raw_test_df = raw_df1.where("va
ue like '%"text":%'").select(
              split("value", " ")).toDF("words")
>>> test_cat_df = raw_test_df.withColumn("category",
        findCategoryUDF("words")).withColumn(
        "label",idxCategoryUDF("category"))
>>> test_cat_df.groupBy("category").count().show()
+--------+---------------
+
|category|count(category)|
+--------+---------------+
| General|              6|
|   event|             11|
+--------+---------------+
```

//Step 5b: Run predictions on test data
```
>>> testResultsDF = p.fit(test_cat_df).transform(test_cat_df)
```
//Step 5c:: Examine results
```
>>> testResultsDF.select("category","predictedCategory").show(3)
+--------+-----------------+
|category|predictedCategory|
+--------+-----------------+
| General|          General|
|   event|            event|
|   event|            event|
+--------+-----------------+
```
//Step 5d: Look for prediction mismatches
```
>>> testResultsDF.filter("category != predictedCategory").select(
        "category","predictedCategory").show()
+--------+-----------------+
|category|predictedCategory|
+--------+-----------------+
|   event|          General|
|   event|          General|
```

```
    +--------+----------------+
```

Once this is done, a model can be trained with the output of this step, which can classify a text blob or file.

Text clustering

Clustering is an unsupervised learning technique. Intuitively, clustering groups objects into disjoint sets. We do not know how many groups exist in the data, or what might be the commonality within these groups (clusters).

Text clustering has several applications. For example, an organizational entity may want to organize its internal documents into similar clusters based on some similarity measure. The notion of similarity or distance is central to the clustering process. Common measures used are TF-IDF and cosine similarity. Cosine similarity, or the cosine distance, is the cos product of the word frequency vectors of two documents. Spark provides a variety of clustering algorithms that can be effectively used in text analytics.

K-means

Perhaps K-means is the most intuitive of all the clustering algorithms. The idea is to segregate data points as K different clusters based on some similarity measure, say cosine distance or Euclidean distance. This algorithm that starts with K random single point clusters, and each of the remaining data points are assigned to nearest cluster. Then cluster centers are recomputed and the algorithm loops through the data points once again. This process continues iteratively until there are no re-assignments or when pre-defined iteration count is reached.

How to fix the number of clusters (K) is not obvious. Identifying the initial cluster centers is also not obvious. Sometimes the business requirement may dictate the number of clusters; for example, partition all existing documents into 10 different sections. But in most of the real world scenarios, we need to find K through trial and error. One way is to progressively increase the K value and compute the cluster quality, such as cluster variance. The quality ceases to improve significantly beyond a certain value of K, which could be your ideal K. There are various other techniques, such as the elbow method, **Akaike information criterion** (**AIC**), and **Bayesian information criterion** (**BIC**).

Likewise, start with different starting points until the cluster quality is satisfactory. Then you may wish to validate your result using techniques such as Silhouette Score. However, these activities are computationally intensive.

Spark provides K-means from MLlib as well as ml packages. You may specify maximum iterations or convergence tolerance to fine tune algorithm performance.

Dimensionality reduction

Imagine a large matrix with many rows and columns. In many matrix applications, this large matrix can be represented by some narrow matrices with small number of rows and columns that still represents the original matrix. Then processing this smaller matrix may yield similar results as that of the original matrix. This can be computationally efficient.

Dimensionality reduction is about finding that small matrix. MLLib supports two algorithms, SVD and PCA for dimensionality reduction on RowMatrix class. Both of these algorithms allow us to specify the number of dimensions we are interested in retaining. Let us look at example first and then delve into the underlying theory .

Example 9: Dimensionality reduction

Scala:

```
scala> import scala.util.Random
import scala.util.Random
scala> import org.apache.spark.mllib.linalg.{Vector, Vectors}
import org.apache.spark.mllib.linalg.{Vector, Vectors}
scala> import org.apache.spark.mllib.linalg.distributed.RowMatrix
import org.apache.spark.mllib.linalg.distributed.RowMatrix

//Create a RowMatrix of 6 rows and 5 columns
scala> var vlist: Array[Vector] = Array()
vlist: Array[org.apache.spark.mllib.linalg.Vector] = Array()
scala> for (i <- 1 to 6) vlist = vlist :+ Vectors.dense(
       Array.fill(5)(Random.nextInt*1.0))
scala> val rows_RDD = sc.parallelize(vlist)
rows_RDD: org.apache.spark.rdd.RDD[org.apache.spark.mllib.linalg.Vector] =
ParallelCollectionRDD[0] at parallelize at <console>:29
scala> val row_matrix = new RowMatrix(rows_RDD)
row_matrix: org.apache.spark.mllib.linalg.distributed.RowMatrix =
org.apache.spark.mllib.linalg.distributed.RowMatrix@348a6639

//SVD example for top 3 singular values
scala> val SVD_result = row_matrix.computeSVD(3)
SVD_result:
org.apache.spark.mllib.linalg.SingularValueDecomposition[org.apache.spark.m
lli
.linalg.distributed.RowMatrix,org.apache.spark.mllib.linalg.Matrix] =
SingularValueDecomposition(null,
```

```
    [4.933482776606544E9,3.290744495921952E9,2.971558550447048E9],
    -0.678871347405378     0.054158900880961904   -0.23905281217240534
    0.2278187940802        -0.6393277579229861     0.078663353163388
    0.48824560481341733    0.3139021297613471     -0.7800061948839081
    -0.4970903877201546    2.366428606359744E-4   -0.3665502780139027
    0.041829015676406664   0.6998515759330556      0.4403374382132576     )

scala> SVD_result.s    //Show the singular values (strengths)
res1: org.apache.spark.mllib.linalg.Vector =
    [4.933482776606544E9,3.290744495921952E9,2.971558550447048E9]

//PCA example to compute top 2 principal components
scala> val PCA_result = row_matrix.computePrincipalComponents(2)
PCA_result: org.apache.spark.mllib.linalg.Matrix =
    -0.663822435334425     0.24038790854106118
    0.3119085619707716     -0.30195355896094916
    0.47440026368044447    0.8539858509513869
    -0.48429601343640094   0.32543904517535094
    -0.0495437635382354    -0.12583837216152594
```

Python:

Not available in Python as of Spark 2.0.0

Singular Value Decomposition

The **Singular Value Decomposition (SVD)** is one of the centerpieces of linear algebra and is widely used for many real-world modeling requirements. It provides a convenient way of breaking a matrix into simpler, smaller matrices. This leads to a low-dimensional representation of a high-dimensional matrix. It helps us eliminate less important parts of the matrix to produce an approximate representation. This technique is useful in dimensionality reduction and data compression.

Let *M* be a matrix of size m-rows and n-columns. The rank of a matrix is the number of rows that are linearly independent. A row is considered independent if it has at least one non-zero element and it is not a linear combination of one or more rows. The same rank will be obtained if we considered columns instead of rows – as in linear algebra.

If the elements of one row are the sum of two rows, then that row is not independent. Then as a result of SVD, we find three matrices, *U*, *Σ*, and *V* that satisfy the following equation:

$M = U \Sigma VT$

These three matrices have the following properties:

- **U**: This is a column-orthonormal matrix with m rows and r columns. An orthonormal matrix implies that each of the columns is a unit vector and the pairwise dot product between any two columns is 0.
- **V**: This is a column-orthonormal matrix with n rows and r columns.
- **Σ**: This is an r x r diagonal matrix with non-negative real numbers as principal diagonal values in descending order. In a diagonal matrix, all elements except the ones on the principal diagonal are zero.

The principal diagonal values in the Σ matrix are called singular values. They are considered as the underlying *concepts* or *components* that connect the rows and columns of the matrix. Their magnitude represents the strength of the corresponding components. For example, imagine that the matrix in the previous example contains ratings of five books by six readers. SVD allows us to split them into three matrices: Σ containing the singular values representing the *strength* of underlying topics; U connecting people to concepts; and V connecting concepts to books.

In a large matrix, we can replace the lower magnitude singular values to zero and thereby reduce the corresponding rows in the remaining two matrices. Note that if we re-compute the matrix product on the right hand side and compare the value with the original matrix on the left hand side, they will be almost similar. We can use this technique to retain the desired number of dimensions.

Principal Component Analysis

Principal Component Analysis (PCA) is a technique that takes n-dimensional data points and project onto a smaller (fewer dimensions) subspace with minimum loss of information. A set of data points in a high dimensional space find the directions along which these tuples line up best. In other words, we need to find a rotation such that the first coordinate has the largest variance possible, and each succeeding coordinate in turn has the largest variance possible. The idea is to treat the set of tuples as a matrix M and find the eigenvectors for MMT.

If A is a square matrix, e is a column matrix with the same number of rows as A, and λ is a constant such that $Me = \lambda e$, then e is called the eigenvector of M and λ is called the eigenvalue of M. In terms of n-dimensional plane, the eigenvector is the direction and the eigenvalue is a measure of variance along that direction. We can drop the dimensions with a low eigenvalue, thereby finding a smaller subspace without loss of information.

Summary

In this chapter, we examined the sources of unstructured data and the motivation behind analyzing the unstructured data. We explained various techniques that are required in pre-processing unstructured data and how Spark provides most of these tools out of the box. We also covered some of the algorithms supported by Spark that can be used in text analytics.

In the next chapter, we will go through different types of visualization techniques that are insightful in different stages of data analytics lifecycle.

References:

The following are the references:

- http://totoharyanto.staff.ipb.ac.id/files/2012/10/Building-Machine-Learning-Systems-with-Python-Richert-Coelho.pdf
- https://www.cs.nyu.edu/web/Research/Theses/borthwick_andrew.pdf
- https://web.stanford.edu/class/cs124/lec/naivebayes.pdf
- http://nlp.stanford.edu/IR-book/html/htmledition/naive-bayes-text-classification-1.html
- http://www.mmds.org/
- http://sebastianraschka.com/Articles/2014_pca_step_by_step.html
- http://arxiv.org/pdf/1404.1100.pdf
- http://spark.apache.org/docs/latest/mllib-dimensionality-reduction.html

Count Vectorizer:

- https://spark.apache.org/docs/1.6.1/api/java/org/apache/spark/ml/feature/CountVectorizer.html

n-gram modeling:

- https://en.wikipedia.org/wiki/N-gram

9
Visualizing Big Data

Proper data visualization has solved many business problems in the past without much statistics or machine learning being involved. Even today, with so many technological advancements, applied statistics, and machine learning, proper visuals are the end deliverables for business users to consume information or the output of some analyses. Conveying the right information in the right format is something that data scientists yearn for, and an effective visual is worth a million words. Also, representing the models and the insights generated in a way that is easily consumable by the business is extremely important. Nonetheless, exploring big data visually is very cumbersome and challenging. Since Spark is designed for big data processing, it also supports big data visualization along with it. There are many tools and techniques that have been built on Spark for this purpose.

The previous chapters outlined how to model structured and unstructured data and generate insights from it. In this chapter, we will look at data visualization from two broad perspectives-one is from a data scientist's perspective—where visualization is the basic need to explore and understand the data effectively, and the other is from a business user's perspective, where the visuals are end deliverables to the business and must be easily comprehendible. We will explore various data visualization tools such as *IPythonNotebook* and *Zeppelin* that can be used on Apache Spark.

As a prerequisite for this chapter, a basic understanding of SQL and programming in Python, Scala, or other such frameworks, is nice to have. The topics covered in this chapter are listed as follows:

- Why visualize data?
    - A data engineer's perspective
    - A data scientist's perspective
    - A business user's perspective

- Data visualization tools
  - IPython notebook
  - Apache Zeppelin
  - Third-party tools

- Data visualization techniques
  - Summarizing and visualizing
  - Subsetting and visualizing
  - Sampling and visualizing
  - Modeling and visualizing

Why visualize data?

Data visualization deals with representing data in a visual form so as to enable people to understand the underlying patterns and trends. Geographical maps, the bar and line charts of the seventeenth century, are some examples of early data visualizations. Excel is perhaps a familiar data visualization tool that most of us have already used. All data analytics tools have been equipped with sophisticated, interactive data visualization dashboards. However, the recent surge in big data, streaming, and real-time analytics has been pushing the boundaries of these tools and they seem to be bursting at the seams. The idea is to make the visualizations look simple, accurate, and relevant while hiding away all the complexity. As per the business needs, any visualization solution should ideally have the following characteristics:

- Interactivity
- Reproducibility
- Control over the details

Apart from these, if the solution allows users to collaborate over the visuals or reports and share with each other, then that would make up an end-to-end visualization solution.

Big data visualization in particular poses its own challenges because we may end up with more data than pixels on the screen. Manipulating large data usually requires memory- and CPU-intensive processing and may have long latency. Add real-time or streaming data to the mix and the problem becomes even more challenging. Apache Spark is designed from the ground up just to tackle this latency by parallelizing CPU and memory usage. Before exploring the tools and techniques to visualize and work with big data, let's first understand the visualization needs of data engineers, data scientists, and business users.

A data engineer's perspective

Data engineers play a crucial role in almost every data-driven requirement: sourcing data from different data sources, consolidating them, cleaning and preprocessing them, analyzing them, and then the final reporting with visuals and dashboards. Their activities can be broadly stated as follows:

- Visualize the data from different sources to be able to integrate and consolidate it to form a single data matrix
- Visualize and find various anomalies in the data, such as missing values, outliers and so on (this could be while scraping, sourcing, ETLing, and so on) and get those fixed
- Advise the data scientists on the properties and characteristics of the dataset
- Explore various possible ways of visualizing the data and finalize the ones that are more informative and intuitive as per the business requirement

Observe here that the data engineers not only play a key role in sourcing and preparing the data, but also take a call on the most suitable visualization outputs for the business users. They usually work very closely to the business as well to have a very clear understanding on the business requirement and the specific problem at hand.

A data scientist's perspective

A data scientist's need for visualizing data is different from that of data engineers. Please note that in some businesses, there are professionals who play a dual role of data engineers and data scientists.

Data scientists need to visualize data to be able to take the right decisions in performing statistical analysis and ensure proper execution of the analytics projects. They would like to slice and dice data in various possible ways to find hidden insights. Let's take a look at some example requirements that a data scientist might have to visualize the data:

- See the data distribution of the individual variables
- Visualize outliers in the data
- Visualize the percentage of missing data in a dataset for all variables
- Plot the correlation matrix to find the correlated variables
- Plot the behavior of residuals after a regression
- After a data cleaning or transformation activity, plot the variable again and see how it behaves

Please note that some of the things just mentioned are quite similar to the case of data engineers. However, data scientists could have a more scientific/statistical intention behind such analyses. For example, data scientists may see an outlier from a different perspective and treat it statistically, but a data engineer might think of the various options that could have triggered this.

A business user's perspective

A business user's perspective is completely different from that of data engineers or data scientists. Business users are usually the consumers of information! They would like to extract more and more information from the data, and for that, the correct visuals play a key role. Also, most business questions are more complex and causal these days. The old-school reports are no longer enough. Let's look at some example queries that business users would like to extract from reports, visuals, and dashboards:

- Who are the high-value customers in so-and-so region?
- What are the common characteristics of these customers?
- Predict whether a new customer would be high-value
- Advertising in which media would give maximum ROI?
- What if I do not advertise in a newspaper?
- What are the factors influencing a customer's buying behavior?

Data visualization tools

Out of the many different visualization options, choosing the right visual depends on specific requirements. Similarly, selecting a visualization tool depends on both the target audience and the business requirement.

Data scientists or data engineers would prefer a more interactive console for quick and dirty analysis. The visuals they use are usually not intended for business users. They would like to dissect the data in every possible way to get more meaningful insights. So, they usually prefer a notebook-type interface that supports these activities. A notebook is an interactive computational environment where they can combine code chunks and plot data for explorations. There are notebooks such as **IPython/Jupyter** or **DataBricks**, to name a few available options.

Business users would prefer a more intuitive and informative visual that they can share with each other or use to generate reports. They expect to receive the end result through visuals. There are hundreds and thousands of tools, including some popular ones such as **Tableau**, that businesses use; but quite often, developers have to custom-build specific types for some unique requirements and expose them through web applications. Microsoft's **PowerBI** and open source solutions such as **Zeppelin** are a few examples.

IPython notebook

The IPython/Jupyter notebook on top of Spark's **PySpark** API is an excellent combination for data scientists to explore and visualize the data. The notebook internally spins up a new instance of the PySpark kernel. There are other kernels available; for example, the Apache **Toree** kernel can be used to support Scala as well.

For many data scientists, it is the default choice because of its capability of integrating text, code, formula, and graphics in one JSON document file. The IPython notebook supports `matplotlib`, which is a 2D visualization library that can produce production-quality visuals. Generating plots, histograms, scatterplots, charts, and so on becomes easy and simple. It also supports the `seaborn` library, which is actually built upon matplotlib but is easy to use as it provides higher level abstraction and hides the underlying complexities.

Apache Zeppelin

Apache Zeppelin is built upon JVM and integrates well with Apache Spark. It is a browser-based or frontend-based open source tool that has its own notebook. It supports Scala, Python, R, SQL, and other graphical modules to serve as a visualization solution not only to business users but also to data scientists. In the following section on visualization techniques, we will take a look at how Zeppelin supports Apache Spark code to generate interesting visuals. You need to download Zeppelin (`https://zeppelin.apache.org/`) in order to try out the examples.

Third-party tools

There are many products that support Apache Spark as the underlying data processing engine and are built to fit in the organizational big data ecosystem. While leveraging the processing power of Spark, they provide the visualization interface that supports a variety of interactive visuals, and they also support collaboration. Tableau is one such example of a tool that leverages Spark.

Data visualization techniques

Data visualization is at the center of every stage in the data analytics life cycle. It is especially important for exploratory analysis and for communicating results. In either case, the goal is to transform data into a format that's efficient for human consumption. The approach of delegating the transformation to client-side libraries does not scale to large datasets. The transformation has to happen on the server side, sending only the relevant data to the client for rendering. Most of the common transformations are available in Apache Spark out of the box. Let's have a closer look at these transformations.

Summarizing and visualizing

Summarizing and visualizing is a technique used by many **Business Intelligence (BI)** tools. Since summarization will be a concise dataset regardless of the size of the underlying dataset, the graphs look simple enough and easy to render. There are various ways to summarize the data such as aggregating, pivoting, and so on. If the rendering tool supports interactivity and has drill-down capabilities, the user gets to explore subsets of interest from the complete data. We will show how to do the summarization rapidly and interactively with Spark through the Zeppelin notebook.

The following image shows the Zeppelin notebook with source code and a grouped bar chart. The dataset contains 24 observations with sales information of two products, **P1** and **P2**, for 12 months. The first cell contains code to read a text file and register data as a temporary table. This cell uses the default Spark interpreter using Scala. The second cell uses the SQL interpreter which is supported by out-of-the-box visualization options. You can switch the chart types by clicking on the right icon. Note that the visualization is similar for either Scala or Python or R interpreters.

Summarization examples are as follows:

1. The source code to read data and register as a SQL View:

   Scala (default):

```
//Read data file                          FINISHED ▷ ╳ 韻 ◎
val sales = spark.read.options(Map(
    {"header"->"true"},{"inferSchema"->"true"})).
        csv("../data/MonthlySales.csv")
//Register data frame as a sql view
sales.createOrReplaceTempView("sales_tbl")

sales: org.apache.spark.sql.DataFrame = [Product: string, Month
: int ... 1 more field]
```
Took 0 sec. Last updated by anonymous at September 17 2016, 11:39:01 PM.

PySpark:

```
%pyspark                                  FINISHED ▷ ╳ 韻 ◎
#Read csv file with proper options
sales  = spark.read.csv("../data/MonthlySales.csv",
        inferSchema=True,header=True)
#Register data frame as a sql view
sales.createOrReplaceTempView("sales_tbl")
```
Took 1 sec. Last updated by anonymous at September 18 2016, 12:03:05 AM.

R:

```
%r                                        FINISHED ▷ ╳ 韻 ◎
#Read file and set column names
sales <- read.df("../data/MonthlySales.csv",source="csv")
colnames(sales) <- c("Product","Month","Sales")
#Remove header row
sales <- filter(sales,sales$Product!="Product")
#Register temporary view
createOrReplaceTempView(sales,"sales_tbl")
```
Took 0 sec. Last updated by anonymous at September 17 2016, 11:42:59 PM.

All three are reading the data file and registering as a temporary SQL view. Note that minor differences exist in the preceding three scripts. For example, we need to remove the header row for R and set the column names. The next step is to produce the visualization, which works from the %sql interpreter. The following first picture shows the script to produce the quarterly sales for each product. It also shows the chart types available out of the box, followed by the settings and their selection. You can collapse the settings after making selections. You can even make use of Zeppelin's in-built dynamic forms, say to accept a product during runtime. The second picture shows the actual output.

2. The script to produce quarterly sales for two products:

3. The output produced:

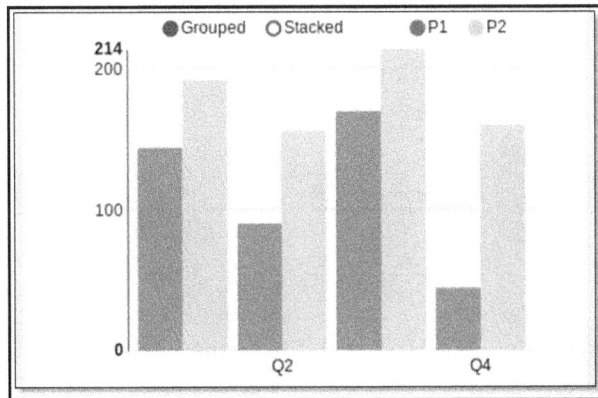

We have seen Zeppelin's inbuilt visualization in the preceding example. But we can use other plotting libraries as well. Our next example utilizes the PySpark interpreter with matplotlib in Zeppelin to draw a histogram. This example code computes bin intervals and bin counts using RDD's histogram function and brings in just this summarized data to the driver node. Frequency is provided as weights while plotting the bins to give the same visual understanding as a normal histogram but with very low data transfer.

The histogram examples are as follows:

```
%pyspark                                    FINISHED
import matplotlib.pyplot as plt
import pylab
import random

#Generate histogram bins and data counts using spark
numRDD = sc.parallelize([random.randint(1,100) for x in
                                       range(1,5000)])
histData = numRDD.histogram(10)
#plot the histogram
plt.clf()
plt.hist(histData[0][1:],10,weights=histData[1],
                facecolor="grey", rwidth=0.6)
pylab.show()

Took 4 sec. Last updated by anonymous at September 19 2016, 11:05:03 PM.
```

This is the generated output (it may come as a separate window):

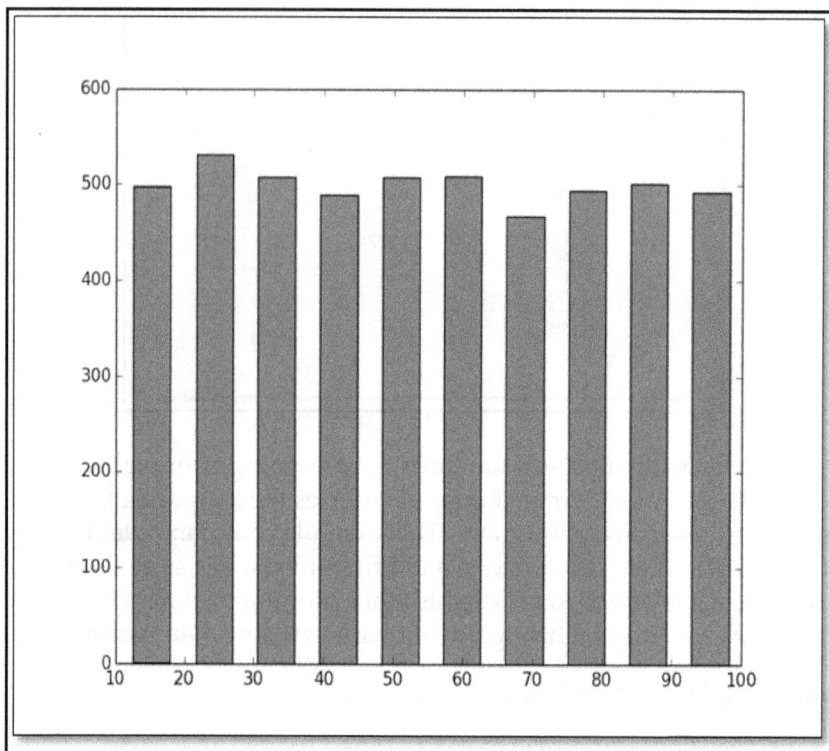

In the preceding example of preparing histograms, note that the bucket counts could be parameterized using the inbuilt dynamic forms support.

Subsetting and visualizing

Sometimes, we may have a large dataset but we may be interested only in a subset of it. Divide and conquer is one approach where we explore a small portion of data at a time. Spark allows data subsetting using SQL-like filters and aggregates on row-column datasets as well as graph data. Let us perform SQL subsetting first, followed by a GraphX example.

The following example takes bank data available with Zeppelin and extracts a few relevant columns of data related to managers only. It uses the `google visualization library` to plot a bubble chart. The data was read using PySpark. Data subsetting and visualization are carried out using R. Note that we can choose any of the interpreters to these tasks and the choice here was just arbitrary.

The data subsetting example using SQL is as follows:

1. Read data and register the SQL view:

```
%pyspark                                    FINISHED ▷ ⟨ 𝄙 ⚙

bank_data = spark.read.csv("../data/bank-full.csv",
        header=True, inferSchema=True, sep=";").select(
        "age","job", "marital","education","balance")
bank_data.createOrReplaceTempView("bank_tbl")

Took 0 sec. Last updated by anonymous at September 18 2016, 12:08:38 AM
```

2. Subset managers' data and show a bubble plot:

```
%r                                          FINISHED ▷ ⟨ 𝄙 ⚙
# Use google Visualization library
library(googleVis)
#Prepare data
managers <- as.data.frame(sql(sqlContext, paste(
    "select education, marital, avg(age) as age, ",
    " avg(balance) as balance, count(*) as freq ",
    "from bank_tbl where job= 'management' and marital !='divorced'",
    " and education != 'unknown' ",
    "group by education, marital")))

#Prepare chart
bubble <- gvisBubbleChart(managers, idvar="education",
                    xvar="age", yvar="balance",
                    colorvar="marital",sizevar="freq" )
#Show the plot
print(bubble, tag = 'chart')
```

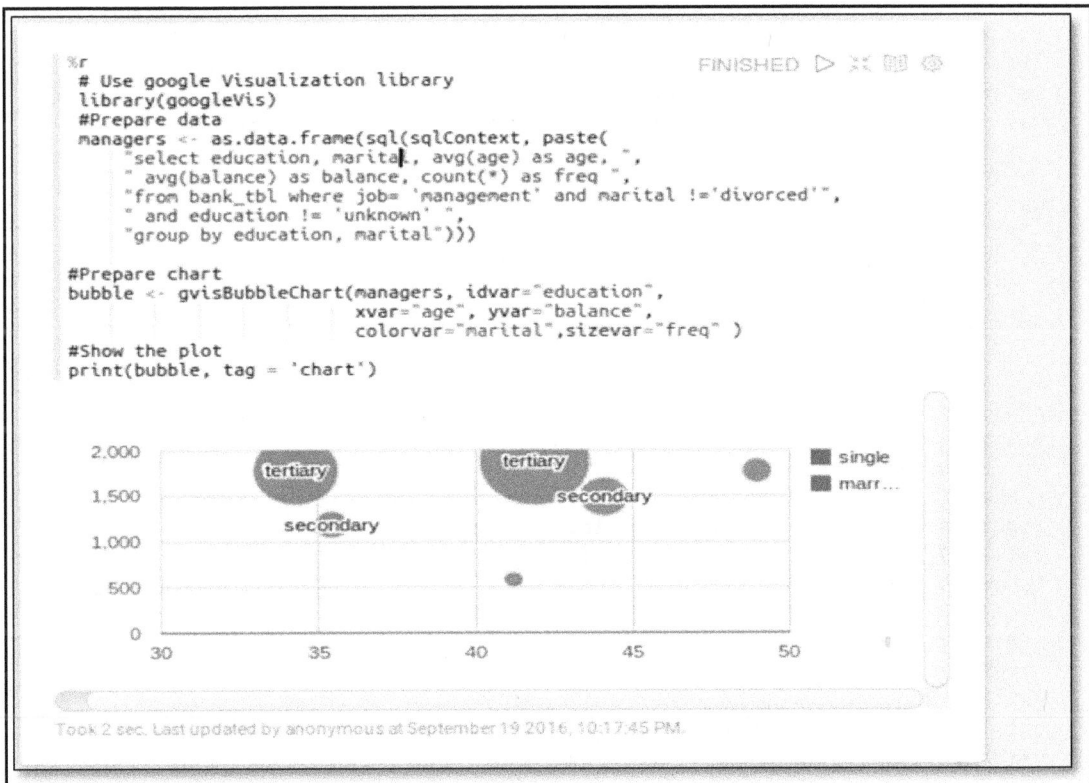

```
Took 2 sec. Last updated by anonymous at September 19 2016, 10:17:45 PM.
```

The next example demonstrates some GraphX processing that uses data provided by the **Stanford Network Analysis Project** (**SNAP**). The script extracts a subgraph covering a given set of nodes. Here, each node represents a Facebook ID and an edge represents a connection between the two nodes (or people). Further, the script identifies direct connections for a given node (id: 144). These are the level 1 nodes. Then it identifies the direct connections to these *level 1 nodes*, which form *level 2 nodes* to the given node. Even though a second-level contact may be connected to more than one first-level contact, it is shown only once thereby forming a connection tree without crisscrossing edges. Since the connection tree may have too many nodes, the script limits up to three connections at level 1 as well as level 2, thereby showing only 12 nodes under the given root node (one root + three level 1 nodes + three of each level 2 nodes).

Scala

```scala
//Subset and visualize
//GraphX subset example
//Datasource: http://snap.stanford.edu/data/egonets-Facebook.html
import org.apache.spark.graphx._
import org.apache.spark.graphx.util.GraphGenerators
//Load edge file and create base graph
val base_dir = "../data/facebook"
val graph = GraphLoader.edgeListFile(sc,base_dir + "/0.edges")

//Explore subgraph of a given set of nodes
val circle = "155  99  327  140  116  147  144  150  270".split("\t").map(
    x=> x.toInt)
val subgraph = graph.subgraph(vpred = (id,name)
    => circle.contains(id))
println("Edges: " + subgraph.edges.count +
    " Vertices: " + subgraph.vertices.count)
//Create a two level contact tree for a given node
//Step1: Get all edges for a given source id
val subgraph_level1 = graph.subgraph(epred= (ed) =>
    ed.srcId == 144)
//Step2: Extract Level 1 contacts
import scala.collection.mutable.ArrayBuffer
val lvl1_nodes : ArrayBuffer[Long] = ArrayBuffer()
subgraph_level1.edges.collect().foreach(x=> lvl1_nodes+= x.dstId)

//Step3: Extract Level 2 contacts, 3 each for 3 lvl1_nodes
import scala.collection.mutable.Map
val linkMap:Map[Long, ArrayBuffer[Long]] = Map() //parent,[Child]
val lvl2_nodes : ArrayBuffer[Long] = ArrayBuffer() //1D Array
var n : ArrayBuffer[Long] = ArrayBuffer()
for (i <- lvl1_nodes.take(3)) {     //Limit to 3
    n = ArrayBuffer()
```

```
    graph.subgraph(epred = (ed) => ed.srcId == i &&
        !(lvl2_nodes contains ed.dstId)).edges.collect().
            foreach(x=> n+=x.dstId)
    lvl2_nodes++=n.take(3)      //Append to 1D array. Limit to 3
  linkMap(i) = n.take(3)   //Assign child nodes to its parent
}
//Print output and examine the nodes
println("Level1 nodes :" + lvl1_nodes)
println("Level2 nodes :" + lvl2_nodes)
println("Link map :" + linkMap)
//Copy headNode to access from another cell
z.put("headNode",144)
//Make a DataFrame out of lvl2_nodes and register as a view
val nodeDF = sc.parallelize(linkMap.toSeq).toDF("parentNode","childNodes")
nodeDF.createOrReplaceTempView("node_tbl")
```

> Note the use of z.put and z.get. This is a mechanism to exchange data between cells/interpreters in Zeppelin.

Now that we have created a data frame with level 1 contacts and their direct contacts, we are all set to draw the tree. The following script uses the graph visualization library igraph and Spark R.

Extract nodes and edges. Plot the tree:

```r
%r                                      FINISHED ▷ ∷ ▦ ⊚
library(igraph)
headNode <- z.get("headNode")

#Create vertex array for level 1 nodes from the nodes_list
lvl1_nodes <- collect(sql("SELECT parentNode FROM node_tbl"))
edges1 <- c(rbind(headNode,lvl1_nodes[,1]))

#Explode childNodes to form one row per list element
#Create vertex array from these elements
lvl2_nodes <- collect(sql(paste(
                "SELECT parentNode, explode(childNodes) ",
                "childNode FROM node_tbl")))

#Get the vertices in desired order
edges2 <- as.numeric(paste(t(lvl2_nodes)))
edges <- c(edges1, edges2)

#Prepare graph and plot
g<-graph(edges, n=max(edges), directed=FALSE)
plot(g,layout=layout_as_tree(g,root=headNode))
```

The preceding script gets parent nodes from the nodes table, which are the parents of level 2 nodes as well as direct connections to the given head node. Ordered pairs of head nodes and level 1 nodes are created and assigned to `edges1`. The next step explodes the array of level 2 nodes to form one row per each array element. The data frame thus obtained is transposed and pasted to form edge pairs. Since paste converts data into strings, they are reconverted to numeric. These are the level 2 edges. The level 1 and level 2 edges are concatenated to form a single list of edges. These are fed to form the graph as shown next. Note that the smudge in `headNode` is 144, though not visible in the following figure:

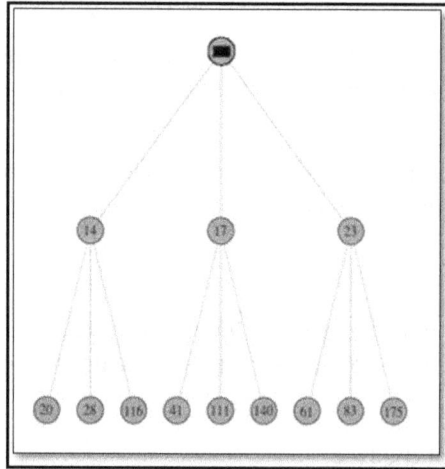

Connection tree for the given node

Sampling and visualizing

Sampling and visualizing has been used by statisticians for a long time. Through sampling techniques, we take a portion of the dataset and work on it. We will show how Spark supports different sampling techniques such as **random sampling, stratified sampling**, and **sampleByKey**, and so on. The following example is created using the Jupyter notebook, PySpark kernel, and `seaborn` library. The data file is the bank dataset provided by Zeppelin. The first plot shows the balance for each education category. The colors indicate marital status.

Read data and take a random sample of 5%:

```
In [177]:  bank_data = sqlContext.read.csv("bank-full.csv",
                       sep=";",header=True,inferSchema=True).select(
              "job","marital","education","balance").where(
              "education!='unknown'")
           #Get 5% random sample data
           sampled_data = bank_data.sample(withReplacement=False,
                       fraction = 0.05, seed=1000).toPandas()
```

Render data using `stripplot`:

```
In [185]:  import seaborn as sns
           sns.set_style("whitegrid")
           ax = sns.stripplot(x="education",y="balance",
                   hue="marital",data=sampled_data,jitter=True)
```

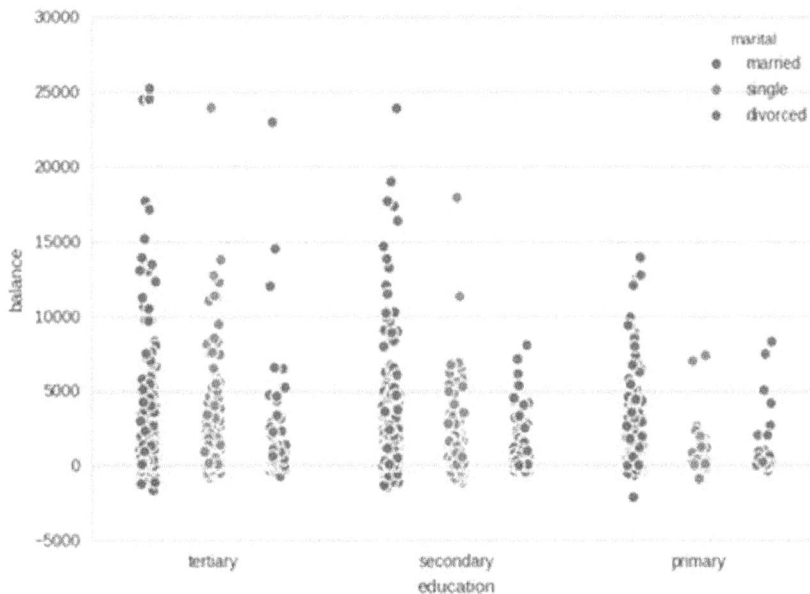

The preceding example showed a random sample of available data, which is much better than completely plotting the population. But if the levels in the categorical variable of interest (in this case, education) are too many, then this plot becomes hard to read. For example, if we want to plot the balance for job instead of education, there will be too many strips, making the picture look cluttered. Instead, we can take desired sample of desired categorical levels only and then examine the data. Note that this is different from subsetting because we will not be able to specify the sample ratio in normal subsetting using SQL WHERE clauses. We need to use sampleByKey for that, as shown next. The following example takes only two jobs and with specific sampling ratios:

```
In [189]: #Stratified sampling
          data_by_key = bank_data.sampleBy("job",
              fractions={'services':0.2,'management': 0.2},
              seed=100).toPandas()
          import seaborn as sns
          ax = sns.stripplot(x="job",y="balance",
                  hue="marital",data=data_by_key,jitter=True)
```

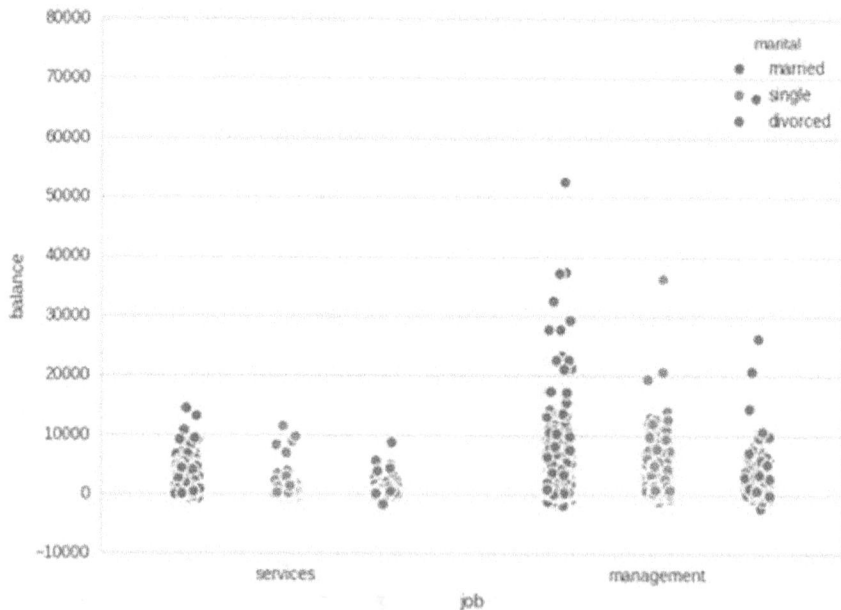

Stratified sampling

Modeling and visualizing

Modeling and visualizing are possible with Spark's **MLLib** and **ML** modules. Spark's unified programming model and diverse programming interfaces enable combining these techniques into a single environment to get insights from the data. We have already covered most of the modeling techniques in the previous chapters. However, here are a few examples for your reference:

- **Clustering**: K-means, Gaussian Mixture Modeling
- **Classification and regression**: Linear model, Decision tree, Naïve Bayes, SVM
- **Dimensionality reduction**: Singular value decomposition, Principal component analysis
- **Collaborative Filtering**
- **Statistical testing**: Correlations, Hypothesis testing

The following example takes a model from the Chapter 7, *Extending Spark with SparkR*, which tries to predict the students' pass or fail results using a Naïve Bayes model. The idea is to make use of the out-of-the-box functionality provided by Zeppelin and inspect the model behavior. So, we load the data, perform data preparation, build the model, and run the predictions. Then we register the predictions as an SQL view so as to harness inbuilt visualization:

```
//Model visualization example using zeppelin visualization
  Prepare Model and predictions
```

```
%r                                                              FINISHED ▷ ⊠ ▦ ⊙
#Read data file and set column
#Data file consists of 20 students, thier marks,attendance and Pass/Fail Result
df <- read.df("../data/StudentsPassFail.csv",source="csv")
colnames(df) <- c("Student_Id","Avg_Marks","Attendance","Result")

#Convert marks to 3 grades A, B and C
df$marks_bkt <- otherwise(when(df$Avg_marks < 40, "C"),
                          when(df$Avg_marks > 60, "A"))
df <- fillna(df,"B",cols="marks_bkt")
#Build naive Bayes model
model <- spark.naiveBayes(Result ~ Attendance + marks_bkt, data = df)
#Run predictions
predictions <- predict(model, newData= df)

#Register temporary view
createOrReplaceTempView(predictions,"predictions_tbl")

Took 3 sec. Last updated by anonymous at September 19 2016, 11:05:04 AM
```

The next step is to write the desired SQL query and define the appropriate settings. Note the use of the UNION operator in SQL and the way the match column is defined.

Define SQL to view model performance:

```
%sql                                                    FINISHED  ▷  ⋊  ▣  ⚙

SELECT student_id, attendance,  marks_bkt, "Match" as match from predictions_tbl
WHERE Result == prediction
UNION
SELECT student_id,attendance, marks_bkt, "Mismatch" as match from predictions_tbl
WHERE Result != prediction
ORDER BY student_id
```

| ⊞ | ∎ | ◐ | ◪ | ◥ | ◺ | | ⬇ ▾ settings ▲

All fields:

| student_id | attendance | marks_bkt | match |

Keys   Groups   Values

attendance ✖   match ✖   student_id COUNT ✖

marks_bkt ✖

The following picture helps us understand where the model prediction deviates from the actual data. Such visualizations are helpful in taking business users' inputs since they do not require any prior knowledge of data science to comprehend:

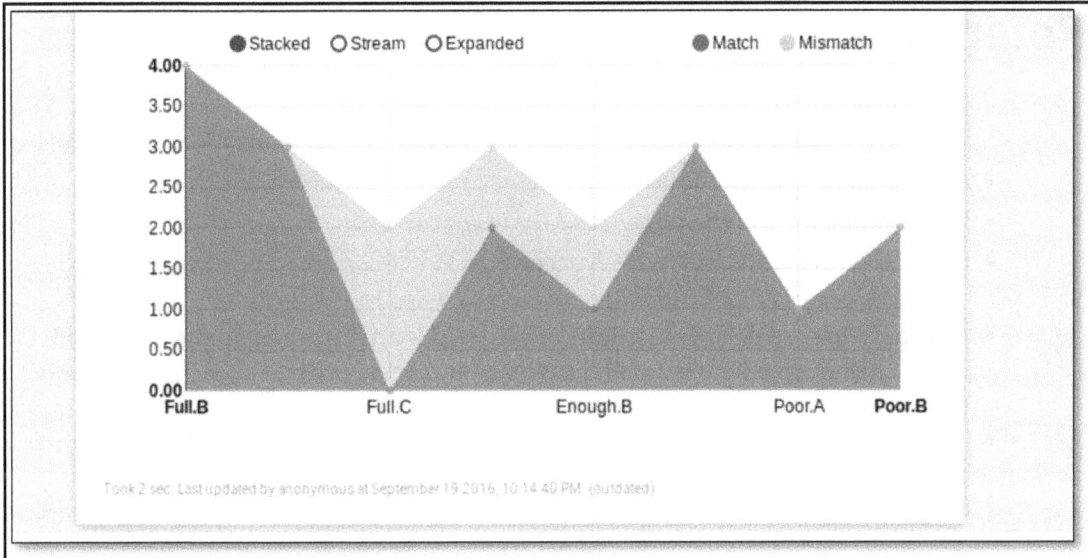

Visualize model performance

We usually evaluate statistical models with error metrics, but visualizing them graphically instead of seeing the numbers makes them more intuitive because it is usually easier to understand a diagram than numbers in a table. For example, the preceding visualization can be easily understood by people outside the data science community as well.

Summary

In this chapter, we explored most of the widely used visualization tools and techniques supported on Spark in a big data setup. We explained some of the techniques with code snippets for better understanding of visualization needs at different stages of the data analytics life cycle. We also saw how business requirements are satisfied with proper visualization techniques by addressing the challenges of big data.

The next chapter is the culmination of all the concepts explained till now . We will walk through the Complete Data Analysis Life Cycle through an example dataset.

References

- 21 Essential Data Visualization Tools:
  http://www.kdnuggets.com/2015/05/21-essential-data-visualization-tools.html
- Apache Zeppelin notebook home page: `https://zeppelin.apache.org/`
- Jupyter notebook home page: `https://jupyter.org/`
- Using IPython Notebook with Apache Spark: `http://hortonworks.com/hadoop-tutorial/using-ipython-notebook-with-apache-spark/`
- Apache Toree, which enables interactive workloads between applications and Spark cluster. Can be used with jupyter to run Scala code: `https://toree.incubator.apache.org/`
- GoogleVis package using R: `https://cran.rproject.org/web/packages/googleVis/vignettes/googleVis_examples.html`
- GraphX Programming Guide: `http://spark.apache.org/docs/latest/graphx-programming-guide.html`
- Going viral with R's igraph package: `https://www.r-bloggers.com/going-viral-with-rs-igraph-package/`
- Plotting with categorical data: `https://stanford.edu/~mwaskom/software/seaborn/tutorial/categorical.html#categorical-tutorial`

Data source citations

Bank data source (citation)

- [Moro et al., 2011] S. Moro, R. Laureano and P. Cortez. Using Data Mining for Bank Direct Marketing: An Application of the CRISP-DM Methodology
- In P. Novais et al. (Eds.), Proceedings of the European Simulation and Modelling Conference – ESM'2011, pp. 117-121, Guimarães, Portugal, October, 2011. EUROSIS
- Available at [pdf] `http://hdl.handle.net/1822/14838`
- [bib] http://www3.dsi.uminho.pt/pcortez/bib/2011-esm-1.txt

Facebook data Source (citation)

- J. McAuley and J. Leskovec. Learning to Discover Social Circles in Ego Networks. NIPS, 2012.

10
Putting It All Together

Big data analytics is revolutionizing the way businesses are run and has paved the way for several hitherto unimagined opportunities. Almost every enterprise, individual researcher, or investigative journalist has lots of data to process. We need a concise approach to start from raw data and arrive at meaningful insights based on the questions at hand.

We have covered various aspects of data science using Apache Spark in previous chapters. We started off discussing big data analytics requirements and how Apache spark fits in. Gradually, we looked into the Spark programming model, RDDs, and DataFrame abstractions and learnt how unified data access is enabled by Spark datasets along with the streaming aspect of continuous applications. Then we covered the entire breadth of the data analysis life cycle using Apache Spark followed by machine learning. We learnt structured and unstructured data analytics on Spark and explored the visualization aspects for data engineers and scientists, as well as business users.

All the previously discussed chapters helped us understand one concise aspect per chapter. We are now equipped to traverse the entire data science life cycle. In this chapter, we shall take up an end-to-end case study and apply all that we have learned so far. We will not introduce any new concepts; this will help apply the knowledge gained so far and strengthen our understanding. However, we have reiterated some concepts without going into too much detail, to make this chapter self-contained. The topics covered in this chapter are roughly the same as the steps in the data analytics life cycle:

- A quick recap
- Introducing a case study
- Framing the business problem
- Data acquisition and data cleansing
- Developing the hypothesis
- Data exploration

- Data preparation
- Model building
- Data visualization
- Communicating the results to business users
- Summary

A quick recap

We already discussed in detail the various steps involved in a typical data science project separately in different chapters. Let us quickly glance through what we have covered already and touch upon some important aspects. A high-level overview of the steps involved may appear as in the following figure:

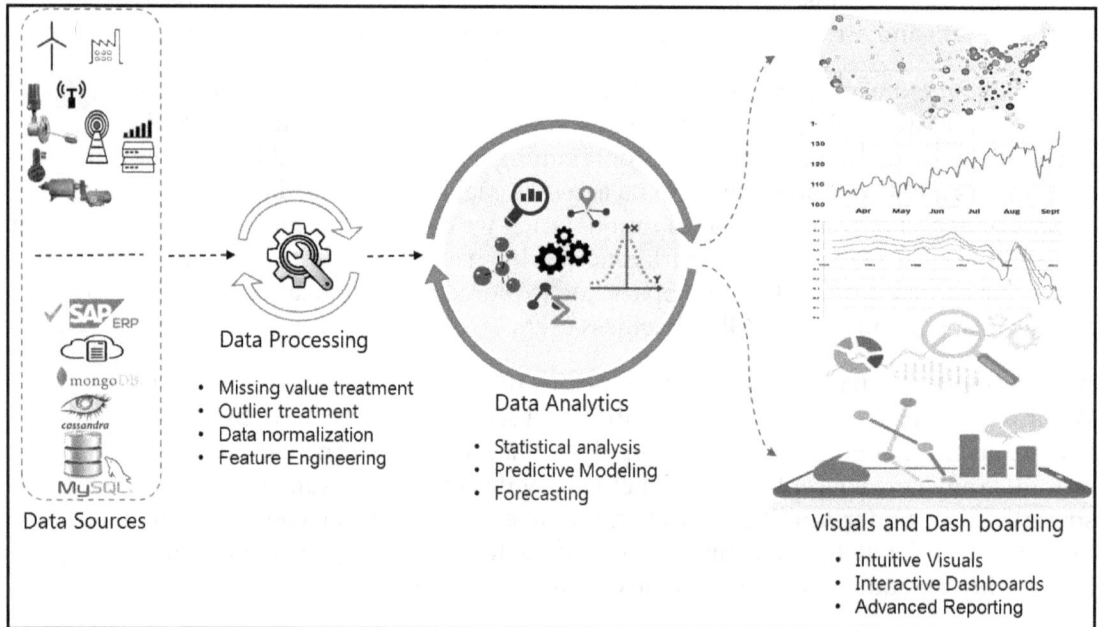

In the preceding pictorial representation, we have tried to explain the steps involved in a data science project at a higher level, mostly generic to many data science assignments. Many more substeps are actually present at every stage, but may differ from project to project.

It is very difficult for data scientists to find the best approach and steps to follow in the beginning. Generally, data science projects do not have a well-defined life cycle such as the **Software Development Life Cycle** (**SDLC**). It is usually the case that data science projects get tramped into delivery delays with repeated hold-ups, as most of the steps in the life cycle are iterative. Also, there could be cyclic dependencies across teams that add to the complexity and cause delay in execution. However, while working on big data analytics projects, it is important as well as advantageous for data scientists to follow a well-defined data science workflow, irrespective of different business cases. This not only helps in an organized execution, but also helps us stay focused on the objective, as data science projects are inherently agile in most cases. Also, it is recommended that you plan for some level of research on data, domain, and algorithms for any given project.

In this chapter, we may not be able to accommodate all the granular steps in a single flow, but will address the important areas to give you a heads-up. We will try to look at some different coding examples that we have not covered in the previous chapters.

Introducing a case study

We will be exploring Academy Awards demographics in this chapter. You can download the data from the GitHub repository at https://www.crowdflower.com/wp-content/uploads/2016/03/Oscars-demographics-DFE.csv.

This dataset is based on the data provided at `http://www.crowdflower.com/data-for-everyone`. It contains demographic details such as race, birthplace, and age. Rows are around 400 and it can be easily processed on a simple home computer, so you can do a **Proof of Concept** (**POC**) on executing a data science project on Spark.

Just start by downloading the file and inspecting the data. The data may look fine but as you take a closer look, you will notice that it is not "clean". For example, the date of birth column does not follow the same format. Some years are in two-digit format whereas some are in four-digit format. Birthplace does not have country for locations within the USA.

Likewise, you will also notice that the data looks skewed, with more "white" race people from the USA. But you might have felt that the trend has changed toward later years. You have not used any tools or techniques so far, just had a quick glance at the data. In the real world of data science, this seemingly trivial activity can be quite helpful further down the life cycle. You get to develop a feel for the data at hand and simultaneously hypothesize about the data. This brings you to the very first step in the workflow.

The business problem

As iterated before, the most important aspect of any data science project is the question at hand. Having a clear understanding on *what problem are we trying to solve?* This is critical to the success of the project. It also drives what is considered as relevant data and what is not. For example, in the current case study, if what we want to look at is the demographics, then movie name and person name are irrelevant. At times, there is no specific question at hand! *What then?* Even when there is no specific question, the business may still have some objective, or data scientists and domain experts can work together to find the area of business to work on. To understand the business, functions, problem statement, or data, the data scientists start with "Questioning". It not only helps in defining the workflow, but helps in sourcing the right data to work on.

As an example, if the business focus is on demographics information, a formal business problem statement can be defined as:

What is the impact of the race and country of origin among Oscar award winners?

In real-world, scenarios this step will not be this straightforward. Framing the right question is the collective responsibility of the data scientist, strategy team, domain experts, and the project owner. Since the whole exercise is futile if it does not serve the purpose, a data scientist has to consult all stakeholders and try to elicit as much information as possible from them. However, they may end up getting invaluable insights or "hunches". All of these combined form the core of the initial hypothesis and also help the data scientist to understand what exactly they should look for.

The situations where there is no specific question at hand that the business is trying to find an answer for are even more interesting to deal with, but can be complex in executing!

Data acquisition and data cleansing

Data acquisition is the logical next step. It may be as simple as selecting data from a single spreadsheet or it may be an elaborate several months project in itself. A data scientist has to collect as much relevant data as possible. 'Relevant' is the keyword here. Remember, more relevant data beats clever algorithms.

We have already covered how to source data from heterogeneous data sources and consolidate it to form a single data matrix, so we will not iterate the same fundamentals here. Instead, we source our data from a single source and extract a subset of it.

Now it is time to view the data and start cleansing it. The scripts presented in this chapter tend to be longer than the previous examples but still are no means of production quality. Real-world work requires a lot more exception checks and performance tuning:

Scala

```
//Load tab delimited file
scala> val fp = "<YourPath>/Oscars.txt"
scala> val init_data = spark.read.options(Map("header"->"true", "sep" ->
"\t","inferSchema"->"true")).csv(fp)
//Select columns of interest and ignore the rest
>>> val awards = init_data.select("birthplace", "date_of_birth",
        "race_ethnicity","year_of_award","award").toDF(
        "birthplace","date_of_birth","race","award_year","award")
awards: org.apache.spark.sql.DataFrame = [birthplace: string,
date_of_birth: string ... 3 more fields]
//register temporary view of this dataset
scala> awards.createOrReplaceTempView("awards")

//Explore data
>>> awards.select("award").distinct().show(10,false) //False => do not
truncate
+----------------------+
|award                 |
+----------------------+
|Best Supporting Actress|
|Best Director         |
|Best Actress          |
|Best Actor            |
|Best Supporting Actor |
+----------------------+
//Check DOB quality. Note that length varies based on month name
scala> spark.sql("SELECT distinct(length(date_of_birth)) FROM awards
").show()
+--------------------+
|length(date_of_birth)|
+--------------------+
|                  15|
|                   9|
|                   4|
|                   8|
|                  10|
|                  11|
+--------------------+

//Look at the value with unexpected length 4 Why cant we show values for
each of the length type ?
scala> spark.sql("SELECT date_of_birth FROM awards WHERE
```

```
length(date_of_birth) = 4").show()
+-------------+
|date_of_birth|
+-------------+
|         1972|
+-------------+
//This is an invalid date. We can either drop this record or give some
meaningful value like 01-01-1972
```

Python

```
    //Load tab delimited file
    >>> init_data =
spark.read.csv("<YOURPATH>/Oscars.txt",sep="\t",header=True)
    //Select columns of interest and ignore the rest
    >>> awards = init_data.select("birthplace", "date_of_birth",
            "race_ethnicity","year_of_award","award").toDF(
            "birthplace","date_of_birth","race","award_year","award")
    //register temporary view of this dataset
    >>> awards.createOrReplaceTempView("awards")
    scala>
    //Explore data
    >>> awards.select("award").distinct().show(10,False) //False => do not
truncate
    +----------------------+
    |award                 |
    +----------------------+
    |Best Supporting Actress|
    |Best Director         |
    |Best Actress          |
    |Best Actor            |
    |Best Supporting Actor |
    +----------------------+
    //Check DOB quality
    >>> spark.sql("SELECT distinct(length(date_of_birth)) FROM awards
").show()
    +--------------------+
    |length(date_of_birth)|
    +--------------------+
    |                  15|
    |                   9|
    |                   4|
    |                   8|
    |                  10|
    |                  11|
    +--------------------+
    //Look at the value with unexpected length 4. Note that length varies
based on month name
```

```
    >>> spark.sql("SELECT date_of_birth FROM awards WHERE
length(date_of_birth) = 4").show()
    +-------------+
    |date_of_birth|
    +-------------+
    |         1972|
    +-------------+
    //This is an invalid date. We can either drop this record or give some
meaningful value like 01-01-1972
```

The preceding code snippet downloads a tab-separated text file, loads the desired columns into a DataFrame, and registers a temporary table. The rest of the code is very similar to basic SQL statements that just explored data.

Most of the datasets contain a `date` field and unless they come from a single, controlled data source, it is highly likely that they will differ in their formats and are almost always a candidate for cleaning.

For the dataset at hand, you might also have noticed that `date_of_birth` and `birthplace` require a lot of cleaning. The following code shows two **user-defined functions** (**UDFs**) that clean `date_of_birth` and `birthplace` respectively. These UDFs work on a single data element at a time and they are just ordinary Scala/Python functions. These user defined functions should be registered so that they can be used from within a SQL statement. The final step is to create a cleaned data frame that will participate in further analysis.

Notice the following logic for cleaning `birthplace`. It is a weak logic because we are assuming that any string ending with two characters is an American state. We have to compare them against a list of valid abbreviations. Similarly, assuming two-digit years are always from the twentieth century is another error-prone assumption. Depending on the use case, a data scientist/data engineer has to take a call whether retaining more rows is important or only quality data should be included. All such decisions should be neatly documented for reference:

Scala:

```
//UDF to clean date
//This function takes 2 digit year and makes it 4 digit
// Any exception returns an empty string
scala> def fncleanDate(s:String) : String = {
  var cleanedDate = ""
  val dateArray: Array[String] = s.split("-")
  try{    //Adjust year
    var yr = dateArray(2).toInt
    if (yr < 100) {yr = yr + 1900 } //make it 4 digit
```

```
    cleanedDate = "%02d-%s-%04d".format(dateArray(0).toInt,
              dateArray(1),yr)
    } catch { case e: Exception => None }
    cleanedDate }
fncleanDate: (s: String)String
```

Python:

```
    //This function takes 2 digit year and makes it 4 digit
    // Any exception returns an empty string
    >>> def fncleanDate(s):
        cleanedDate = ""
        dateArray = s.split("-")
        try:    //Adjust year
          yr = int(dateArray[2])
          if (yr < 100):
              yr = yr + 1900 //make it 4 digit
          cleanedDate = "{0}-{1}-{2}".format(int(dateArray[0]),
              dateArray[1],yr)
        except :
          None
        return cleanedDate
```

The UDF to clean date accepts a hyphenated date string and splits it. If the last component, which is the year, is two digits long, then it is assumed to be a twentieth-century date and 1900 is added to bring it to four-digit format.

The following UDF appends the country as USA if the country string is either New York City or the last component is two characters long, where it is assumed to be a state in the USA:

```
//UDF to clean birthplace
// Data explorartion showed that
// A. Country is omitted for USA
// B. New York City does not have State code as well
//This function appends country as USA if
// A. the string contains New York City  (OR)
// B. if the last component is of length 2 (eg CA, MA)
scala> def fncleanBirthplace(s: String) : String = {
        var cleanedBirthplace = ""
        var strArray : Array[String] =  s.split(" ")
        if (s == "New York City")
           strArray = strArray ++ Array ("USA")
        //Append country if last element length is 2
        else if (strArray(strArray.length-1).length == 2)
           strArray = strArray ++ Array("USA")
        cleanedBirthplace = strArray.mkString(" ")
        cleanedBirthplace }
```

Python:

```
>>> def fncleanBirthplace(s):
        cleanedBirthplace = ""
        strArray = s.split(" ")
        if (s == "New York City"):
            strArray += ["USA"]  //Append USA
        //Append country if last element length is 2
        elif (len(strArray[len(strArray)-1]) == 2):
            strArray += ["USA"]
        cleanedBirthplace = " ".join(strArray)
        return cleanedBirthplace
```

The UDFs should be registered if you want to access them from SELECT strings:

Scala:

```
//Register UDFs
scala> spark.udf.register("fncleanDate",fncleanDate(_:String))
res10: org.apache.spark.sql.expressions.UserDefinedFunction =
UserDefinedFunction(<function1>,StringType,Some(List(StringType)))
scala> spark.udf.register("fncleanBirthplace", fncleanBirthplace(_:String))
res11: org.apache.spark.sql.expressions.UserDefinedFunction =
UserDefinedFunction(<function1>,StringType,Some(List(StringType)))
```

Python:

```
>>> from pyspark.sql.types import StringType
>>> sqlContext.registerFunction("cleanDateUDF",fncleanDate,
StringType())
>>> sqlContext.registerFunction(
"cleanBirthplaceUDF",fncleanBirthplace, StringType())
```

Clean the data frame using the UDFs. Perform the following cleanup operations:

1. Call UDFs `fncleanDate` and `fncleanBirthplace` to fix birthplace and country.
2. Subtract birth year from `award_year` to get `age` at the time of receiving the award.
3. Retain `race` and `award` as they are.

Scala:

```
//Create cleaned data frame
scala> var cleaned_df = spark.sql (
        """SELECT fncleanDate (date_of_birth) dob,
            fncleanBirthplace(birthplace) birthplace,
            substring_index(fncleanBirthplace(birthplace),' ',-1)
```

```
                            country,
                (award_year - substring_index(fncleanDate( date_of_birth),'-
',-1)) age, race, award FROM awards""")
cleaned_df: org.apache.spark.sql.DataFrame = [dob: string, birthplace:
string ... 4 more fields]
```

Python:

```
//Create cleaned data frame
>>> from pyspark.sql.functions import substring_index>>> cleaned_df =
spark.sql (           """SELECT cleanDateUDF (date_of_birth) dob,
cleanBirthplaceUDF(birthplace) birthplace,
substring_index(cleanBirthplaceUDF(birthplace),' ',-1) country,
(award_year - substring_index(cleanDateUDF( date_of_birth),
'-',-1)) age, race, award FROM awards""")
```

The last line requires some explanation. The UDFs are used similar to SQL functions and the expressions are aliased to meaningful names. We have added a computed column `age` because we would like to validate the impact of age also. The `substring_index` function searches the first argument for the second argument. `-1` indicates to look for the first occurrence from the right.

Developing the hypothesis

A hypothesis is your best guess about what the outcome will be. You form your initial hypothesis based on the question, conversations with stakeholders, and also by looking at the data. You may form one or more hypotheses for a given problem. This initial hypothesis serves as a roadmap that guides you through the exploratory analysis. Developing a hypothesis is very important to statistically approve or not approve a statement, and not just by looking at the data as a data matrix or even through visuals. This is because our perception built by just looking at the data may be incorrect and rather deceptive at times.

Now you know that your final result may or may not prove the hypothesis to be correct. Coming to the case study we have considered for this lesson, we arrive at the following initial hypotheses:

- Award winners are mostly white
- Most of the award winners are from the USA
- Best actors and actresses tend to be younger than best directors

Now that we have formalized our hypotheses, we are all set to move forward with the next steps in the life cycle..

Data exploration

Now that we have a clean data frame with relevant data and the initial hypothesis, it is time to really explore what we have. The DataFrames abstraction provides functions such as `group by` out of the box for you to look around. You may register the cleaned data frame as a table and run the time-tested SQL statements to do just the same.

This is also the time to plot a few graphs. This phase of visualization is the exploratory analysis mentioned in the data visualization chapter. The objectives of this exploration are greatly influenced by the initial information you garner from the business stakeholders and the hypothesis. In other words, your discussions with the stakeholders help you know what to look for.

There are some general guidelines that are applicable for almost all data science assignments, but again subjective to different use cases. Let us look at some generic ones:

- Look for missing data and treat it. We have already discussed various ways to do this in `Chapter 5`, *Data Analysis on Spark*.
- Find the outliers in the dataset and treat them. We have discussed this aspect as well. Please note that there are cases where what we think of as outliers and normal data points may change depending on the use case.
- Perform univariate analysis, wherein you explore each variable in the dataset separately. Frequency distribution or percentile distribution are quite common. Perhaps plot some graphs to get a better idea. This will also help you prepare your data before getting into data modeling.
- Validate your initial hypothesis.
- Check minimum and maximum values of numerical data. If the variation is too high in any column, that could be a candidate for data normalization or scaling.

- Check distinct values in categorical data (string values such as city names) and their frequencies. If there are too many distinct values (aka levels) in any column, you may have to look for ways to reduce the number of levels. If one level is occurring almost always, then this column is not helping the model to differentiate between the possible outcomes. Such columns are likely candidates for removal. At the exploration stage, you just figure out such candidate columns and let the data preparation phase take care of the actual action.

In our current dataset, we do not have any missing data and we do not have any numerical data that might create any challenge. However, some missing values might creep in when invalid dates are processed. So, the following code covers the remaining action items. This code assumes that `cleaned_df` is already created:

Scala/Python:

```
cleaned_df = cleaned_df.na.drop //Drop rows with missing values
cleaned_df.groupBy("award","country").count().sort("country","award","count
").show(4,False)
+--------------------+---------+-----+
|award               |country  |count|
+--------------------+---------+-----+
|Best Actor          |Australia|1    |
|Best Actress        |Australia|1    |
|Best Supporting Actor   |Australia|1    |
|Best Supporting Actress|Australia|1    |
+--------------------+---------+-----+
//Re-register data as table
cleaned_df.createOrReplaceTempView("awards")
//Find out levels (distinct values) in each categorical variable
spark.sql("SELECT count(distinct country) country_count, count(distinct
race) race_count, count(distinct award) award_count from awards").show()
+-------------+----------+-----------+
|country_count|race_count|award_count|
+-------------+----------+-----------+
|           34|         6|          5|
+-------------+----------+-----------+
```

The following visualizations correspond to the initial hypotheses. Note that two of our hypotheses were found to be correct but the third one was not. These visualizations are created using zeppelin:

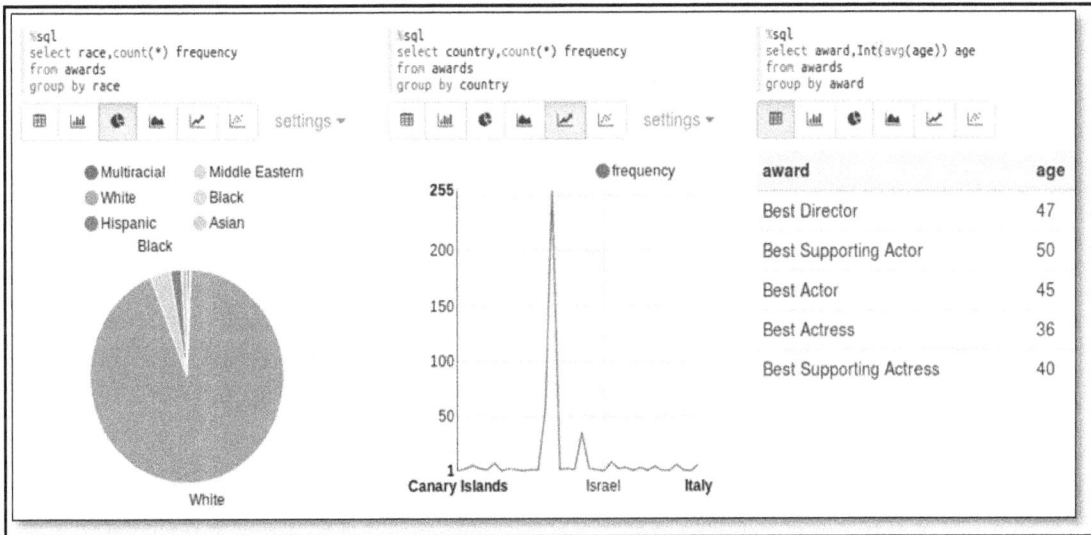

Note here that the all hypotheses cannot just be validated through visuals, as they can be deceptive at times. So proper statistical tests such as t-tests, ANOVA, Chi-squared tests, correlation tests, and so on need to be performed as applicable. We will not get into the details in this section. Please refer to Chapter 5, *Data Analysis on Spark*, for further details.

Data preparation

The data exploration stage helped us identify all the issues that needed to be fixed before proceeding to the modeling stage. Each individual issue requires careful thought and deliberation to choose the best fix. Here are some common issues and the possible fixes. The best fix is dependent on the problem at hand and/or the business context.

Too many levels in a categorical variable

This is one of the most common issues we face. The treatment of this issue is dependent on multiple factors:

- If the column is almost always unique, for example, it is a transaction ID or timestamp, then it does not participate in modeling unless you are deriving new features from it. You may safely drop the column without losing any information content. You usually drop it during the data cleansing stage itself.
- If it is possible to replace the levels with coarser-grained levels (for example, state or country instead of city) that make sense in the current context, then usually that is the best way to fix this issue.
- You may want to add dummy columns with 0 or 1 values for each distinct level. For example, if you have 100 levels in a single column, you add 100 columns instead. At most, one column will have 1 at any observation (row). This is called **one-hot encoding** and Spark provides this out of the box through the `ml.features` package.
- Another option is to retain the most frequent levels. You may even attach each of these levels to one of the dominant levels that is somehow considered "nearer" to this level. Also, you may bundle up the remaining into a single bucket, say, `Others`.
- There is no hard and fast rule for an absolute limit to the number of levels. It depends on what granularity you require in each individual feature and the performance constraints.

The current dataset has too many levels in the categorical variable `country`. We chose to retain the most frequent levels and bundle the remaining into `Others`:

Scala:

```
//Country has too many values. Retain top ones and bundle the rest
//Check out top 6 countries with most awards.
scala> val top_countries_df = spark.sql("SELECT country, count(*) freq FROM
awards GROUP BY country ORDER BY freq DESC LIMIT 6")
top_countries_df: org.apache.spark.sql.DataFrame = [country: string, freq:
bigint]
scala> top_countries_df.show()
+-------+----+
|country|freq|
+-------+----+
|    USA| 289|
|England|  57|
| France|   9|
```

```
| Canada|    8|
|  Italy|    7|
|Austria|    7|
+-------+----+
//Prepare top_countries list
scala> val top_countries =
top_countries_df.select("country").collect().map(x => x(0).toString)
top_countries: Array[String] = Array(USA, England, New York City, France,
Canada, Italy)
//UDF to fix country. Retain top 6 and bundle the rest into "Others"
scala> import org.apache.spark.sql.functions.udf
import org.apache.spark.sql.functions.udf
scala > val setCountry = udf ((s: String) =>
        { if (top_countries.contains(s)) {s} else {"Others"}})
setCountry: org.apache.spark.sql.expressions.UserDefinedFunction =
UserDefinedFunction(<function1>,StringType,Some(List(StringType)))
//Apply udf to overwrite country
scala> cleaned_df = cleaned_df.withColumn("country",
setCountry(cleaned_df("country")))
cleaned_df: org.apache.spark.sql.DataFrame = [dob: string, birthplace:
string ... 4 more fields]
```

Python:

```
//Check out top 6 countries with most awards.
>>> top_countries_df = spark.sql("SELECT country, count(*) freq FROM
awards GROUP BY country ORDER BY freq DESC LIMIT 6")
>>> top_countries_df.show()
+-------+----+
|country|freq|
+-------+----+
|    USA| 289|
|England|  57|
| France|   9|
| Canada|   8|
|  Italy|   7|
|Austria|   7|
+-------+----+
>>> top_countries = [x[0] for x in
top_countries_df.select("country").collect()]
//UDF to fix country. Retain top 6 and bundle the rest into "Others"
>>> from pyspark.sql.functions import udf
>>> from pyspark.sql.types import StringType
>>> setCountry = udf(lambda s: s if s in top_countries else "Others",
StringType())
//Apply UDF
>>> cleaned_df = cleaned_df.withColumn("country",
setCountry(cleaned_df["country"]))
```

Numerical variables with too much variation

Sometimes numerical data values may vary by several orders of magnitude. For example, if you are looking at the annual income of individuals, it may vary a lot. Z-score normalization (standardization) and min-max scaling are two popular choices to deal with such data. Spark includes both of these transformations out of the box in the `ml.features` package.

Our current dataset does not have any such variable. The only numerical variable we have is age and its value is uniformly two digits. That's one less issue to fix.

Please note that it is not always necessary to normalize such data. If you are comparing two variables that are in two different scales, or if you are using a clustering algorithm or SVM classifier, or any other scenario where there is really a need to normalize the data, you may normalize the data.

Missing data

This is a major area of concern. Any observations where the target itself is missing should be removed from the training data. The remaining observations may be retained with some imputed values or removed as per the requirements. You should be very careful in imputing the missing values; it may lead to misleading output otherwise! It may seem very easy to just go ahead and substitute average values in the blank cells of a continuous variable, but this may not be the right approach.

Our current case study does not have any missing data so there is no scope for treating it. However, let us look at an example.

Let's assume you have a student's dataset that you are dealing with, and it has data from class-1 to class-5. If there are some missing `Age` values and you just find the average of the whole column and substitute, then that would rather become an outlier and could lead to vague results. You may choose to find the average of only the class that the student is in, and then impute that value. This is at least a better approach, but may not be a perfect one. In most of the cases, you will have to give weightage to other variables as well. If you do so, you may end up building a predictive model to find the missing values and this can be a great approach!

Continuous data

Numerical data is often continuous and must be discretized because it is a prerequisite to some of the algorithms. It is usually split into different buckets or ranges of values. However, there could be cases where you may not just uniformly bucket based on the range of your data, you may have to consider the variance or standard deviation or any other applicable reason to bucket properly. Now, deciding the number of buckets is also at the discretion of the data scientist, but that too needs careful analysis. Too few buckets reduces granularity and too many buckets is just about the same as having too many categorical levels. In our case study, `age` is an example of such data and we need to discretize it. We split it into different buckets. For example, look at this pipeline stage, which converts `age` to 10 buckets:

Scala:

```
scala> val splits = Array(Double.NegativeInfinity, 35.0, 45.0, 55.0,
            Double.PositiveInfinity)
splits: Array[Double] = Array(-Infinity, 35.0, 45.0, 55.0, Infinity)
scala> val bucketizer = new Bucketizer().setSplits(splits).
                setInputCol("age").setOutputCol("age_buckets")
bucketizer: org.apache.spark.ml.feature.Bucketizer =
bucketizer_a25c5d90ac14
```

Python:

```
>>> splits = [-float("inf"), 35.0, 45.0, 55.0,
                float("inf")]
>>> bucketizer = Bucketizer(splits = splits, inputCol = "age",
                outputCol = "age_buckets")
```

Categorical data

We have discussed the need for discretizing continuous data and converting it to categories or buckets. We have also discussed the introduction of dummy variables, one for each distinct value of a categorical variable. There is one more common data preparation practice where we convert categorical levels to numerical (discrete) data. This is required because many machine learning algorithms work with numerical data, integers, and real-valued numbers, or some other situation may demand it. So, we need to convert categorical data into numerical data.

There can be downsides to this approach. Introducing an order into inherently unordered data may not be logical at times. For example, assigning numbers such as 0, 1, 2, 3 to the colors "red", "green", "blue", and "black", respectively, does not make sense. This is because we cannot say that red is one unit distant from "green" and so is "green" from "blue"! If applicable, introducing dummy variables makes more sense in many such cases.

Preparing the data

Having discussed the common issues and possible fixes, let us see how to prepare our current dataset. We have already covered the too many levels issue related code fix. The following example shows the rest. It converts all the features into a single features column. It also sets aside some data for testing the models. This code heavily relies on the `ml.features` package, which was designed to support the data preparation phase. Note that this piece of code is just defining what needs to be done. The transformations are not carried out as yet. These will become stages in subsequently defined pipelines. Execution is deferred as late as possible, until the actual model is built. The Catalyst optimizer finds the optimal route to implement the pipeline:

Scala:

```
//Define pipeline to convert categorical labels to numerical labels
scala> import org.apache.spark.ml.feature.{StringIndexer, Bucketizer,
VectorAssembler}
import org.apache.spark.ml.feature.{StringIndexer, Bucketizer,
VectorAssembler}
scala> import org.apache.spark.ml.Pipeline
import org.apache.spark.ml.Pipeline
//Race
scala> val raceIdxer = new StringIndexer().
          setInputCol("race").setOutputCol("raceIdx")
raceIdxer: org.apache.spark.ml.feature.StringIndexer = strIdx_80eddaa022e6
//Award (prediction target)
scala> val awardIdxer = new StringIndexer().
          setInputCol("award").setOutputCol("awardIdx")
awardIdxer: org.apache.spark.ml.feature.StringIndexer = strIdx_256fe36d1436
//Country
scala> val countryIdxer = new StringIndexer().
          setInputCol("country").setOutputCol("countryIdx")
countryIdxer: org.apache.spark.ml.feature.StringIndexer =
strIdx_c73a073553a2

//Convert continuous variable age to buckets
scala> val splits = Array(Double.NegativeInfinity, 35.0, 45.0, 55.0,
          Double.PositiveInfinity)
splits: Array[Double] = Array(-Infinity, 35.0, 45.0, 55.0, Infinity)
```

```scala
scala> val bucketizer = new Bucketizer().setSplits(splits).
                setInputCol("age").setOutputCol("age_buckets")
bucketizer: org.apache.spark.ml.feature.Bucketizer =
bucketizer_a25c5d90ac14

//Prepare numerical feature vector by clubbing all individual features
scala> val assembler = new VectorAssembler().setInputCols(Array("raceIdx",
        "age_buckets","countryIdx")).setOutputCol("features")
assembler: org.apache.spark.ml.feature.VectorAssembler =
vecAssembler_8cf17ee0cd60

//Define data preparation pipeline
scala> val dp_pipeline = new Pipeline().setStages(
            Array(raceIdxer,awardIdxer, countryIdxer, bucketizer, assembler))
dp_pipeline: org.apache.spark.ml.Pipeline = pipeline_06717d17140b
//Transform dataset
scala> cleaned_df = dp_pipeline.fit(cleaned_df).transform(cleaned_df)
cleaned_df: org.apache.spark.sql.DataFrame = [dob: string, birthplace:
string ... 9 more fields]
//Split data into train and test datasets
scala> val Array(trainData, testData) =
        cleaned_df.randomSplit(Array(0.7, 0.3))
trainData: org.apache.spark.sql.Dataset[org.apache.spark.sql.Row] = [dob:
string, birthplace: string ... 9 more fields]
testData: org.apache.spark.sql.Dataset[org.apache.spark.sql.Row] = [dob:
string, birthplace: string ... 9 more fields]
```

Python:

```python
    //Define pipeline to convert categorical labels to numcerical labels
    >>> from pyspark.ml.feature import StringIndexer, Bucketizer,
VectorAssembler
    >>> from pyspark.ml import Pipelin
    //Race
    >>> raceIdxer = StringIndexer(inputCol= "race", outputCol="raceIdx")
    //Award (prediction target)
    >>> awardIdxer = StringIndexer(inputCol = "award",
outputCol="awardIdx")
    //Country
    >>> countryIdxer = StringIndexer(inputCol = "country", outputCol =
"countryIdx")
    //Convert continuous variable age to buckets
    >>> splits = [-float("inf"), 35.0, 45.0, 55.0,
                    float("inf")]
    >>> bucketizer = Bucketizer(splits = splits, inputCol = "age",
                        outputCol = "age_buckets")
    >>>
    //Prepare numerical feature vector by clubbing all individual features
```

```
>>> assembler = VectorAssembler(inputCols = ["raceIdx",
        "age_buckets","countryIdx"], outputCol = "features")
//Define data preparation pipeline
>>> dp_pipeline = Pipeline(stages = [raceIdxer,
        awardIdxer, countryIdxer, bucketizer, assembler])
//Transform dataset
>>> cleaned_df = dp_pipeline.fit(cleaned_df).transform(cleaned_df)
>>> cleaned_df.columns
['dob', 'birthplace', 'country', 'age', 'race', 'award', 'raceIdx',
'awardIdx', 'countryIdx', 'age_buckets', 'features']
//Split data into train and test datasets
>>> trainData, testData = cleaned_df.randomSplit([0.7, 0.3])
```

After carrying out all data preparation activity, you will end up with a completely numeric data with no missing values and with manageable levels in each attribute. You may have already dropped any attributes that may not add much value to the analysis on hand. This is what we call the **final data matrix**. You are all set now to start modeling your data. So, first you split your source data into train data and test data. Models are "trained" using train data and "tested" using test data. Note that the split is random and you may end up with different train and test partitions if you redo the split.

Model building

A model is a representation of things, a rendering or description of reality. Just like a model of a physical building, data science models attempt to make sense of the reality; in this case, the reality is the underlying relationships between the features and the predicted variable. They may not be 100 percent accurate, but still very useful to give some deep insights into our business space based on the data.

There are several machine learning algorithms that help us model data and Spark provides many of them out of the box. However, which model to build is still a million dollar question. It depends on various factors, such as interpretability-accuracy trade-off, how much data you have at hand, categorical or numerical variables, time and memory constraints, and so on. In the following code example, we have just trained a few models at random to show you how it can be done.

We'll be predicting the award type based on race, age, and country. We'll be using the DecisionTreeClassifier, RandomForestClassifier, and OneVsRest algorithms. These three are chosen arbitrarily. All of them work with multiclass labels and are simple to understand. We have used the following evaluation metrics provided by the `ml` package:

- **Accuracy**: The ratio of correctly predicted observations.

- **Weighted Precision**: Precision is the ratio of correct positive observations to all positive observations. Weighted precision takes the frequency of individual classes into account.
- **Weighted Recall**: Recall is the ratio of positives to actual positives. Actual positives are the sum of true positives and false negatives. Weighted Recall takes the frequency of individual classes into account.
- **F1**: The default evaluation measure. This is the weighted average of Precision and Recall.

Scala:

```
scala> import org.apache.spark.ml.Pipeline
import org.apache.spark.ml.Pipeline
scala> import org.apache.spark.ml.classification.DecisionTreeClassifier
import org.apache.spark.ml.classification.DecisionTreeClassifier

//Use Decision tree classifier
scala> val dtreeModel = new DecisionTreeClassifier().
          setLabelCol("awardIdx").setFeaturesCol("features").
          fit(trainData)
dtreeModel:
org.apache.spark.ml.classification.DecisionTreeClassificationModel =
DecisionTreeClassificationModel (uid=dtc_76c9e80680a7) of depth 5 with 39
nodes

//Run predictions using testData
scala> val dtree_predictions = dtreeModel.transform(testData)
dtree_predictions: org.apache.spark.sql.DataFrame = [dob: string,
birthplace: string ... 12 more fields]

//Examine results. Your results may vary due to randomSplit
scala> dtree_predictions.select("award","awardIdx","prediction").show(4)
+--------------------+--------+----------+
|               award|awardIdx|prediction|
+--------------------+--------+----------+
|       Best Director|     1.0|       1.0|
|        Best Actress|     0.0|       0.0|
|        Best Actress|     0.0|       0.0|
|Best Supporting A...|     4.0|       3.0|
+--------------------+--------+----------+

//Compute prediction mismatch count
scala> dtree_predictions.filter(dtree_predictions("awardIdx") =!=
dtree_predictions("prediction")).count()
res10: Long = 88
scala> testData.count
```

```
res11: Long = 126
//Predictions match with DecisionTreeClassifier model is about 30%
((126-88)*100/126)


//Train Random forest
scala> import org.apache.spark.ml.classification.RandomForestClassifier
import org.apache.spark.ml.classification.RandomForestClassifier
scala> import
org.apache.spark.ml.classification.RandomForestClassificationModel
import org.apache.spark.ml.classification.RandomForestClassificationModel
scala> import org.apache.spark.ml.feature.{StringIndexer, IndexToString,
VectorIndexer}
import org.apache.spark.ml.feature.{StringIndexer, IndexToString,
VectorIndexer}

//Build model
scala> val RFmodel = new RandomForestClassifier().
        setLabelCol("awardIdx").
        setFeaturesCol("features").
        setNumTrees(6).fit(trainData)
RFmodel: org.apache.spark.ml.classification.RandomForestClassificationModel
= RandomForestClassificationModel (uid=rfc_c6fb8d764ade) with 6 trees
//Run predictions on the same test data using Random Forest model
scala> val RF_predictions = RFmodel.transform(testData)
RF_predictions: org.apache.spark.sql.DataFrame = [dob: string, birthplace:
string ... 12 more fields]
//Check results
scala> RF_predictions.filter(RF_predictions("awardIdx") =!=
RF_predictions("prediction")).count()
res29: Long = 87 //Roughly the same as DecisionTreeClassifier

//Try OneVsRest Logistic regression technique
scala> import org.apache.spark.ml.classification.{LogisticRegression,
OneVsRest}
import org.apache.spark.ml.classification.{LogisticRegression, OneVsRest}
//This model requires a base classifier
scala> val classifier = new LogisticRegression().
          setLabelCol("awardIdx").
          setFeaturesCol("features").
          setMaxIter(30).
          setTol(1E-6).
          setFitIntercept(true)
classifier: org.apache.spark.ml.classification.LogisticRegression =
logreg_82cd24368c87

//Fit OneVsRest model
scala> val ovrModel = new OneVsRest().
```

```
                setClassifier(classifier).
                setLabelCol("awardIdx").
                setFeaturesCol("features").
                fit(trainData)
ovrModel: org.apache.spark.ml.classification.OneVsRestModel =
oneVsRest_e696c41c0bcf
//Run predictions
scala> val OVR_predictions = ovrModel.transform(testData)
predictions: org.apache.spark.sql.DataFrame = [dob: string, birthplace:
string ... 10 more fields]
//Check results
scala> OVR_predictions.filter(OVR_predictions("awardIdx") =!=
OVR_predictions("prediction")).count()
res32: Long = 86 //Roughly the same as other models
```

Python:

```
    >>> from pyspark.ml import Pipeline
    >>> from pyspark.ml.classification import DecisionTreeClassifier
    //Use Decision tree classifier
    >>> dtreeModel = DecisionTreeClassifier(labelCol = "awardIdx",
featuresCol="features").fit(trainData)
    //Run predictions using testData
    >>> dtree_predictions = dtreeModel.transform(testData)
    //Examine results. Your results may vary due to randomSplit
    >>> dtree_predictions.select("award","awardIdx","prediction").show(4)
    +--------------------+--------+----------+
    |               award|awardIdx|prediction|
    +--------------------+--------+----------+
    |       Best Director|     1.0|       4.0|
    |       Best Director|     1.0|       1.0|
    |       Best Director|     1.0|       1.0|
    |Best Supporting A...|     4.0|       3.0|
    +--------------------+--------+----------+
    >>> dtree_predictions.filter(dtree_predictions["awardIdx"] !=
dtree_predictions["prediction"]).count()
    92
    >>> testData.count()
    137
    >>>
    //Predictions match with DecisionTreeClassifier model is about 31%
((133-92)*100/133)
    //Train Random forest
    >>> from pyspark.ml.classification import RandomForestClassifier,
RandomForestClassificationModel
    >>> from pyspark.ml.feature import StringIndexer, IndexToString,
VectorIndexer
    >>> from pyspark.ml.evaluation import MulticlassClassificationEvaluator
```

```
    //Build model
    >>> RFmodel = RandomForestClassifier(labelCol = "awardIdx", featuresCol
= "features", numTrees=6).fit(trainData)
    //Run predictions on the same test data using Random Forest model
    >>> RF_predictions = RFmodel.transform(testData)
    //Check results
    >>> RF_predictions.filter(RF_predictions["awardIdx"] !=
RF_predictions["prediction"]).count()
    94      //Roughly the same as DecisionTreeClassifier
    //Try OneVsRest Logistic regression technique
    >>> from pyspark.ml.classification import LogisticRegression, OneVsRest
    //This model requires a base classifier
    >>> classifier = LogisticRegression(labelCol = "awardIdx",
featuresCol="features",
                    maxIter = 30, tol=1E-6, fitIntercept = True)
    //Fit OneVsRest model
    >>> ovrModel = OneVsRest(classifier = classifier, labelCol =
"awardIdx",
                    featuresCol = "features").fit(trainData)
    //Run predictions
    >>> OVR_predictions = ovrModel.transform(testData)
    //Check results
    >>> OVR_predictions.filter(OVR_predictions["awardIdx"] !=
OVR_predictions["prediction"]).count()
    90  //Roughly the same as other models
```

So far, we have tried a few models and found that they gives us roughly the same performance. There are various other ways to validate the model performance. This again depends on the algorithm you have used, the business context, and the outcome produced. Let us look at some metrics that are offered out of the box in the spark.ml.evaluation package:

Scala:

```
scala> import
org.apache.spark.ml.evaluation.MulticlassClassificationEvaluator
import org.apache.spark.ml.evaluation.MulticlassClassificationEvaluator
//F1
scala> val f1_eval = new MulticlassClassificationEvaluator().
                    setLabelCol("awardIdx") //Default metric is F1
f1_eval: org.apache.spark.ml.evaluation.MulticlassClassificationEvaluator =
mcEval_e855a949bb0e

//WeightedPrecision
scala> val wp_eval = new MulticlassClassificationEvaluator().
setMetricName("weightedPrecision").setLabelCol("awardIdx")
wp_eval: org.apache.spark.ml.evaluation.MulticlassClassificationEvaluator =
```

```
mcEval_44fd64e29d0a

//WeightedRecall
scala> val wr_eval = new MulticlassClassificationEvaluator().
setMetricName("weightedRecall").setLabelCol("awardIdx")
wr_eval: org.apache.spark.ml.evaluation.MulticlassClassificationEvaluator =
mcEval_aa341966305a
//Compute measures for all models
scala> val f1_eval_list = List (dtree_predictions, RF_predictions,
OVR_predictions) map (
          x => f1_eval.evaluate(x))
f1_eval_list: List[Double] = List(0.2330854098674473, 0.2330854098674473,
0.2330854098674473)
scala> val wp_eval_list = List (dtree_predictions, RF_predictions,
OVR_predictions) map (
          x => wp_eval.evaluate(x))
wp_eval_list: List[Double] = List(0.2661599224979506, 0.2661599224979506,
0.2661599224979506)

scala> val wr_eval_list = List (dtree_predictions, RF_predictions,
OVR_predictions) map (
          x => wr_eval.evaluate(x))
wr_eval_list: List[Double] = List(0.31746031746031744, 0.31746031746031744,
0.31746031746031744)
```

Python:

```
    >>> from pyspark.ml.evaluation import MulticlassClassificationEvaluator
    //F1
    >>> f1_eval = MulticlassClassificationEvaluator(labelCol="awardIdx")
//Default metric is F1
    //WeightedPrecision
    >>> wp_eval = MulticlassClassificationEvaluator(labelCol="awardIdx",
metricName="weightedPrecision")
    //WeightedRecall
    >>> wr_eval = MulticlassClassificationEvaluator(labelCol="awardIdx",
metricName="weightedRecall")
    //Accuracy
    >>> acc_eval = MulticlassClassificationEvaluator(labelCol="awardIdx",
metricName="Accuracy")
    //Compute measures for all models
    >>> f1_eval_list = [ f1_eval.evaluate(x) for x in [dtree_predictions,
RF_predictions, OVR_predictions]]
    >>> wp_eval_list = [ wp_eval.evaluate(x) for x in [dtree_predictions,
RF_predictions, OVR_predictions]]
    >>> wr_eval_list = [ wr_eval.evaluate(x) for x in [dtree_predictions,
RF_predictions, OVR_predictions]]
    //Print results for DecisionTree, Random Forest and OneVsRest
```

```
>>> f1_eval_list
[0.2957949866055487, 0.2645186821042419, 0.2564967990214734]
>>> wp_eval_list
[0.3265407181548341, 0.31914852065228005, 0.25295826631254753]
>>> wr_eval_list
[0.3082706766917293, 0.2932330827067669, 0.3233082706766917]
```

Output:

	Decision tree	Random Forest	OneVsRest
F1	0.29579	0.26451	0.25649
WeightedPrecision	0.32654	0.26451	0.25295
WeightedRecall	0.30827	0.29323	0.32330

Upon validating the model performance, you will have to tune the model as much as possible. Now, tuning can happen both ways, at the data level and at the algorithm level. Feeding the right data that an algorithm expects is very important. The problem is that whatever data you feed in, the algorithm may still give some output – it never complains! So, apart from cleaning the data properly by treating missing values, treating univariate and multivariate outliers, and so on, you can create many more relevant features. This feature engineering is usually treated as the most important aspect of data science. Having decent domain expertise helps to engineer better features. Now, coming to the algorithmic aspect of tuning, there is always scope for working on optimizing the parameters that we pass to an algorithm. You may choose to use grid search to find the optimal parameters. Also, data scientists should question themselves on which loss function to use and why, and, out of GD, SGD, L-BFGS, and so on, which algorithm to use to optimize the loss function and why.

Please note that the preceding approach is intended just to demonstrate how to perform the steps on Spark. Selecting one algorithm over the other by just looking at the accuracy level may not be the best way. Selecting an algorithm depends on the type of data you are dealing with, the outcome variable, the business problem/requirement, computational challenges, interpretability, and many others.

Data visualization

Data visualization is something which is needed every now and then from the time you take on a data science assignment. Before building any model, preferably, you will have to visualize each variable to see their distributions to understand their characteristics and also find outliers so you can treat them. Simple tools such as scatterplot, box plot, bar chart, and so on are a few versatile, handy tools for such purposes. Also, you will have to use the visuals in most of the steps to ensure you are heading in the right direction.

Every time you want to collaborate with business users or stakeholders, it is always a good practice to convey your analysis through visuals. Visuals can accommodate more data in them in a more meaningful way and are inherently intuitive in nature.

Please note that most data science assignment outcomes are preferably represented through visuals and dashboards to business users. We already have a dedicated chapter on this topic, so we won't go deeper into it.

Communicating the results to business users

In real-life scenarios, it is mostly the case that you have to keep communicating with the business intermittently. You might have to build several models before concluding on a final production-ready model and communicate the results to the business.

An implementable model does not always depend on accuracy; you might have to bring in other measures such as sensitivity, specificity, or an ROC curve, and also represent your results through visuals such as a Gain/Lift chart or an output of a K-S test with statistical significance. Note that these techniques require business users' input. This input often guides the way you build the models or set thresholds. Let us look at a few examples to better understand how it works:

- If a regressor predicts the probability of an event occurring, then blindly setting the threshold to 0.5 and assuming anything above 0.5 is 1 and less than 0.5 is 0 may not be the best way! You may use an ROC curve and take a rather more scientific or logical decision.
- False-negative predictions for diagnosis of a cancer test may not be desirable at all! This is an extreme case of life risk.

- E-mail campaigning is cheaper compared to delivery of hard copies. So the business may decide to send e-mails to the recipients who are predicted with less than 0.5 (say 0.35) probability.

Notice that the preceding decisions are influenced heavily by business users or the problem owners, and data scientists work closely with them to take a call on such cases.

Again, as discussed already, the right visuals are the most preferred way to communicate the results to the business.

Summary

In this chapter, we have taken up a case study and completed the data analytics life cycle end to end. During the course of building a data product, we have applied the knowledge gained so far in the previous chapters. We have stated a business problem, formed an initial hypothesis, acquired data, and prepared it for model building. We have tried building multiple models and found a suitable model.

In the next chapter, which is also the final chapter, we will discuss building real-world applications using Spark.

References

http://www2.sas.com/proceedings/forum2007/073-2007.pdf.

https://azure.microsoft.com/en-in/documentation/articles/machine-learning-al gorithm-choice/.

http://www.cs.cornell.edu/courses/cs578/2003fa/performance_measures.pdf.

11
Building Data Science Applications

Data science applications are garnering a lot of excitement, mainly because of the promise they hold in harnessing data and extracting consumable results. There are already several successful data products that have had a transformative effect on our daily lives. The ubiquitous recommender systems, e-mail spam filters, and targeted advertisements and news content have become part and parcel of life. Music and movies have become data products streaming from providers such as iTunes and Netflix. Businesses, especially in the domains such as retail, are actively pursuing ways to gain a competitive advantage by studying the market and customer behavior using a data-driven approach.

We have discussed the data analytics workflow up to the model building phase so far in the previous chapters. But the real value of a model is when it is actually deployed in a production system. The end product, the fruit of a data science workflow, is an operationalized data product. In this chapter, we discuss this culminating stage of the data analytics workflow. We will not get into actual code snippets but take a step back to get the complete picture, including the non-technical aspects.

The complete picture is not limited to the development process alone. It comprises the user application, developments in Spark itself, as well as rapid changes happening in the big data landscape. We'll start with the development process of the user application first and discuss various options at each stage. Then we'll delve into the features and enhancements in the latest Spark 2.0 release and future plans. Finally, we'll attempt to give a broad overview of the big data trends, especially the Hadoop ecosystem. References and useful links are included in individual sections in addition to the end of the chapter for further information about the specific context.

Scope of development

Data analytics workflow can be roughly divided into two phases, the build phase and the operationalization phase. The first phase is usually a one-time exercise, with heavy human intervention. Once we've attained reasonable end results, we are ready to operationalize the product. The second phase starts with the models generated in the first phase and makes them available as a part of some production workflow. In this section, we'll discuss the following:

- Expectations
- Presentation options
- Development and testing
- Data quality management

Expectations

The primary goal of data science applications is to build "actionable" insights, actionable being the keyword. Many use cases such as fraud detection need the insights to be generated and made available in a consumable fashion in near real time, if you expect any action-ability at all. The end users of the data product vary with the use case. They may be customers of an e-commerce site or a decision maker of a major conglomerate. The end user need not always be a human being. It could be a risk assessment software tool in a financial institution. A one-size-fits-all approach does not fit in with many software products, and data products are no exception. However, there are some common expectations for data products, as listed here:

- The first and foremost expectation is that the insight generation time frame based on real-world data should be within "actionable" timeframes. The actual time frame varies based on the use case.
- The data product should integrate into some (often already existing) production workflow.
- The insights should be translated into something that people can use instead of obscure numbers or hard-to-interpret charts. The presentation should be unobtrusive.
- The data product should have the ability to fine-tune itself (self-adapting) based on the incoming data inputs.
- Ideally, there has to be some way to receive human feedback, which can be used as a source for self-tuning.

- There should be a mechanism that quantitatively assesses its effectiveness periodically and automatically.

Presentation options

The varied nature of data products calls for varied modes of presentation. Sometimes the end result of a data analytics exercise is to publish a research paper. Sometimes it could be a part of a dashboard, where this becomes one of several sources publishing results on a single web page. They may be overt and targeted for human consumption, or covert and feeding into some other software application. You may use a general-purpose engine such as Spark to build your solution, but the presentation must be highly aligned to the targeted user base.

Sometimes all you need to do is write an e-mail with your findings or just export a CSV file of insights. Or you may have to develop a dedicated web application around your data product. Some other common options are discussed here, and you have to choose the right one that fits the problem on hand.

Interactive notebooks

Interactive notebooks are web applications that allow you to create and share documents that contain code chunks, results, equations, images, videos, and explanation text. They may be viewed as executable documents or REPL shells with visualization and equation support. These documents can be exported as PDFs, Markdown, or HTML. Notebooks contain several "kernels" or "computational engines" that execute code chunks.

Interactive notebooks are the most suitable choice if the end goal of your data analytics workflow is to generate a written report. There are several notebooks and many of them have Spark support. These notebooks are useful tools during the exploration phase also. We have already introduced IPython and Zeppelin notebooks in previous chapters.

References

- The IPython Notebook: A Comprehensive Tool for Data Science: http://conferences.oreilly.com/strata/strata2013/public/schedule/detail/27233
- Sparkly Notebook: Interactive Analysis and Visualization with Spark: `http://www.slideshare.net/felixcss/sparkly-notebook-interactive-analysis-and-visualization-with-spark`

Web API

An **Application Programming Interface** (**API**) is a software-to-software interfaceâ®® a specification that describes the available functionality, how it must be used, and what the inputs and outputs are. The software (service) provider exposes some of its functionality as an API. A developer may develop a software component that consumes this API. For example, Twitter offers APIs to get or post data onto Twitter or to query data programmatically. A Spark enthusiast may write a software component that automatically collects all tweets on #Spark, categorizes according to their requirements, and publishes that data on their personal website. Web APIs are a type of APIs where the interface is defined as a set of **Hypertext Transfer Protocol** (**HTTP**) request messages along with a definition of the structure of response messages. Nowadays REST-ful (Representational State Transfer) have become the de facto standard.

You can implement your data product as an API, and perhaps this is the most powerful option. It can then be plugged into one or more applications, say the management dashboard as well as the marketing analytics workflow. You may develop a domain specific "insights-as-a-service" as a public Web API with a subscription model. The simplicity and ubiquity of Web APIs make them the most compelling choice for building data products.

References

- Application programming interface: `https://en.wikipedia.org/wiki/Application_programming_interface`
- Ready for APIs? Three steps to unlock the data economy's most promising channel: http://www.forbes.com/sites/mckinsey/2014/01/07/ready-for-apis-three-steps-to-unlock-the-data-economys-most-promising-channel/#61e7103b89e5
- How Insights-as-a-service is growing based on big data: http://www.kdnuggets.com/2015/12/insights-as-a-service-big-data.html

PMML and PFA

Sometimes you may have to expose your model in a way that other data mining tools can understand. The model and the complete pre- and post-processing steps should be converted into a standard format. PMML and PFA are two such standard formats in the data mining domain.

Predictive Model Markup Language (**PMML**) is an XML-based predictive model interchange format and Apache Spark API convert models into PMML out of the box. A PMML message may contain a myriad of data transformations as well as one or more predictive models. Different data mining tools can export or import PMML messages without the need for custom code.

Portable Format for Analytics (**PFA**) is the nextgeneration of predictive model interchange format. It exchanges JSON documents and straightaway inherits all advantages of JSON documents as against XML documents. In addition, PFA is more flexible than PMML.

References

- PMML FAQ: Predictive Model Markup Language: http://www.kdnuggets.com/2013/01/pmml-faq-predictive-model-markup-language.html
- Portable Format for Analytics: moving models to production: http://www.kdnuggets.com/2016/01/portable-format-analytics-models-production.html
- What is PFA for?: http://dmg.org/pfa/docs/motivation/

Development and testing

Apache Spark is a general-purpose cluster computing system that can run both by itself or over several existing cluster managers such as Apache Mesos, Hadoop, Yarn, and Amazon EC2. In addition, several big data and enterprise software companies have already integrated Spark into their offerings: Microsoft Azure HDInsight, Cloudera, IBM Analytics for Apache Spark, SAP HANA, and the list goes on. Databricks, a company founded by the creators of Apache Spark, have their own product for data science workflow, from ingestion to production. Your responsibility is to understand your organizational requirements and existing talent pool and decide which option is the best for you.

Regardless of the option chosen, follow the usual best practices in any software development life cycle, such as version control and peer reviews. Try to use high-level APIs wherever applicable. The data transformation pipelines used in production should be the same as the ones used in building the model. Document any questions that arise during the data analytics workflow. Often these may result in business process improvements.

As always, testing is extremely important for the success of your product. You have to maintain a set of automated scripts that give easy-to-understand results. The test cases should cover the following at the minimum:

- Adherence to timeframe and resource consumption requirements
- Resilience to bad data (for example, data type violations)
- New value in a categorical feature that was not encountered during the model building phase
- Very little data or too heavy data that is expected in the target production system

Monitor logs, resource utilization, and so on to uncover any performance bottlenecks. The Spark UI provides a wealth of information to monitor Spark applications. The following are some common tips that will help you improve performance:

- Cache any input or intermediate data that might be used multiple times.
- Look at the Spark UI and identify jobs that are causing a lot of shuffle. Check the code and see whether you can reduce the shuffles.
- Actions may transfer the data from workers to the driver. See that you are not transferring any data that is not absolutely necessary.
- Stragglersâ◎◎tasks that run slower than othersâ◎◎may increase the overall job completion time. There may be several reasons for a straggler. If a job is running slow due to a slow node, you may set `spark.speculation` to `true`. Then Spark automatically relaunches such a task on a different node. Otherwise, you may have to revisit the logic and see whether it can be improved.

References

- Investigating Spark's performance: http://radar.oreilly.com/2015/04/investigating-sparks-performance.html
- Tuning and Debugging in Apache Spark by Patrick Wendell: `https://sparkhub.databricks.com/video/tuning-and-debugging-apache-spark/`
- How to tune your Apache Spark jobs: http://blog.cloudera.com/blog/2015/03/how-to-tune-your-apache-spark-jobs-part-1/ and part 2

Data quality management

At the outset, let's not forget that we are trying to build fault-tolerant software data products from unreliable, often unstructured, and uncontrolled data sources. So data quality management gains even more importance in a data science workflow. Sometimes the data may solely come from controlled data sources, such as automated internal process workflows in an organization. But in all other cases, you need to carefully craft your data cleansing processes to protect the subsequent processing.

Metadata consists of the structure and meaning of data, and obviously the most critical repository to work with. It is the information about the structure of individual data sources and what each component in that structure means. You may not always be able to write some script and extract this data. A single data source may contain data with different structures or an individual component (column) may mean different things during different times. A label such as owner or high may mean different things in different data sources. Collecting and understanding all such nuances and documenting is a tedious, iterative task. Standardization of metadata is a prerequisite to data transformation development.

Some broad guidelines that are applicable to most use cases are listed here:

- All data sources must be versioned and timestamped
- Data quality management processes often require involvement of the highest authorities
- Mask or anonymize sensitive data
- One important step that is often missed out is to maintain traceabilityâ®®a link between each data element (say a row) and its original source

The Scala advantage

Apache Spark allows you to write applications in Python, R, Java, or Scala. With this flexibility comes the responsibility of choosing the right language for your requirements. But regardless of your usual language of choice, you may want to consider Scala for your Spark-powered application. In this section, we will explain why.

Let's digress to gain a high-level understanding of imperative and functional programming paradigms first. Languages such as C, Python, and Java belong to the imperative programming paradigm. In the imperative programming paradigm, a program is a sequence of instructions and it has a program state. The program state is usually represented as a set of variables and their values at any given point in time. Assignments and reassignments are fairly common. Variable values are expected to change over the period of execution by one or more functions. Variable value modification in a function is not limited to local variables. Global variables and public class variables are some examples of such variables.

In contrast, programs written in functional programming languages such as Erlang can be viewed as stateless expression evaluators. Data is immutable. If a function is called with the same set of input arguments, then it is expected to produce the same result (that is, referential transparency). This is possible due to the absence of interference from a variable context in the form of global variables and the like. This implies that the sequence of function evaluation is of little importance. Functions can be passed as arguments to other functions. Recursive calls replace loops. The absence of state makes parallel programming much easier because it eliminates the need for locking and possible deadlocks. Coordination gets simplified when the execution order is less important. These factors make the functional programming paradigm a neat fit for parallel programming.

Pure functional programming languages are hard to work with because most of the programs require state changes. Most functional programming languages, including good old Lisp, do allow storing of data in variables (side-effects). Some languages such as Scala draw from multiple programming paradigms.

Returning to Scala, it is a JVM-based, statically typed multi-paradigm programming language. Its built-in-type inference mechanism allows programmers to omit some redundant type information. This gives a feel of the flexibility offered by dynamic languages while retaining the robustness of better compile time checks and fast runtime. Scala is an object-oriented language in the sense that every value is an object, including numerical values. Functions are first-class objects, which can be used as any data type, and they can be passed as arguments to other functions. Scala interoperates well with Java and its tools because Scala runs on JVM. Java and Scala classes can be freely mixed. That implies that Scala can easily interact with the Hadoop ecosystem.

All of these factors should be taken into account when you choose the right programming language for your application.

Spark development status

Apache Spark has become the most currently active project in the Hadoop ecosystem in terms of the number of contributors by the end of 2015. Having started as a research project at UC Berkeley AMPLAB in 2009, Spark is still relatively young when compared to projects such as Apache Hadoop and is still in active development. There were three releases in the year 2015, from 1.3 through 1.5, packed with features such as DataFrames API, SparkR, and Project Tungsten respectively. Version 1.6 was released in early 2016 and included the new Dataset API and expansion of data science functionality. Spark 2.0 was released in July 2016, and this being a major release has a lot of new features and enhancements that deserve a section of their own.

Spark 2.0's features and enhancements

Apache Spark 2.0 included three major new features and several other performance improvements and under-the-hood changes. This section attempts to give a high-level overview yet step into the details to give a conceptual understanding wherever required.

Unifying Datasets and DataFrames

DataFrames are high-level APIs that support a data abstraction conceptually equivalent to a table in a relational database or a DataFrame in R and Python (the pandas library). Datasets are an extension of the DataFrame API that provide a type-safe, object-oriented programming interface. Datasets add static types to DataFrames. Defining a structure on top of DataFrames provides information to the core that enables optimizations. It also helps in catching analysis errors early on, even before a distributed job starts.

RDDs, Datasets, and DataFrames are interchangeable. RDDs continue to be the low-level API. DataFrames, Datasets, and SQL share the same optimization and execution pipeline. Machine learning libraries take either DataFrames or Datasets. Both DataFrames and Datasets run on Tungsten, an initiative to improve runtime performance. They leverage Tungsten's fast in-memory encoding, which is responsible for converting between JVM objects and Spark's internal representation. The same APIs work on streams also, introducing the concept of continuous DataFrames.

Structured Streaming

Structure Streaming APIs are high-level APIs that are built on the Spark SQL engine and extend DataFrames and Datasets. Structured Streaming unifies streaming, interactive, and batch queries. In most use cases, streaming data needs to be combined with batch and interactive queries to form continuous applications. These APIs are designed to address that requirement. Spark takes care of running the query incrementally and continuously on streaming data.

The first release of structured streaming will be focusing on ETL workloads. Users will be able to specify the input, query, trigger, and type of output. An input stream is logically equivalent to an append-only table. Users define queries just the way they would on a traditional SQL table. The trigger is a timeframe, say one second. The output modes offered are complete output, deltas, or updates in place (for example, a DB table).

Take this example: you can aggregate the data in a stream, serve it using the Spark SQL JDBC server, and pass it to a database such as MySQL for downstream applications. Or you could run ad hoc SQL queries that act on the latest data. You can also build and apply machine learning models.

Project Tungsten phase 2

The central idea behind project Tungsten is to bring Spark's performance closer to bare metal through native memory management and runtime code generation. It was first included in Spark 1.4 and enhancements were added in 1.5 and 1.6. It focuses on substantially improving the efficiency of memory and CPU for Spark applications, primarily by the following ways:

- Managing memory explicitly and eliminating the overhead of JVM object model and garbage collection. For example, a four-byte string would occupy around 48 bytes in the JVM object model. Since Spark is not a general-purpose application and has more knowledge about the life cycle of memory blocks than the garbage collector, it can manage memory more efficiently than JVM.
- Designing cache-friendly algorithms and data structures.
- Spark performs code generation to compile parts of queries to Java bytecode. This is being broadened to cover most built-in expressions.

Spark 2.0 rolls out phase 2, which is an order of magnitude faster and includes:

- Whole stage code generation by removing expensive iterator calls and fusing across multiple operators so that the generated code looks like hand-optimized code
- Optimized input and output

What's in store?

Apache Spark 2.1 is expected to have the following:

- **Continuous SQL (CSQL)**
- BI application integration
- Support for more streaming sources and sinks
- Inclusion of additional operators and libraries for structured streaming
- Enhancements to a machine learning package
- Columnar in-memory support in Tungsten

The big data trends

Big data processing has been an integral part of the IT industry, more so in the past decade. Apache Hadoop and other similar endeavors are focused on building the infrastructure to store and process massive amounts of data. After being around for over 10 years, the Hadoop platform is considered mature and almost synonymous with big data processing. Apache Spark, a general computing engine that works well with is and not limited to the Hadoop ecosystem, was quite successful in the year 2015.

Building data science applications requires knowledge of the big data landscape and what software products are available out of that box. We need to carefully map the right blocks that fit our requirements. There are several options with overlapping functionality, and picking the right tools is easier said than done. The success of the application very much depends on assembling the right mix of technologies and processes. The good news is that there are several open source options that drive down the cost of doing big data analytics; and at the same time, you have enterprise-quality end-to-end platforms backed by companies such as Databricks. In addition to the use case on hand, keeping track of the industry trends in general is equally important.

The recent surge in NOSQL data stores with their own interfaces are adding SQL-based interfaces even though they are not relational data stores and may not adhere to ACID properties. This is a welcome trend because converging to a single, age-old interface across relational and non-relational data stores improves programmer productivity.

The operational (OLTP) and analytical (OLAP) systems were being maintained as separate systems over the past couple of decades, but that's one more place where convergence is happening. This convergence brings us to near-real-time use cases such as fraud prevention. Apache Kylin is one open source distributed analytics engine in the Hadoop ecosystem that offers an extremely fast OLAP engine at scale.

The advent of the Internet of Things is accelerating real-time and streaming analytics, bringing in a whole lot of new use cases. The cloud frees up organizations from the operations and IT management overheads so that they can concentrate on their core competence, especially in big data processing. Cloud-based analytic engines, self-service data preparation tools, self-service BI, just-in-time data warehousing, advanced analytics, rich media analytics, and agile analytics are some of the commonly used buzzwords. The term big data itself is slowly evaporating or becoming implicit.

There are plenty of software products and libraries in the big data landscape with overlapping functionalities, as shown in this infographic (http://matturck.com/wp-content/uploads/2016/02/matt_turck_big_data_landscape_v11.png). Choosing the right blocks for your application is a daunting but very important task. Here is a short list of projects to get you started. The list excludes popular names such as Cassandra and tries to include blocks with complementing functionality and mostly from Apache Software Foundation:

- **Apache Arrow** (https://arrow.apache.org/) is an in-memory columnar layer used to accelerate analytical processing and interchange. It is a high-performance, cross-system, and in-memory data representation that is expected to bring in 100 times the performance improvements.
- **Apache Parquet** (https://parquet.apache.org/) is a columnar storage format. Spark SQL provides support for both reading and writing parquet files while automatically capturing the structure of the data.
- **Apache Kafka** (http://kafka.apache.org/) is a popular, high-throughput distributed messaging system. Spark streaming has a direct API to support streaming data ingestion from Kafka.

- **Alluxio** (`http://alluxio.org/`), formerly called Tachyon, is a memory-centric, virtual distributed storage system that enables data sharing across clusters at memory speed. It aims to become the de facto storage unification layer for big data. Alluxio sits between computation frameworks such as Spark and storage systems such as Amazon S3, HDFS, and others.

- **GraphFrames** (https://databricks.com/blog/2016/03/03/introducing-graphframes.html) is a graph processing library for Apache spark that is built on top of DataFrames API.

- **Apache Kylin** (`http://kylin.apache.org/`) is a distributed analytics engine designed to provide SQL interface and multidimensional analysis (OLAP) on Hadoop, supporting extremely large datasets.

- **Apache Sentry** (`http://sentry.apache.org/`) is a system for enforcing fine-grained role-based authorization to data and metadata stored on a Hadoop cluster. It is in the incubation stage at the time of writing this book.

- **Apache Solr** (`http://lucene.apache.org/solr/`) is a blazing fast search platform. Check this `presentation` for integrating Solr and Spark.

- **TensorFlow** (`https://www.tensorflow.org/`) is a machine learning library with extensive built-in support for deep learning. Check out this `blog` to learn how it can be used with Spark.

- **Zeppelin** (`http://zeppelin.incubator.apache.org/`) is a web-based notebook that enables interactive data analytics. It is covered in the data visualization chapter.

Summary

In this final chapter, we discussed how to build real-world applications using Spark. We discussed the big picture consisting of technical and non-technical aspects of data analytics workflows.

References

- The Spark Summit site has a wealth of information on Apache Spark and related projects from completed events
- Interview with *Matei Zaharia* by KDnuggets
- *Why Spark Reached the Tipping Point* in 2015 from KDnuggets by *Matthew Mayo*
- Going Live: Preparing your first Spark production deployment is a very good starting point
- *What is Scala?* from the Scala home page
- *Martin Odersky*, creator of Scala, explains the reasons why Scala fuses together imperative and functional programming

Index

www.ingramcontent.com/pod-product-compliance
Lightning Source LLC
Chambersburg PA
CBHW080916220326
41598CB00034B/5583